W9-ABP-733

IDEAS IN THINGS

IDEAS IN THINGS

The Poems
of William Carlos Williams

Donald W. Markos

Rutherford ● Madison ● Teaneck
Fairleigh Dickinson University Press
London and Toronto: Associated University Presses

Associated University Presses
440 Forsgate Drive
Cranbury, NJ 08512

Associated University Presses
25 Sicilian Avenue
London WC1A 2QH, England

Associated University Presses
P.O. Box 338, Port Credit
Mississauga, Ontario
Canada L5G 4L8

The paper used in this publication meets the requirements
of the American National Standard for Permanence of Paper
for Printed Library Materials Z39.48-1984.

Library of Congress Cataloging-in-Publication Data

Markos, Donald W., 1933–
    Ideas in things : the poems of William Carlos Williams / Donald W. Markos.
        p.   cm.
    Includes bibliographical references and index.
    ISBN 0-8386-3518-0
    1. Williams, William Carlos, 1883–1963—Criticism and interpretation.   I. Title.
    PS3545.I544Z6265   1994
    811'.52—dc20   92-55037
                                                        CIP

PRINTED IN THE UNITED STATES OF AMERICA

To my mother, Rosemarie.

CONTENTS

ABBREVIATIONS

The following abbreviations, adopted by the *William Carlos Williams Review,* are used for parenthetical citations to Williams' works. All books listed are published by New Directions unless otherwise stated:

A	*The Autobiography of William Carlos Williams* (1951)
AG	*In the American Grain* (1925)
BU	*The Build-Up* (1952)
CP1	*The Collected Poems,* Volume One, A. Walton Litz and Christopher MacGowan, eds. (1986)
CP2	*The Collected Poems,* Volume Two, Christopher MacGowan, ed. (1988)
EK	*The Embodiment of Knowledge,* Ron Loewinsohn, ed. (1974)
I	*Imaginations,* Webster Shott, ed. (1970: contains *Kora in Hell: Improvisations,* 1920; *Spring and All,* 1923; *The Great American Novel,* 1923; *The Descent of Winter,* 1928; *A Novelette [January] and other Prose,* 1932)
Int	*Speaking Straight Ahead: Interviews with William Carlos Williams,* Linda Welshimer Wagner, ed. (1976)
IWWP	*I Wanted to Write a Poem: the Autobiography of the Works of a Poet,* reported and edited by Edith Heal. Boston: Beacon Press, 1958.
ML	*Many Loves and Other Plays* (1961)
P	*Paterson* (1963; contains books 1–5 and notes for book 6)
PB	*Pictures from Brueghel and Other Poems* (1962: includes *The Desert Music,* 1954, and *Journey to Love,* 1955)
RI	*A Recognizable Image: William Carlos Williams on Art and Artists,* Bram Dijkstra, ed. (1978)
SE	*Selected Essays of William Carlos Williams* (1954)
SL	*Selected Letters of William Carlos Williams,* John C. Thirlwall, ed. (1957)

ACKNOWLEDGMENTS

I am deeply indebted to Douglas L. Peterson at Michigan State University for his editorial help in the early stages of this book and his conviction that its premises would bring a fresh perspective to many of Williams' most familiar poems. I am also grateful to my colleagues John Manion, Mark Van Aken, and Marcelline Krafchick for reading portions of the work in progress and to James Breslin at Berkeley, who graciously agreed to read a stranger's lengthy manuscript and who gave me good advice on making it more publishable. Finally, I am grateful to my wife, Carol, for her editorial help and encouragement, as well as for her tolerance of having the kitchen table so often spread with books, draft pages, and folders.

Grateful acknowledgment is given to New Directions Publishing Corporation for permission to quote from the following copyrighted works of William Carlos Williams: *The Autobiography of William Carlos Williams.* Copyright 1948, 1951 by William Carlos Williams. *The Build-Up.* Copyright 1946, 1952 by William Carlos Williams. *Collected Poems: Volume I, 1909–1939.* Copyright 1938 by New Directions Publishing Corporation. Copyright © 1982, 1986 by William Eric Williams and Paul H. Williams. *Collected Poems: Volume II, 1939–1962.* Copyright 1944, 1953. Copyright © 1962, by William Carlos Williams. Copyright © 1988 by William Eric Williams and Paul H. Williams. *The Embodiment of Knowledge.* Copyright © 1974 by Florence H. Williams. *I Wanted to Write A Poem.* Copyright © 1958 by William Carlos Williams. *Imaginations.* Copyright © 1970 by Florence H. Williams. *In the American Grain.* Copyright 1925 by James Laughlin. Copyright 1933 by William Carlos Williams. *Many Loves & Other Plays.* Copyright 1948 by William Carlos Williams. *Paterson.* Copyright © 1946, 1948, 1948, 1949, 1958 by William Carlos Williams. *Pictures from Brueghel.* Copyright 1954, 1955, 1962 by William Carlos Williams. *A Recognizable Image: William Carlos Williams on Art and Artists.* Copyright © 1978 by the Estate of Florence H. Williams. *Selected Essays.* Copyright 1954 by

IDEAS IN THINGS

It isn't what he *says* that counts as a work of art, it's what he makes. . . .
> —W. C. Williams, "Author's Introduction" to *The Wedge*

It is substance that makes their work important. Technique is part of it—new technique; technique is itself substance . . . but it is the substance under that, forming that, giving it its reason for existence which must be the final answer and source of reliance.
> —W. C. Williams, "Caviar and Bread Again"

1

WILLIAMS: A VISIONARY POET

Despite his claims that he had nothing to do with metaphysics or philosophy, William Carlos Williams was nevertheless something of a closet Platonist, deeply rooted in a platonic-based romantic tradition, including the militantly individualistic and optimistic American transcendentalism. In the foreword to his *Autobiography,* Williams writes: "We always try to hide the secret of our lives from the general stare. What I believe to be the hidden core of my life will not easily be deciphered." The evidence indicates that this hidden core is platonic—the result perhaps of sublimated eros, but still platonic. In the same paragraph Williams states "that from [sexual desire] arises the drive which empowers us all. . . . In the manner in which he directs that power lies his secret."

The "secret" that Williams refers to appears to have its origin in a childhood religious experience or moment of illumination— a modern version of Jonathan Edwards' "divine and supernatural light," but without religious belief attached to it. This unforgettable illumination occurred much earlier than the more often discussed "nameless religious experience" that Williams described to Marianne Moore, and it persisted through the temporary despair of the later experience. Williams alludes to this early moment in both poems and prose. In his essay "Revelation" (1947), he writes that when a child

> through fortuitous circumstances . . . can preserve some rare, unblemished area of the first revelation hidden in his secret heart, it is there that he will live and most beautifully blossom. . . . It is in fact the history of everyone that his whole infancy is spent in a mad attempt to rescue what he can for himself from his first revelation. (*SE* 270)

The "first revelation" is represented in the image of light in "Choral: The Pink Church":

> the thrust of that first light
> was to me
> as through a heart
> of jade

And in *Paterson,* it is "a first beauty," a platonic "flower within a flower" (*P* 22).

Williams comes close to disclosing his "secret" in his play *A Dream of Love,* in which Doc (easily identifiable as Williams) is trying to justify his infidelities as the consequence of a search for a supreme beauty glimpsed, for example, in women. The language here stresses the transcendent nature of beauty:

> He interests his wife in this—she follows his vision—or she does not. She joins him—or she doesn't—in the search for that divine beauty which is not theirs, to be sure, but moves them both together—or it does not. It is supremely detached from their acts, from all infidelities. It stands in the full light, APART. (*ML* 210)

Doc then recalls being confused during his school days about the nature of the thing that haunted him and that he feared to lose. Its chief enemies were the authority exerted by "our masters, who suppress us," and "the fake of sex." "And this something else in my mind grew and grew, mushroomed up in me until I was a small-time Emerson of ideas and determinations gone sour" (*ML* 203). The only person, he feels, who could have given him some reassurance about the "something I instinctively wanted" was "my baldheaded Sunday School teacher, poor guy—who used to read from Plato's Dialogues to us. If I could only have known what his poor dried-up life found there in those days!" (*ML* 203). Williams, the schoolboy, could not respond to the abstract language in which the platonic vision was presented: "He couldn't put it over—not in the way I wanted it put over" (*ML* 203). Any acceptable account of a transcendent beauty would have to do justice to the immediacy of its presence: "Damned if I knew what it was. How could I—it was right in front of me?" (*ML* 203).

The platonic sense of an ideal Beauty is only one component of Williams' vision, for he was a man very much in time and of the world, but, thanks to his sense of the ideal, not imprisoned by time and place. Williams is not the simpleminded imagist he has often been taken for, content to celebrate the immediacy of experience. Like his romantic and transcendentalist predecessors—especially Coleridge, Wordsworth, Emerson, and Whitman—Williams was a visionary poet with an intuitive sense of ideal value beyond but also within the world that appears to the senses. The romantic and transcendentalist influences on Williams are manifest in the life-affirming mood of his work. Pleasure, gratitude, curiosity, wonder, trust—these are the fundamental emotions in Williams' poetry, encompassing anger and despair. But his basic optimism, along with his lively sensory response to the world he lives in, is more than a matter of mood or temperament. It is an integral part of a deeply thought-out worldview: an organic vision of man and nature, of the human potential that can be realized through the imagination as it allows the creative individual both a fuller participation in nature and yet a freedom from naturalistic determinism. Furthermore, Williams' organicism involves an attempt to reconcile the reality of the flux with the reality of permanent and transcendent universal essences.

The question of Williams' relation to romantic and transcendental idealism is still a live issue, as the following survey of critical responses to Williams' work shows. This survey will place the present approach to Williams in perspective, for it is contended here that Williams' body of work as a whole, and individual poems in particular, take on a special richness of meaning when read in the light of his complex idealist vision.

As early as 1946, Vivienne Koch noted that the "cultural roots of Williams' upbringing were closer to Emerson's transcendentally oriented Unitarianism" than to any other tradition.[1] But most criticism in the following decades, including Koch's book-length study of Williams in 1950, did not follow Koch's lead into a thoroughgoing investigation of the latent transcendentalism in Williams' work.[2] When Williams' debt to Emerson has been acknowledged, it has usually been for Williams' self-reliant individualism or his insistence on seeing the "thing" freshly, not for any metaphysical idealism.

With some exceptions, critics in the 1960s formulated the dominant image of Williams as a thorough antiromantic empiricist and democratic celebrant of this world. Kenneth Burke, for example, saw Williams' "observations about animals or things" as essentially "statements about notable traits in people,"[3] but Burke did not press further into the question of whether such metaphorical resemblance was arbitrary or whether it was based on an Emersonian sense of correspondence rooted in a unity of being. Richard Macksey claimed that all that remained of Williams' early "romantic idealism" was "a certain generosity and spontaneity of the affections," while "any transcendence beyond the immediate field of experience is unthinkable."[4] Macksey does see a transcendence of sorts in Williams' emphasis on the poem as an object in itself: "The poem . . . alone promises a momentary stay against the ceaseless cycle of change."[5] But, while there is a strong element of aestheticism in Williams, to view his poems as providing "mastery"—a term used often in Macksey's essay—"over the sprawling chaos of universal flux" seems both to limit the cognitive functions of Williams' poetry and to view him as essentially a dualist, like Robert Frost.

Perhaps the most influential treatment of Williams as antiplatonic and antitranscendental is to be found in Joseph Hillis Miller's *Poets of Reality* (1965). Here Miller noted a special "drama" in Williams arising from the poet's struggle to bring into equilibrium three contrary elements of the universe: the "formless ground, origin of all things"; the "formed thing"; and beauty, "a nameless presence hidden in all things." Miller describes the "ground," the ultimate source of all being, as "chaotic, senseless, absurd, but fecund, holding within itself the possibility of all forms." It is both "generative source" and "drag toward formlessness"—paradoxically the origin of form but "radically opposed" to form, although "any form must continue to draw its energy from the living earth."[6] Miller sums up this dilemma by saying that "the achievement of form of whatever sort is subject to a double jeopardy. If the generative urge remains buried in the earth, it is not form at all . . . but as soon as it rises altogether free of the ground it becomes a hollow shell."[7] The reason conventional forms become empty has to do with the third element of Williams' cosmos, the "nameless presence," or beauty,

> present in the ground but invisible, and present too in every form but covered up as soon as the form gets fixed in a shape. Only in the moment when the flower rises from the ground is a brief glimpse of the presence released. For this reason validity lies in the process of flowering and not in the flower full blown.[8]

Miller's perception of a three-part cosmos—ground, form, presence—provides a valuable insight into Williams' world. But Miller acknowledges no traditional precedent for Williams' cosmology, though such precedent, as shall be seen, is clearly there—in romantic and transcendentalist thought and their platonic antecedents.

By denying Williams' roots in the romantic tradition, Miller neglects important features of Williams' cosmos, as well as of his poems. For example, although it may be implicit in Miller's discus-

sion of the "ground," Miller does not explicitly state that one of
Williams' deepest assumptions about the universe is that it is, as
A. N. Whitehead has argued, alive throughout and permeated by
a teleological drive (Eros) in man and nature toward self-realiza-
tion. This assumption is present in "Spring and All," "Rain," "The
Injury," "A Unison," and other poems.

Miller also ignores the organic correspondences between man
and nature and between one part of nature with another, as in
"Flowers by the Sea" or "The Botticellian Trees," correspondences
testifying to the unity and harmony of the universe—not, as will
be argued later, merely to the power of the human mind to *impose*
resemblances and analogies. Instead of noting interrelationships,
Miller stresses only Williams' focus on objects in isolation. Thus,
in his otherwise illuminating commentary on "Young Sycamore,"
Miller states that the tree

> is an object in space, separated from other objects in space, with its
> own sharp edges, its own innate particularity. The tree stands "be-
> tween" the pavement and the gutter, but there is no assertion of an
> interchange between the three objects, no flow of an ubiquitous na-
> ture-spirit binding all things together.[9]

It is true that there is no obvious interchange between man-made
pavement or gutter and the living tree, but there is, as Miller
acknowledges, an interchange between Williams and the tree: "the
tree is described as though its life were taking place inside his
own life," and the poem "is an object which has the same kind of
life as the tree."[10] But the creative force that generates both the
"undulant thrust" of the tree and the poem inspired by it is no
isolated force but rather the same that, in "Spring and All,"
"quickens" the interrelated mass of mud, water, decayed leaves,
seeds, and shrubs to new growth and brings definition and unconscious volition to matter that "grips down and begins to awaken."

As for gutter and pavement, there is, at some deep level in
Williams' thinking, no absolute separation between so-called animate and inanimate matter (see chapter 5). Nowhere in Miller's
extensive analysis is there any mention of water trickling in the
gutter or the fact that the pavement is "wet," details that have at
least a slight degree of suggestiveness in so far as the image of
water (one of Williams' symbols for the "ground," or generative
source) reminds one that the tree does not really exist in isolation
from the rest of the world, although the mind, for the moment,
might focus on its singularity.

Stressing only Williams' focus on the uniqueness and separateness of all things, Miller accordingly construes Williams as a nominalist—one who believes that only particular things or particular moments of perception are real. Consequently Miller, like many critics, ignores the reality for Williams of universal essences—stable, timeless, but active forms within the flux of experience.

While Miller rescues Williams from Cartesian dualism, he distorts Williams' place in American literature by cutting him off from transcendentalist and romantic predecessors. As a result, he can treat Williams only as a kind of revolutionary celebrant of sensibility. Miller accords Williams' work the highest praise because it "expresses, quietly and without fanfare, a revolution in human sensibility."[11] This revolution consists in Williams' having arrived at a position not only beyond Cartesian dualism, which places consciousness and physical reality into separate spheres, but also beyond the romantic effort to bridge the separation by finding a spiritual presence in nature or by finding the phenomena of nature to be symbolic of a spiritual reality. In Miller's view of Williams, there is simply no longer any subject/object distinction. The self and the world are not separate; there is only "one realm" and "space and the mind are identical."[12] This total fusion of self and world in the monism that Miller attributes to Williams supposedly leaves nothing for the mind to transcend to: "since there is no 'behind' or 'beyond' in Williams' world, no depth or transcendence, there can be no symbolic meaning in things, no reference to a secret heaven of ideal values."[13] Yet Miller brings back into this detranscendentalized world something extraordinary and not easily attained: "The ultimate source of measure is no longer a transcendent God. It is an immanent presence, the radiant gist hidden everywhere in the soil, manifesting itself differently every time a new form emerges from the dark."[14] Williams, for Miller, therefore represents a complete break with the past, not only with the tradition of Cartesian-Lockean dualism but also with the subsequent romantic effort to overcome this dualism.

Miller ignores, however, the extent to which the encompassing unity he attributes to Williams—based on the "ground" as the common origin of all things, including consciousness itself—was central to the experience and thinking of many of the romantic poets. Coleridge, for example, says of the poet that "his spirit . . . has the same ground with nature."[15] Miller also neglects the extent to which the "rare presence" points to a dimension of transcendence, an object of desire and striving in Williams as in the Romantics.

Evidently, the view of Williams as a poet of things, a poet of the isolated moment, seems to be undergoing a change. Hyatt Waggoner's *American Poets: the Puritans to the Present* (1968) was atypical in its treatment of Williams as being in the Emersonian camp. Waggoner presented Williams as a poet divided by the anti-romantic modernism of Pound and Eliot and a more deeply felt, more authentic side of himself that had strong affinities with Emerson and Whitman. Although Williams does go so far in one poem, "A Unison," as to be "thoroughly Emersonian . . . in spirit and theme and attitude,"[16] Waggoner stops short of ascribing a transcendental metaphysics to Williams: "Except for Whitman's religious views and his Transcendental metaphysics, most of what William James said about Whitman could be said about Williams."[17]

In his more recent treatment of Williams in *American Visionary Poetry* (1982), Waggoner includes a small portion of Williams' poems as belonging to a visionary mode that begins in *literal* seeing but includes "the positive implications of better, deeper, truer, more imaginative perception, with the consequent discovery of patterns of meaning and value not easily perceived by most of us most of the time."[18] The patterns of meaning that Waggoner finds in Emerson, Whitman, Williams, Roethke, and Ammons turn out to be characteristic of the "Romantic and post-Romantic phenomenon,"[19] for the Romantics sought to replace the mechanistic-dualistic view of mind and nature with an organic and unitary vision, "thus narrowing the Descartean gulf between the two, between perceiver and perceived."[20]

Waggoner, however, persists, wrongly it would seem, in denying any metaphysical commonality between Williams and Whitman and Emerson; yet Waggoner's own analysis of "Spring and All" as countering "the 'alien universe' and 'dead nature' notions that haunted so many of his contemporaries,"[21] implicitly imputes a common metaphysical ground that Williams shares with his romantic and transcendental predecessors, namely the assumption of a living universe. In fact, one could carry it a step further and say that Williams finds not only "life and value implicit in nature,"[22] but also sentience and intelligence that form a continuum between the natural and the human. Thus, while Waggoner's view of Williams as in the Emerson-Whitman tradition is wholly in accord with the treatment of Williams in this book, it is necessary to show that the tradition involves underlying metaphysical assumptions for Williams, and not just values and attitudes.

Joseph Hillis Miller's more recent discussion of Williams seems to involve something very like the idealism in Williams that his earlier writings denied. (In fact, even in Miller's original discussion of the generative force of nature and imagination and of a *universal* beauty revealing the world's plenitude, there are the seeds of an interpretation that goes counter to his main thrust.) In *The Linguistic Moment* (1985), Miller seems even closer to some version of idealism. Miller states that the purpose of his book is to search "for a ground within, beneath, above, before, or after time, something that will support time" and thus be "a ground beyond language for the linguistic patterns present in my [chosen] poems."[23] Miller, in effect, attributes a theological dimension to this ground when he personifies it as "some anonymous power of or in language that is urgently affirming its need to establish a strange sort of 'I-thou' relationship with the reader." He adds that in Williams "this compulsion to . . . allow the words to write themselves through the poet is a little like glossolalia."[24] Miller finds in the "curious immediacy" of Williams' words as jostling, dynamic "objects"—apart from their referential or mimetic function—a manifestation of a "nameless" something that makes the poet and the poem its instrument.[25] Miller's affirmation of this "ubiquitous force"[26] does not seem compatible with his earlier assertion (repeated verbatim in *The Linguistic Moment*) that in Williams' poetry there is "no flow of an ubiquitous nature-spirit binding all things together."[27]

James Breslin is another Williams scholar whose stance towards Williams has undergone a notable change. In *William Carlos Williams: an American Artist* (1970), Breslin had declared Williams to be part of the modernist "repudiation of the romantic ego and the idealistic philosophy that supports it."[28] But in the preface to a 1985 reissue of his book, Breslin believes that "a sacred principle clearly resides at the center of Williams' poetics."[29] Furthermore, in *From Modern to Contemporary* (1984), Breslin states, with evident approval, that the *value* which Denise Levertov finds in Williams' fragmentary imagistic poems presupposes "some external (and prior) framework from which it derives," a framework that "she has come to identify . . . as 'supernatural.'"[30]

The most compelling evidence of a changing view of Williams, however, has been Carl Rapp's *William Carlos Williams and Romantic Idealism* (1984), which places Williams in an idealist tradition that includes Hegel, Coleridge, and Emerson and reaches back to

Plato and to aspects of Christianity. Rapp's interpretation is much closer to the one presented in this book—except for one crucial difference: Rapp regards Williams (and Emerson) as a subjective idealist: "It is the subject that constitutes the essence of the object."[31] According to Rapp, Williams' Emersonian position, while allowing him to "countenance an extraordinary interest in the ... phenomenal world," turns out to be a "thoroughly consistent egoism in which the soul makes everything into a vehicle for itself."[32] Williams' closeness to things is the result not of abandoning ego (as Miller believes) but of expanding ego "to the point where it now contains everything within it."[33] This, however, sounds less characteristic of Williams than of Whitman who, in section 33 of "Song of Myself," describes his expansive self in gigantic terms: "my elbows rest in sea-gaps, / I skirt sierras, my palms cover continents." Whether the self expands to include everything or whether, through an outgoing, noninterfering empathy (which Miller ascribes to Williams), the self becomes part of everything is perhaps only a matter of accent or emphasis within a basically monistic perspective. Nevertheless, the language Rapp uses in discussing Williams often makes him seem unattractively solipsistic.

Rapp's central insight is that, for both Emerson and Williams, the soul has priority over things. Rapp argues that, on the one hand, Williams "needs appearances, for they are the means whereby he comes to know himself"; the "world becomes intensely interesting ... because it ... is capable of reflecting back to him the depths of his own mind."[34] On the other hand, the mind must avoid the idolatry of mistaking any particular reflection of itself as final: "In contemplating the nature of its own transcendence, the ego must also insist that nothing in the phenomenal world is really adequate to represent that which exceeds all phenomena—namely, itself."[35]

This point is well made, but in developing it Rapp often makes Williams seem narcissistic in his appropriation of phenomena for his own purposes without regard to the intrinsic qualities or values of the things so used. He likewise neglects the extent to which Williams' "precursor"—Emerson—valued the intrinsic qualities of things as playing their part to give delight and instruction to man. Like Wordsworth, who believed that what the eye sees and the ear hears is half created, half perceived, Emerson affirms a dialectic between man and nature. In part 1 of *Nature*, Emerson speaks of how the woods and fields give him a delightful sense of correspondence between the human and the natural: "Yet it is certain that the power to produce this delight does not reside in nature, but in man, *or in a harmony of both*"[36] (italics added).

And in "The American Scholar" Emerson describes how "the young mind" develops by "discovering roots running under ground whereby contrary and remote things cohere and flower out from one stem" and by "perceiving that these objects are not chaotic, and are not foreign, but have a law which is also a law of the human mind" (65–66).

The seeming egocentricity Rapp finds in Williams is significantly modified when he summarizes Williams' belief "that in coming to know itself, the mind may also come to know the nature of mind in general or the nature of the one mind, which is God."[37] One of the most important claims Rapp makes is that Williams

> did come to believe in the existence of something like a universal spirit or a universal mind in which all finite minds necessarily participate. Though he generally shied away from using terms like "God," he was still impelled to acknowledge the ultimate source of his own creative power in language unmistakably associated with religious mysticism.[38]

Granted that Rapp has touched upon the central (and hidden) assumption behind Williams' work, it does not follow that a belief in the universal mind relegates external nature to the arbitrary use of the individual human mind. If man is to "come to know . . . the nature of the one mind," the objects of creation must be seen as *objectively* manifesting charm, charisma, uniqueness, vitality, interesting formal features—qualities that might arouse wonder in the viewer's mind.

But Rapp, construing Williams as a subjective idealist, rejects the common view that Williams' imagist poetry is "a defense of the independence and objectivity of that which has been described."[39] Instead, "the imagist poem has little or nothing to do with the intrinsic importance of the things themselves. Rather it signalizes a momentary intensification of the mental powers of the poet."[40] Close description is not "undertaken for the sake of the persons and objects described," but "as a method of indirectly indicating the emotions of the person doing the describing."[41] The "objective correlative" in Williams really becomes a subjective correlative, "object-ive" only in that objects are used to externalize unparaphrasable emotion: "Williams seizes the object of his immediate attention . . . and identifies it as the perfect receptacle of his innermost feelings."[42] Thus Rapp approvingly finds "pathetic fallacy" in many of Williams' poems. In "Spring Strains," for example, the "blue-grey buds" are "erect with desire."[43]

Rapp's view of Williams leads to a kind of tautology: if the mind is not constrained by the intrinsic qualities of those phenomena it uses as occasions to display its own power or to objectify its emotion, then every poem winds up meaning the same thing. Perhaps this is why Rapp discusses so few of Williams' poems in any detail; the real subject of the poem is always the poet's exercise of the unique power within him. Granted that the external world provides a way for Williams to know himself and ultimately to know the larger mystery of which he is part, nevertheless it is important that Williams discover something extraordinary about the objective character of the phenomenal world in order to better know the rare mystery that it manifests.

Furthermore, Williams' immediate, intense response to an object is often linked to or has as its background a coherent view of nature. To take the example of the buds "erect with desire," the image is not merely an objectification of Williams' own sexual feelings at the moment, so that the image is, as Rapp says any Williams Imagist image is, "merely . . . the end point of an action which cannot, by the very nature of the case, appear *within* the poem and of which the poet himself is the protagonist."[44] An alternative view is proposed here: that the "desire" is *in* the buds and is a manifestation of a force that the Greeks mythologized as Eros and that Williams sees as the basic creative energy in man and nature, although manifest more complexly in man than in nature. If it can be shown that Williams celebrates the power of Eros in many different poems (and in prose), then the "image" becomes less the random and arbitrary equation of the poet's momentary emotion and more a component in a symbology that reflects a well thought-out view of nature (see chapter 5).

According to this view, Williams is not wholly or consistently a subjective idealist. A more accurate account of Williams' position is provided by Alfred North Whitehead's notion of "objective idealism." Whitehead differentiates objective idealism from both "subjective idealism" ("the dependence of the world of sense on the individual percipient") and "realism" (based on the assumption of a fundamentally material universe from which "cognitive mentality" is excluded):

The distinction between realism and idealism does not coincide with that between objectivism and subjectivism. Both realists and idealists can start from an objective standpoint. . . . In the past, the objectivist position has been distorted by the supposed necessity of accepting the classical scientific materialism, with its doctrine of simple location.[45]

For Whitehead, the universe is *ideal* in that it is not made of life-less, mindless matter. Furthermore, whatever name is given to its substance, the universe has an *objective* character of its own, and this character can in some sense be known because consciousness and the external world do not occupy separate spatial locations:

> my theory involves the entire abandonment of the notion that simple location is the primary way in which things are involved in space-time. In a certain sense, everything is everywhere at all times. For every location involves an aspect of itself in every other location. Thus every spatio-temporal standpoint mirrors the world.[46]

Whitehead's objective idealism, in which consciousness does not constitute the essence of the world and yet is an integral part of the world in which perception takes place is, it would seem, a more accurate account of Williams, who refers often to a dialectic between himself and external reality as when he says, for example, of a man's relation to the city that it is "an identity . . . / an / interpenetration both ways" (*P* 3).

While Rapp's identification of Williams with romantic idealism marks an important shift from viewing Williams merely as a poet of things, or a poet exclusively of immanence, Rapp goes too far in negating the importance of things-in-themselves in order to emphasize the priority of the perceiving mind. Rather than oblit-erating the object in order to assert the priority of mind, Williams most typically regards nature and the external world as, initially, something other than himself, so that contact with otherness brings excitement, shock, discovery, or exhilaration, as in "Sea-farer" and "Labrador" (discussed in chapter 2). But ultimately Williams finds a basis of oneness with the other—a common ground.

Like Emerson, the fountainhead of organic-transcendentalist thought in American literature, Williams holds basically to an or-ganic conception of the universe. In Emerson's cosmology, both the Me (human consciousness) and the not-Me (external world) are embodiments of a living third substance or fundamental activ-ity—a World Spirit or Oversoul that inexhaustibly overflows into and through man and nature, linking the two in a spiritual bond. Williams, in commenting on St. Francis of Assisi as someone awake to the immediate presence of nature, makes a rare explicit state-ment of the spiritual cosmology he shares with Emerson. In "the word of God," Williams says, St. Francis found "a common stem where all were one and from which every paired characteristic branched" (*SE* 28). Since these paired characteristics—inclusively mind and matter—originate from a common source, the relationship between them is not arbitrary. Nature is an index to mind, and both are manifestations of their common source.

But the bond between them could be broken, as Emerson emphasized, by "specialization," a reductive attention to limited aspects of both self and nature. "A man is a god in ruins," Emerson said in *Nature*, and "the blank that we see when we look at nature, is in our own eye" (53, 55). Similarly, Williams states that "the so-called . . . scientific array becomes fixed, the walking devil of modern life," and the result is a form of "despair" (*SE* 11–12). The thrust of Williams' poetry, as will be demonstrated, is an effort to unfix the "scientific array," the mechanistic view of the universe, and thus to overcome despair. Williams recovers much of the idealism of Emerson and Whitman, but brings it into a tougher modernistic medium that all but disguises the spiritual vision at the core of his worldview.

Another clue to Williams' underlying (or overlying) transcendental idealism is to be found in *Poems* (1909), his first book of poems, self-published and derivative in style. A brief glance at the cliché romanticism of this premodern book highlights the idealism buried in his later modernist poetry in which ideal value is located in unexpected particulars. In *Poems,* the ideal and the real exist in two separate realms, and poetry is considered a means for entertaining thoughts of the ideal and for providing a beauty of the imagination that is lacking in the real world. While some of the early poems express delight in the conventionally picturesque aspects of nature—"December in a weave / Of blanched crystal," "lush high grasses," "gaudy winged flies"—others assert that the things of earth are imperfect and that perfection is to be sought elsewhere. In "The Folly of Preoccupation," Williams urges his reader to contemplate perfection in God, who sees all imperfections but stands above them:

> Yet to man's eyes, He who, all these can see,
> Constrained to throb in just apportioned space,
> Should all-pervading perfection be.

The "all-pervading perfection" of God will be replaced in Williams' modernist poetry with epiphanies of a rare presence that flames out in such unlikely situations as "a semcircle of dirt-colored men / about a fire bursting from an old ash can" (*CPI* 101). Another early poem, "The Bewilderment of Youth," supports the

notion of a transcendent absolute. According to this poem, man
is "perplexed by detail in his youth" and "amazed, unknit / By
wonder" at the "fresh variety" of things in the world. But the
mature man finds out that "these but aspects are of scant things
true." As he ages, he is less engrossed with the particular beauties
of the world and comes to contemplate, as Socrates had urged in
Plato's *Symposium,* an absolute beauty:

> Until he sees, when life is almost done,
> These final few go mingling into one.

In these early poems, poetry itself is a way of turning from the
imperfect actual world to contemplate an ideal that exists only in
the imagination. In "The Uses of Poetry," Williams imagines a
pleasant day spent reading "a lady poesy" while they glide on a
"leafy bay" and take in the charming sights of nature. But then,
lest their rural peace be spoiled by imperfections, they will "close
the door of sense" and "wend, / On poesy's transforming giant
wing, / To worlds afar whose fruits all anguish mend." One can
hardly imagine the later Williams—whose "bony nose" delights in
the odor of "souring flowers"—wanting to "close the door of
sense"! After his "nameless religious experience" dispossesses Williams of his early genteel idealism, he comes to disdain "those
who permit their senses to be despoiled of the things under their
nose by stories of all manner of things removed and unattainable"
(*SE* 15).

The naive, escapist idealism expressed in *Poems* (1909) was soon
to be submerged in the vivid actualities of the everyday world and
expressed in a contemporary idiom and a semiprivate symbolism.
Yet Williams' intoxication with platonic beauty did not end with
the transformation of himself from a Keatsian-imbued idealist to
a twentieth-century modernist influenced by the earthiness of
Whitman, the imagist concreteness of Pound, and the revolutions
in modern painting. Rather, beauty was now to be sought within
the immediate sensory experience of local realities. Nevertheless,
beauty continued to have, even in its new immanence, a transcendent dimension for Williams as it had had before—only now its
manifestations derived less from romantic literature and more
from life, and from a wider area of life than his genteel poems
had been capable of absorbing. Furthermore, the static idealism
of his early youth was transformed into the more evolutionary
organicism of his modernist poetry according to which beauty
was revealed in the processes of growth and creation.

Besides being influenced by Whitman, Pound, and the movements in modern painting, Williams' style was also undoubtedly
affected by his personal circumstances: the realities of a medical
internship in a city hospital, disappointment in a romantic infatuation, and a kind of redemption-in-reverse that Williams referred
to as his "nameless religious experience," a kind of despair he
experienced when he was twenty-two and that left him with a
sense that "heaven was impossible"—that there was nothing but
the actual world before his eyes. His new style—colloquial, disjunctive, and often symbolic—all but disguised the fact that, despite
the despair, the idealism was still with him, that there was, for lack
of a better phrase, a spiritual dimension to his worldview.

As the following chapters should make more clear, Williams
inherits the romantic conception of man and nature—an organicism imbued with idealism. Emerson, both directly and through
Whitman, is an important influence on Williams. Just as Emerson
called the ultimate ground of being "oversoul" to remove much
of the anthropomorphic and theological connotation associated
with "God," so Williams—by calling the living origin "ground"
and symbolizing it by such fundamental aspects of nature as earth,
soil, ocean, and clouds—removes it even further from theological
associations. It is the premise of this interpretation of Williams
that he sought to name "divinity" with other words, to find a
language for the perennial experience of ultimate mystery that
in the past had generated a God-language—which in turn became
institutionalized, abstract, and empty. This interpretation of Williams places him as continuing what M. H. Abrams calls "the Romantic endeavor to salvage traditional [religious] experience and
values by accommodating them to premises tenable to a later
age."[47]

The remaining chapters of this book are an exposition of Williams' largely implicit romantic-transcendentalist assumptions
about man and nature. This book is not a chronological study of
Williams' development as an artist, nor is it primarily an influence
study (though many parallels are drawn between Williams and his
key predecessors). Rather, it is devoted to an exposition of the
different components of Williams' largely implicit romantic idealism and how this worldview is manifest in particular poems. Chapter 2, "Overcoming Dualism," deals with Williams' sense of kinship
or unity with nature, in opposition to the inherited scientific world
picture that has left modern man feeling estranged in an alien
universe. This chapter also deals with the role imagination plays
in creating a renewed perception of the external world and thus

in discovering the universal in the immediacy of fresh contact
with concrete particulars. Chapter 3, "Language and the Renewal
of Perception," is a study of Williams' stylistic innovations as an
outgrowth of his view that the poetic imagination, working
through the medium of words, gives man a renewed perception of
value in the universe—of "ideas" in "things." Here again Williams
continues the romantic program of renewing the world dulled
to the senses by habit and deprived of value by the mechanistic
assumptions of pre-Einsteinian science. Chapter 4, "Imagination:
A Force of Nature," turns from the cognitive function of the
imagination to its creative function. This chapter discusses Williams' theory that the imagination advances the creativity of nature itself, producing poems that are not merely statements about
or copies of existing reality, but new "objects" added to the totality
of things that exist. It includes a study of poems in manuscript
to demonstrate the working principles by which Williams' imagination took the formless matter of raw experience and shaped
it into the formed poem. Chapter 5, "Nature: An Overview of
Organicism," deals with Williams' vision of the universe as alive
and, in some sense, purposeful—not entropic or totally alien. Like
Emerson, Williams sees correspondences between man and nature
that serve as a basis for metaphor and symbol. And though he
sees the visible universe as an evolving process, it is a process
through which shine permanent universals. Chapter 6 concludes
with a look at the very latest poems of Williams' old age when he
seems to have retreated from the confident transcendentalism of
his main years to an aestheticism in which art is asserted to be
the only order that man can know, although even within this aes-
theticist stance, elements of the earlier transcendentalist faith
still linger.

2

OVERCOMING DUALISM

1. Alienation and the Dualist Legacy

One of the long-range effects of Cartesian dualism has been the modernist sense of cosmic isolation—a mood that Hyatt Waggoner finds epitomized in the wonderfully apt expression, "the cosmic chill." The phrase comes from John Burroughs, who wrote at the end of the century: "Feeling, emotion falls helpless before the revelations of science. The universe is going its own way with no thought of us. . . . This discovery sends the cosmic chill, with which so many of us are familiar these days."[1] While Waggoner discusses E. A. Robinson as the first important modern American writer to reflect the cosmic chill in his work, the prospect of an indifferent universe exerted its pressure on subsequent modern writers either as a condition to be tragically resigned to, retreated from, or resisted and fought on grounds other than those laid down by nineteenth-century science. Robert Frost, for example, expressed the chilling view of an alien universe in such poems as "Design," "An Old Man's Winter Night," "Acquainted with the Night," and "The Most of It," a poem in which the protagonist, crying out for a human response from nature, is greeted only by brute reality—"a great buck" that "stumbled through the rocks with horny tread, / And forced the underbrush."

The cosmic chill appears in fiction too. F. Scott Fitzgerald's Gatsby, after his dream fails—and therefore fails subjectively to infuse his universe with life and value—looks upon a "new world, material without being real."[2] More recently, Saul Bellow's narrator in *Humboldt's Gift* attributes the modern disease of boredom to "lack of a *personal* connection with the external world":

> I wasn't seeing what was there but only what everyone sees under a common directive. By this is implied that our world-view has used up nature. The rule of this view is that I, a subject, see the phenomena,

the world of objects. . . . The educated speak of the disenchanted (boring) world. But it is not the world, it is my own head that is disenchanted. The world *cannot* be disenchanted.[3]

Bellow's narrator complains that he is screened off from nature
by "a common directive," perhaps the dualism that since the sev-
enteeth century, has so insinuated itself that it has come to seem
the commonsense view. Separated from nature, the Cartesian ego
of modern man, the "I," has become too dominant and self-impos-
ing in perception, so that, as Bellow's narrator complains, things
do not "speak to him about themselves."

According to Joseph Wood Krutch, the combination of dualism
and scientific materialism had created a crisis of values for the
modern age. Krutch felt that mankind had neither fully absorbed
nor courageously faced the consequences of dualism and materialism. Science offered no objective verification of values that former generations had deemed essential for human nobility: "The
world [of values] which our minds have created to meet our desires and our need exists precariously and on sufferance: it is
shadowy and insubstantial for the very reason that there is nothing outside of itself to correspond with it."[4] Given empirical and
quantitative verification as the only criteria for truth, one is left
with a bifurcated universe: consciousness and its created world of
culture versus the alien material processes of nature.

All modern writers of major stature have confronted the threat
to human values posed by the loss of traditional meaning—by the
nothingness that lies behind the impressive facade of Progress,
waiting to leap out, like James's beast in the jungle, as a huge
emptiness. However, few major writers have been willing to accept
the loss of value as irrevocable fact or to accept consciousness as
absolutely confined to itself. T. S. Eliot persisted through the
doubt and longing of *The Waste Land* to a chastened faith in the
Logos, the transcendent-immanent principle that makes the
world intelligible. But Eliot's belief in an ultimate order led him
to the enshrinement of that order in institutional worship. Yeats,
influenced by the visionary Blake, wanted to reach an ideal order
through an aestheticism employing occult symbols by means of
which he felt he could communicate with spiritual reality. Wallace
Stevens represented the opposite response. While he often celebrated the nominalist's vivid sense of the particular, he could
never quite bring himself to believe that a principle of transcendent order informed the external world, organizing particulars into
a coherent whole. As a nominalist, he believed that order had to

be supplied by the mind in the form of a "supreme fiction" that could become either an individual or a collective myth and could be accepted as such without guarantee of its objective status.

William Carlos Williams took a position different from Eliot's transcendent but institutionalized Logos, from Yeats's occult symbolism as means of reaching the Ideal, and from Stevens' wholly subjective (although perhaps collective) imagination—derived from Coleridge but without Coleridge's religious belief that both nature and the human imagination were embedded in the divine. Williams, however, shared with his contemporaries their realization that science had undermined the spiritual foundations of Western man. Williams was a trained physician and respectful of science within its limited area, but he rejected the notion that science could explain all that is essential about nature and ourselves.

Perhaps of all the major modernists, Williams was willing to let things speak for themselves, to bridge the gap between the self and the world. He characteristically respects the objective existence of nature—a premise that he shares with science; but he goes beyond science in his conviction that objects perceived with sympathetic imagination reveal *value*—a quality that science, since Descartes, has increasingly relegated to subjective status. Approached with the right kind of attention, things and people reveal to Williams a special beauty and worth, "not for him alone," as Bellow's narrator complained, "but also for them." While Williams appreciates the independent status of nature, he intuits a larger unity embracing both man and nature—a unity that the imagination can grasp and, in so doing, can also grasp values which are potentially present in things. Williams' complex sense of oneness with a nature that has its own objective existence and integrity might be substantiated by a close examination of several poems.

"At Night" (*CP1* 251), for example, establishes that nature has an existence apart from humanized perceptions of it:

> The stars, that are small lights—
> now that I know them foreign,
> uninterfering, like nothing
> in my life—I walk by their sparkle
> relieved and comforted. Or when
> the moon moves slowly up among them
> with flat shine then the night
> has a novel light in it—curved
> curiously in a thin half-circle

To a disillusioned romantic or a naturalist, such as Sylvia Plath, the stars might be reminders only of the cold indifference of the universe, but Williams feels a quiet and satisfying wonder in the face of their alien beauty. The poem gains much of its effect from a deliberately flat diction and unromantic attitude. Williams avoids metaphor here because the stars are "like nothing / in my life." Whereas a romantic poet or a religious mystic, regarding the stars as divine wonders, might be uplifted and reassured, Williams paradoxically is "relieved" of the burden of beholding the stars through the accumulated weight of romantic diction and expectations. He need not make an effort to possess what he sees in nature or to reach beyond appearances to spiritual reality.

Were we to define Williams by this one poem alone, we might agree with Miller that Williams is not a romantic. Although Williams does express a tone of romantic wonder and delight, he does not postulate either a sense of oneness with nature or a transcendent realm beyond appearances. But even a romantic who desires, like Wordsworth or Emerson, to find something akin to human presence in nature recognizes an alien aspect that is necessary to complement what Emerson called nature's "consanguinity." If nature had no independent existence, it could not be an influence on the mind: "the first in importance of the influences upon the mind is that of nature" (65). Further, although Emerson dwelled on the "radical correspondence between visible things and human thoughts" (33), he also stressed the importance of seeing nature accurately in itself so that the correspondences, or analogies, would be just. Williams, too, wants to keep mind and nature as two distinct but related realities: "Nature is the hint to composition not because it is familiar to us . . . but because it possesses the quality of independent existence, of reality which we feel in ourselves" (*I* 121). Recognizing the independence of nature frees and encourages the poet to find his own independence, not by trying to copy the external forms but by imitating the inner creative energies behind the appearances of nature. Or as Williams says, it is only through the imagination that a work of art "escapes plagiarism after nature and becomes a creation" (*I* 111).

While "At Night" shows Williams' respect for the foreignness of nature, other poems celebrate an interchange between mind and nature, an experience in which the barrier between inner and outer worlds seems to be overcome. This kind of mind-matter relationship, common to romantic poets, was most strikingly formulated by an early progenitor of romantic thought, the German idealist F. W. Schelling:

> If consciousness were something absolutely inward and no unmedi-
> ated contact between it and outward things could be conceived, we
> would find that we do not at all see things outside of us . . . but that
> we simply see them in ourselves. If this were so, there could be no
> possible separation between inner and outer worlds. And since inner
> is only distinguishable in contrast to outer, the inner along with the
> outer world would unavoidably collapse.[5]

The passage first emphasizes that consciousness is not "absolutely inward," but is spread outward, occupying, so to speak, the same space as things themselves. Such interpenetration of mind and thing, a basic premise of organicism, makes possible an "unmediated contact" with external reality. But Schelling adds that there must also be a "separation" between consciousness and outward things in order to guarantee the integrity of both. Respect for the reality of things-in-themselves is necessary to avoid a complete collapse into solipsism.

Williams' poem, "Sea-Trout and Butterfish" (*CP1* 353), illustrates the romantic paradox of separateness within unity and the consequent excitement the mind has in perceiving something other than itself, yet part of the totality that includes the mind itself:

> The contours and the shine
> hold the eye—caught and lying
>
> orange-finned and the two
> half its size, pout-mouthed
>
> beside it on the white dish—
> silver scales, the weight
>
> quick tails
> whipping the streams aslant—
>
> the eye comes down eagerly
> unravelled of the sea
>
> separates this from that
> and the fine fins' sharp spines

By themselves, the first four couplets comprise an imagist poem—the kind of poem that embodies a special moment of perception in a vivid image, as if the poet were trying to fuse himself with the object perceived. The last four lines, however, extend the moment into a more reflective consideration of the mind/object relationship; they illustrate in small compass what Wordsworth meant when he proclaimed how "exquisitely" the mind and the external world are "fitted" to each other.[6] The objects—the fish on the white plate—"hold the eye" with a special fascination. The eye comes "down" because, as in John Dewey's words, "Experience . . . reaches down into nature; it has depth," bridging the distance between perceiver and perceived.[7]

The vividness, accuracy, and excited, disjunctive order of the details are testimony to the eye's direct contact with the thing it sees and, even deeper, with what the philosopher Whitehead would call its "intrinsic reality" and the poet Hopkins would call its "inscape." What excites Williams here is a quality that is of no practical use to the scientist, the fisherman, or the food vendor, although it is an actual quality of the thing observed. This quality is what Kant, according to Mary Warnock, calls an "aesthetic idea" or "finality."[8] Warnock's *Imagination,* a study of the role that imagination plays in the acquisition of knowledge, is helpful toward understanding Williams' lively, imaginative response to things as having intrinsic worth. According to Warnock's explanation of Kant, the beauty one perceives in a natural object or a work of art results from the object's having an intrinsic design, as if it had been put together in a purposeful way but not for any utilitarian purpose:

> *Something* can be envisaged and represented by imagination as that feature of the object which makes us say it is beautiful, even though that something is not something which falls under any known scientific category, nor is it to be referred to an external end or function. . . . In general, finality means intelligibility; it means an object's seeming significant, but not of anything outside itself.[9]

The objects in many of Williams' poems are not symbols, but have their own intrinsic interest. Not only do the fish in "Sea-Trout" stand out in their separate individuality, but particular features—"the fine fins' sharp spines"—are isolated for special appreciation. The vividness of detail is evidence that the mind has encountered something real outside itself and has a true perception of that reality. But more is involved than sensory realism; through the senses the poet has apprehended the object's inner form, its fittedness of parts. This intrinsic design, which excites pleasure in the poet, is as real as any of the object's physical or quantitative qualities. Furthermore, the beauty the poet experiences is potentially there for everyone; it is not merely subjective ("in the eye of the beholder"). Again, Warnock's comments on Kant are relevant to this point:

> For we expect, and to some extend demand, that if we judge an object to be beautiful . . . other people shall agree with us. There is a kind of universalization, or objectivity, implied in our use of what Kant regards as the central aesthetic word "beautiful", which, while it entails the existence of pleasure in ourselves, entails much more besides.[10]

What excites Williams in "Sea-Trout" as much as the object itself is the way the mind, through sense perception, reaches down into things and the way things reach out to be taken up and vividly realized in the mind. The poem is as much about the mind as it is about the natural facts upon which the mind seizes. It asserts that the mind knows itself more fully as it "unravels" the reality of which it is, in some potential sense, already a part. The key to this reading of the poem is the tenth line in which the "eye" is said to be "unravelled of the sea." The line is syntactically confusing, for one would normally expect the sea to be unravelled *by* (not *of*) the eye. The eye, after all, has "unravelled," or isolated, the sea trout from the butterfish and the entire group on the white dish from its surroundings. Yet to have the sea unravelled *by* the eye would be to give external reality (the sea) a passive role in perception and imply a total separation between eye and sea. Williams' unusual syntax is very likely a way of implying that the "eye" is already, in some sense, a part of that which it unravels: it is "of" the sea of total reality. The metaphor implies that the perceiving eye itself becomes disentangled, or focused and clarified, in the act of perception.[11] Since self and world are interpenetrating dimensions of each other, knowledge of the world is in some way knowledge of the self. To unravel, in the figurative sense of the word, is to separate and clarify the elements of something baffling or mysterious. There is a discipline involved in aesthetic perception, a discipline of attention, and the goal is ultimately a kind of knowledge.

The eagerness the mind has for a reality independent of itself can be further illustrated by two related poems, "Seafarer" and "Labrador," both of which involve images of the sea. The independent status of perceiver and object, each with a tropism for the other, makes their coming together in perception an exhilarating event (one reason for the frequent exclamations in Williams' poetry). In "Seafarer" (*CP2* 114) man is symbolized as the "rocks" jutting out into the sea and washed over by the waves:

The sea will wash in
but the rocks—jagged ribs
riding the cloth of foam
or a knob or pinnacles
            with gannets—
are the stubborn man.

He invites the storm, he
lives by it! instinct
with fears that are not fears
but prickles of ecstasy,
a secret liquor, a fire
that inflames his blood to
coldness so that the rocks
seem rather to leap
at the sea than the sea
to envelope them. They strain
forward to grasp ships
or even the sky itself that
bends down to be torn
upon them. To which he says,
It is I! I who am the rocks!
Without me nothing laughs.

Although nature takes some initiative—the sea washes in on the
rocks, and the sky bends down to them—the primary active force
is the human consciousness symbolized by the sturdy but sentient
rocks which are "instinct / with fears that are not fears / but prickles of ecstasy." Without initial separation and difference to be
overcome, the encounter between knower and known would not
be the invigorating, dramatic experience that it is. Furthermore,
as the final assertion proclaims, nature as well as man is more fully
actualized in perception: "Without me nothing laughs." Laughter
here is a symbol of fulfillment. (In the Prologue to *Kora*, Williams
claims that "laughter is the reverse of aspiration," in a context
wherein laughter is the accompaniment of fulfillment [*SE* 15]).
In the poem, Williams' choice of *nothing* rather than *no one* is
deliberate, to indicate that nature reaches its fullest realization
and expression in human consciousness.[12]

A passage in Emerson's essay "Nature" (*Essays: Second Series,*
1844) may well be the unconscious source for some aspects of
tone and imagery in this poem:

We come to our own, and make friends with matter, which the ambi-
tious chatter of the schools would persuade us to despise. We never

can part with it; the mind loves its old home: as water to our thirst, so is the rock, the ground, to our eyes, and hands, and feet. It is firm water: it is cold flame: what health, what affinity![13]

To Emerson's enthusiasm for contact, Williams adds also a tone of defiance and self-assertion. Though Emerson's "rock" (matter) becomes, reversely, Williams' symbol for consciousness, Emerson's rock metaphorically takes on the qualities or effects of Williams' sea of reality: "It is firm water: it is cold flame."

Whereas in "Seafarer" man is present as the "stubborn rocks," in "Labrador" (*CP2* 124) man is a bather in the sea of reality:

> How clean these shallows
> how firm these rocks stand
> about which wash the waters of the world
>
> It is ice to this body
> that unclothes its pallors
> to thoughts
> of an immeasurable sea,
>
> unmarred, that as it lifts
> encloses this
> straining mind, these
> limbs in a single gesture.

"Labrador" is less triumphant and defiant in tone than "Seafarer," but it more clearly emphasizes the unity that obtains between mind and reality. The "waters of the world" are "ice"—bracing, invigorating, incapable of not being felt—"to this body / that unclothes its pallors / to thoughts / of an immeasurable sea." An earlier title given to the poem, "The Bath,"[14] makes explicit the metaphor of the poem: man or the mind bathing in the sea of reality.

Williams' use of the sea here is opposite that of Wallace Stevens in "The Idea of Order at Key West" where the singer-poet, though within proximity of the sea, imposes a separation between herself and it: regardless of the sea's intrinsic nature, it becomes "the self / That was her song, for she was the maker." Order here is imposed on nature, rather than discovered after an initial immersion in otherness. Stevens' singer walks *beside* the sea; Williams' perceiver is bathed *in* it. Consciousness, as Williams conceives it, is eager for the naked embrace of the sea, and the sea itself is in some active sense willing to oblige. Consciousness without immediate contact with things as they are would be a pallid solipsism. The sea, for Williams, sometimes represents the totality of things and, at other times, the ultimate source of these things, the "formless ground" in Williams' three-part cosmos. It is akin to William James's concept of "Pure Experience" or Schelling's *natura naturans*—the primal, active, living unity from which both matter and consciousness arise: the sea "encloses this / straining mind, these / limbs in a single gesture."

2. Philosophical Precedent for the Ground

Images of unity are frequent in Williams, some of them in rather strange poems. For example, in "The Avenue of Poplars" (*CP1* 228), Williams says:

> He who has kissed
> a leaf
>
> need look no further—
> I ascend
>
> through
> a canopy of leaves
>
> and at the same time
> I descend
>
> for I do nothing
> unusual . . .

This sense of fusion with nature (where even "the leaves embrace") is not "unusual," because man and nature are part of each other through the common ground they share. To "ascend" into the "wordless realm" of nature through a feeling of oneness with it is not to enter a void, but to "descend" back into the expansive self. That is, abandoning oneself to nature is not "unusual" since it is self, or part of self. In another poem, "Winter Quiet" (*CP1* 84), Williams describes the mist making love to the earth: "limb to limb, mouth to mouth." The ground (female) "has humped / an aching shoulder for / the ecstasy." The bizarre sexual imagery of this poem expresses the exhilaration of contact and unity with nature. Similarly, in "January Morning" (*CP1* 100), the sky (male) comes down to kiss the waters (female): "exquisite brown waves."

In both poems, images of sky or mist uniting with earth or sea suggest the romantic "marriage" of man and nature (and perhaps an even older myth of the union of Uranus and Gaia).

The unity Williams suggests in these and other poems has its precedent in the romantic reaction to the disunity resulting from Cartesian dualism. Philosophically, what distinguishes Williams from Yeats, Frost, Eliot, and Stevens but links him to Pound, Whitman, Emerson, and Coleridge is his belief that human creative powers are an extension of nature's, that "the work of the imagination [is] transfused with the same forces which transfuse the earth" (*I* 121). Through this belief, or ingrained assumption, Williams not only sweeps aside Cartesian dualism, but also empowers himself as a poet and gives a kind of cosmic sanction to his endeavors.

Descartes's separation of mind and matter into unrelated entities had created an almost insuperable obstacle to the human desire to know reality, for there is an axiom in philosophy that only "like knows like." If Descartes is right, there is no way for objects to come within the "space" of the mind nor for the mind to initiate actions in the field of objects. But poets and philosophers of the organic view of reality feel that there is something false in thinking of mind and matter as absolutely separate.

Schelling, for example, by establishing that perception was an activity of nature but transcending nature, provided a fruitful approach to the problem of dualism; and Schelling's view of man and nature as copresences within a living, organic unity was influential in shaping romanticism in general. According to Frederick Copleston, Schelling tried to show how "Nature is . . . a unified dynamic and teleological system which develops upwards, so to speak, to the point at which it returns upon itself in and through the human spirit."[15]

Just as Williams often sees nature as a symbol and source of human creativity, so Schelling, according to John Herman Randall, found in nature a vital link with human life,

> . . . something already able to respond to man and his purposes, something whose impulses he can both imitate and bring to a happy fruition. The subject does not "oppose" its object, it actualizes and fulfills what is potential in it. And when Schelling . . . went on to find this human Self intelligible and significant only as manifesting a larger Self and a deeper Life, Nature too had to be an expression of the same Life that appears in man.[16]

Schelling's view that the generative force in nature, *natura natu-*

rans, reaches its highest expression in human consciousness is central to romantic thought. According to Coleridge, for example, the artist, instead of merely copying the external forms of nature *(natura naturata),* "must master the essence, the *natura naturans,* which presupposes a bond between nature in the higher sense and the soul of man"; therefore, "genius must act on the feeling, that body is but a striving to become mind,—that it is mind in its essence!"[17]

Schelling's "unified dynamic and teleological system" and Coleridge's *natura naturans* are essentially the same as Williams' "forces" that transfuse both the earth and the imagination. And Coleridge's notion—in W. J. Bates's explanation—that "man's mind serves as a focal point at which the unfolding processes of nature can become awake"[18]—has its counterpart in Williams: ". . . in great works of the imagination A CREATIVE FORCE IS SHOWN AT WORK MAKING OBJECTS WHICH ALONE COMPLETE SCIENCE AND ALLOW INTELLIGENCE TO SURVIVE" (*I* 112).

Williams goes on to say that a true work of imagination "lives anew" by its "power TO ESCAPE ILLUSION and stand between man and nature as saints once stood between man and sky" (*I* 112). Williams' "CREATIVE FORCE" is present both in nature, as *natura naturans,* and in man, as the power of the imagination. The works of authentic imagination form a bond between man and nature as saints once mediated between man and heaven. The result of the creative process in Schelling, Coleridge, and Williams is also a greater fulfillment of nature itself, or in Williams' words:

> Thus a poem is tough by no quality it borrows from a logical recital of events nor from the events themselves but solely from that attenuated power which draws perhaps many broken things into a dance giving them thus a full being. (*SE* 14)

Schelling's view of nature, besides its influence on early nineteenth-century romanticism, anticipated and perhaps influenced similar views held by William James and Alfred North Whitehead, whose modern organicist thinking provides a further context for understanding William Carlos Williams. James, for example, in order to solve the problem of how an object can be located in space and yet be "in" the mind that perceives it, derived both mind and object from a fundamental process he called "Pure Experience." James used the term to suggest that the ultimate ground of being was neither matter (as the materialists held) nor a static absolute (as the idealists held), but something like experience itself, or the flow of consciousness—a process. To explain how something apparently "out there" could be perceived "in here," James used the example of a person sitting in a room and perceiving the room and its contents. How could one account for the "paradox that what is evidently one reality should be in two places at once, both in outer space and in a person's mind"? To resolve the paradox, James compared the room to a geometrical point—as having a double existence at the intersection of two lines:

> and similarly, if the "pure experience" of the room were a place of intersection of two processes ... it could be counted twice over ... and spoken of loosely as existing in two places, although it would remain all the time numerically a single thing. ... In one of these contexts it is your "field of consciousness"; in another it is "the room in which you sit," and it enters both contexts in its wholeness.[19]

James's view of both the room and consciousness as coinciding or interpenetrating processes—rather than the room as a static, bounded, impervious thing and consciousness as a mirror reflecting it—anticipated Whitehead's philosophy of organicism with its rejection of "simple location."

Whitehead's organicism, like that of Schelling and James, places perception within nature; it does not make perception, as Locke did, a mirroring act in which an unknowable external substance impresses "ideas" of itself on a passively recording mind that then knew the ideas but not the things-in-themselves. Whitehead abandons the notion of "simple location" according to which consciousness is located inside the head and objects exist outside that consciousness:

> In a certain sense, everything is everywhere at all times. For every location involves an aspect of itself in every other location. ... You are in a certain place perceiving things. Your perception takes place where you are, and is entirely dependent on how your body is functioning. But this functioning of the body in one place, exhibits for your cognisance an aspect of the distant environment. ... If this cognisance conveys knowledge of a transcendent [objective] world, it must be because the event which is the bodily life unifies in itself aspects of this universe.[20]

Whitehead finds the doctrine of interpenetration "extremely consonant with the vivid expression of personal experience which we

find in the nature-poetry of imaginative writers such as Wordsworth and Shelley. The brooding, immediate presences of things
are an obsession to Wordsworth." Whitehead denies that "cognitive mentality," mind itself, is all one knows in perception; instead,
he asserts that the unity of mind and object is "now placed in an
event."[21] Implicitly rejecting Kant, Whitehead says that it is not
the mind, considered as a separate entity, that imposes its order
on impulses received from nature, but that both mind and nature
are processes unified in the "event" of perception.

To abandon the notion of "simple location" is to depart from
Locke's long-standing view that secondary qualities (smell, color,
sound, tactile qualities) do not exist in things but are produced in
the mind by "powers" in the object affecting the mind:

> Such Qualities . . . in truth are nothing in the Objects themselves, but
> Powers to produce various Sensations in us by their *primary qualities,*
> i.e., by the Bulk, Figure, Texture, and Motion of their insensible parts,
> as Colors, Sounds, Tastes, etc.[22]

Today, the textbook explanation of sight, for example, is essentially
a more scientific version of the Lockean view. One distinguishes,
say, the color green from the frequency of light waves that strike
the retina, sending impulses through the optic nerve to the brain
where they are "interpreted" as color. Hence one thinks that green
is only the subjective experience of neural activity, that it is only
an illusion that the color is located in the leaf, which in itself is
colorless and quality-less. Nature, as Ishmael speculates, "paints
like the harlot whose allurements cover nothing but the charnel-
house within." For Whitehead, however, the green, since it is an
"eternal object," or platonic form, has more than one "mode of
location"; it really is in the leaf and, in the act of perception, in
the mind too.

James's location of perception at the "intersection" of simultaneous aspects of "pure experience" and Whitehead's in the "unity
of an event" has its counterpart in Williams' view of perception as
"interpenetration": "the city / the man, an identity—it can't be /
otherwise—an / interpenetration, both ways" (*P* 3). Interpenetration (the eye unravalled "of" the sea) is possible because mind and
nature exist in a common "ground." As noted earlier, Williams in
one instance identifies the ground with God: "The only possible
way that St. Francis could be on equal footing with the animals
was through the word of God. . . . Here was a common stem where
all   were   one   and   from   which   every   paired   characteristic

branched" (*SE* 28). It is noteworthy that Williams here uses organic imagery ("stem," "branched") to suggest that both matter and consciousness, the most fundamental of the "paired characteristics," are not radically divorced from their origin nor totally alien to each other. Williams intuitively holds a view of consciousness consistent with those more systematically set forth by William James and Alfred North Whitehead, according to which mind and external reality, neither one reducible to the other, occupy the same "space."

The conception of the perceiver as in some sense already one with the context in which perception takes place helps to clarify an otherwise strangely obscure ending to a poem called "Wild Orchard" (*CP1* 239), in which, after a description of a particular apple tree as "a formal grandeur," the unidentified narrator adds:

> Among the savage
>
> aristocracy of rocks
> one, risen as a tree,
> has turned
> from his repose . . .

The rock—already seen as an image of the stubbornness and durability of consciousness in "Seafarer"—is a person, probably the narrator, who is very much a natural part of the scene observed. His transformation from "rock" (inanimate) to "tree" (animate) suggests the interpenetration of consciousness and matter. The ability of the "rock" to rise and move after its unconscious immersion in nature ("repose") marks off its distinctiveness from the rest of nature. This provisional dualism within the larger monism is necessary in order for there to be perception at all.

3. Innocence: The Descent into the Ground

Williams believes that a kind of innocence is a necessary precondition for maintaining contact with the "ground" as it manifests itself in immediate sensory awareness. In an essay called "The Importance of Place," Williams holds that the ground, although inaccessible to knowledge, can at least be approached if one's mind is in the right "place":

> There is a certain position of the understanding anterior to all systems of thought, as well as of fact and of deed—that is common to

all: it is that in which the thinker places himself on the near side of reality—abjures the unknowable and begins *within* a certain tacitly limited field of human possibility to seek wisdom. (*EK* 132)

The "near side of reality" would be reality in its simplest, least mediated state—such as a child might perceive—but still real and palpable, not totally undifferentiated and beyond human perception.

Very early in his career Williams realized the importance of maintaining an innocent sense of wonder. In his premodernist *Poems* (1909), Williams pledged himself to "innocence" and "simplicity," words that formed the titles of the first two poems in the book. In the first poem, Williams declared that innocence and wonder kept one in touch with "mystery," and he hoped that "wonders" would "still with age increase." His wish was largely fulfilled. Williams knew, even in 1909, that some part of himself must be kept free from enculturation, from what Wordsworth called the "shades of the prison house," and that an innocence— not of ignorance but of trust and humility—would be his weapon and his ally.

Many later poems attest for Williams that innocence makes possible a deeper plunge into the sea of immediate sensation, the raw source against which, and with which, culture and knowledge are built. In "The Sun," innocence is the virtue by which children, playing near the sea, "go / down past knowledge" into "the penetrable / nothingness"—the sea of pure experience—"whose heavy body / opens / to their leaps / without a wound" (*CP1* 446). In "The Visit," the gulls, representing the "naive,"

> dip
> into the featureless surface.
> It is fish they are after,
> fish—and get them.
>
> (*CP2* 130)

The intimate identification with things, the sense of sure contact with the outer world that is the mark of Williams' poetry, seems to have its psychological origin, as several critics have noted, in a kind of religious experience, which Williams explained in a letter to Marianne Moore. Moore had recognized the "inner security" evident in Williams' work, by which she meant, apparently, the poet's firm sense of knowing who he was and exactly how he felt at any given moment. The experience leading to this inner security

involved an abandonment of an ideal or transcendent realm beyond the senses. "The inner security," he told Moore, was the
result of

> something which occurred once when I was about twenty, a sudden
> resignation to existence, a despair—if you wish to call it that, but a
> despair which made everything a unit and at the same time a part
> of myself. I suppose it might be called a sort of nameless religious
> experience. I resigned, I gave up. I decided there was nothing else in
> life for me but to work. . . . Things have no names for me and places
> have no significance. As a reward for this anonymity I feel as much a
> part of things as trees and stones. Heaven seems frankly impossible.
> (*SL* 147)

If this is a religious conversion, it is in a direction away from
"heaven" or the notion of some postmortal happiness. Instead of
the joy normally expected to follow conversion, there is despair—
at the realization that the actual is all that is left, that there is no
ideal realm (or so Williams felt at the time) transcending the actual. But, by desiring no mystical transport from the world of
senses, Williams finds himself at home everywhere, "a part of
things as trees and stones," like the rock that rises from "repose"
in "Wild Orchard."

The abandonment of "heaven" in this "nameless religious experience" coincides with another abandonment Williams made in
his early or midtwenties when he gave up his shy pursuit of Charlotte Herman for her plainer but sexually attractive sister, Florence. In *The Build-Up,* Williams gives a fictionalized account of his
disappointment at being rejected by Charlotte, followed by his
abrupt proposal on the rebound to the younger sister. Throughout the novel, Charlotte has been associated with genteel romanticism—through her music, her "mysterious" beauty, her physical
ethereality, her dark hair, and her nostalgia for the romantic Germany of Beethoven. Her sister, on the other hand, is more down
to earth and has "shapely legs," a feature mentioned often in the
narrative. Williams' persona declares that he is not "in love" with
her, but they can be happy without romantic love. He is through
with romance; the love he offers would be, like the resignation he
describes in the letter to Moore, "founded on . . . a passion of
despair, as all life is despair." Although "difficult" to achieve, it
would not be lacking in passion; it would be "passionate, passionate as one says of a saint" (*BU* 262).

If this fictional portrayal accurately reflects the poet's state of
mind circa 1909, it indicates that Williams was ready to turn away

from both the poetic conventions of nineteenth-century poetry and its genteel notions of conventionally picturesque beauty. Williams turned from the romantic yearning for the infinite typical of much of Shelley, Keats, Poe, and Hart Crane to a more earthbound romanticism typified by Wordsworth and Whitman, a romanticism emphasizing that the most common objects and events might reveal the blessedness that the more platonized idealist seeks beyond the world. Like Wordsworth, Emerson, and Whitman—who represent not the negations of otherworldly romanticism but rather a *via affirmativa*—Williams committed himself to discovering the ideal in the actual. Giving up both the diluted romantic diction of *Poems* (1909) and the exalted conception of romantic love meant abandoning the search for happiness in narrowly idealized portions of experience—the dreamy picturesqueness of genteel nineteenth-century poetry and the aching infatuation with a beautiful but unattainable woman.

The most decisive evidence of the change that was occurring roughly between 1909 and 1914 in Williams' attitude toward language, beauty, and reality is the poem "The Wanderer" (first published in *The Egoist,* March 1914), in which Williams, using a blank verse modified by the influence of Whitman, describes symbolically the "nameless religious experience" and his resignation to an unidealized reality as a plunge into the polluted Passaic River, or as a mutual interpenetration of river and consciousness:

> "Enter, youth, into this bulk!
> Enter, river, into this young man!"
>
> Then the river began to enter my heart,
> Eddying back cool and limpid
> Into the crystal beginning of its days.
> But with the rebound it leaped forward:
> Muddy, then black and shrunken
> Till I felt the utter depth of its rottenness
> The vile breadth of its degradation
> And dropped down knowing this was me now.
>
> *(CP1* 116)

This is not merely the literal Passaic, but also the river of life and consciousness that enters each heart in purity and innocence until the shock of experience causes it to "rebound and leap forward" into the imperfect actualities of existence. The baptism is both disheartening—in that it cuts off access to a conventionalized realm of the ideal—and exhilarating—in that it opens up new areas of experience for the poet who, initially, finds only crude energies in the common world and common people: "Nowhere / The subtle! Everywhere the electric!" (*CP1* 111). Later he will find the "subtle" (the rare presence in things), and, reciprocally, there is promise that the river of unidealized life, now that it has absorbed its poet, will be enriched: "Live, river, live in luxuriance / Remembering this our son" (*CP1* 117). The river of life, an outpouring of whatever nameless source, reaches its most conscious level in the poet.

4. The Revolt against Scientific Materialism

The human relation to nature is, for Williams, inadequately understood without the imagination—the faculty or activity of the mind that makes possible a richer comprehension of both inner and outer reality than science can give. Like the romantics before him, Williams distinguishes between a superficial or empty perception of reality given by scientific abstraction and a deeper, more complete knowledge given by the imagination, a mode of perception that grasps the object whole, with its own charm and beauty. Although Williams came to reject romantic diction and versification, his opposition of the poetic imagination to scientific rationalism establishes him as continuing what Whitehead calls "the romantic reaction" to the mechanistic science that resulted in the clockwork universe of the eighteenth century. With some modification, one can say of Williams what Whitehead says of Wordsworth, that "in his whole being [he] expresses a conscious reaction against the mentality of the eighteenth century." Wordsworth's felt experience of nature convinced him that in scientific description "something had been left out and what had been left out comprised everything that was most important."[23] The omissions included the "mysterious presence of surrounding things" (the way the whole of nature seems to be present in any one part), the "value" of an object as "being an end in itself," and the "aesthetic intuitions of mankind," which resisted the abstractions of science.[24]

Williams, too, feels that the scientific method, with its "gross and minute codifications of the perceptions" (*I* 305), leaves something out. He frequently objects to what Whitehead calls the "fallacy of misplaced concreteness," a perceptual error in which those qualities of things abstracted and formulated by science come to stand for the whole of the thing itself. In Williams' words:

The senses witnessing what is immediately before them in detail see a finality which they cling to in despair, not knowing which way to turn. Thus the so-called natural or scientific array becomes fixed, the walking devil of modern life. He who even nicks the solidity of this apparition does a piece of work superior to that of Hercules when he cleaned the Augean stables. (*SE* 11–12)

Williams' witty and apt oxymoron ("solid apparition") undercuts both the scientific and the habitual commonsense view of reality in so far as these presume that the most usable or measurable features of nature are the only real ones. The difference between the scientific and the poetic perception of reality is what Williams has in mind when he says that

. . . certain laws discovered by analysis, arranging themselves in more gross forms are called "truths," and can be expressed in words and other trite terms but . . . the more impalpable laws felt are called "beauty," and cannot be expressed in words as terms but must be symbolized with direct figures. (*EK* 167)

The fuller truth of nature cannot be expressed in formulas or in words used discursively as "terms," but must be expressed symbolically with "direct figures" (images, metaphors), and this requires the operation of imagination.

5. Imagination and the Renewal of Perception

Williams' trust in the imagination's ability to free perception from custom, including the custom of science, links him with what Abrams sees as a program essential to the Romantics: to remake the world by seeing it with freshened perception. This desire for renewal, according to Abrams, accounts for "the extraordinary emphasis throughout the era on the eye and the object and the relation between them."[25] For the Romantics, "the perception of a new world was the criterion of success in life."[26] Abrams identifies three particular but interrelated modes of perception prized by the Romantics in their progress of transforming "a discrete, dead, alien milieu into a human, integral, and companionable milieu in which man finds himself thoroughly at home."[27] These modes—"visual transvaluations," "moments of illumination," and "freshness of sensation"—are all found in Williams' poetry.

Transvaluations, or reversals of value, are an obvious aspect of Williams' poetic world in which the sparrow is exalted over the

nightingale and the street cleaner, over the Episcopal minister—
and in which common objects and people are seen to possess
dignity, worth, and beauty. Abrams argues that such transvaluations as Wordsworth's elevation of beggars, farm maids, and ordinary flowers to exalted status are a secularized version of
transvaluations in Scripture where the meek are blessed and the
last shall be first.[28] Williams' transvaluations include aspects of
nature that Wordsworth might never have appreciated, as when
Williams praises a rotting apple—"what a / deep and suffusing
brown / mantles that / unspoiled surface" (*CP2* 80). Williams, like
Whitman in his time, extends this romantic attitude to new aspects
of contemporary life:

> Things, things unmentionable,
> the sink with the waste farina in it and
> lumps of rancid meat, milk-bottle tops: have
> here a tranquility and loveliness
> Have here (in his thoughts)
> a complement tranquil and chaste.
>
> (*P* 39)

Romantic transvaluations, according to Abrams, involve the discovery of "sublimity" and "charismatic power" in the lowly and
the common.[29] A good example of this is Williams' "The Dance"
(*CP2* 58), which holds in tension the almost demonic energy of
the sturdy peasants and their sense of pride and worth as human
beings who "prance as they dance."

Moments of illumination also occur throughout Williams' poetry, often signaled and symbolized by images of light when the
third element of Williams' cosmos, the "hidden flame," reveals
itself at unexpected times—in people, objects, music, and gestures.
According to Abrams, these special moments are those "in which
an instant of consciousness, or else an ordinary object or event,
suddenly blazes into revelation."[30] These "gleams" or "spots of
time," as in Wordsworth, are essential to the romantic poet's sense
of liberation from the inherited scheme of a mechanistic universe,
a view imposed by science and built up by stale habits of thought.

Freshness of sensation requires that accustomed ways of perceiving the world be subverted so that new attributes and perspectives might emerge. The classic statement on freshness of
sensation, according to Abrams, is Coleridge's account in *Bio-
graphica Literaria* of Wordworth's primary aim in the 1798 *Lyrical
Ballads*. What Coleridge has to say about Wordworth in chapter

XIV amounts to an apt description of Williams' intentions as well:
". . . to give the charm of novelty to things of every day, and to
excite a feeling analogous to the supernatural, by awakening the
mind's attention to the loveliness and the wonders of the world
before us."[31] When Coleridge's statement is placed beside the following passage from Williams, one sees how closely Williams identifies with romantic aims:

> The true value [of a work of art] is that peculiarity which gives an
> object a character by itself. The associational or sentimental value is
> the false. Its imposition is due to lack of imagination, to an easy lateral
> sliding. . . . The imagination goes from one thing to another. Given
> many things of nearly totally divergent natures but possessing one-
> thousandth part of a quality in common, provided that be new, distin-
> guished, these things belong in an imaginative category and not in a
> gross natural array. . . . But the thing that stands eternally in the way
> of really good writing is always one: the virtual impossibility of lifting
> to the imagination those things which lies under the direct scrutiny
> of the senses, close to the nose (SE 11)

Poetry has value when it reveals the familiar in an unfamiliar way,
when it reveals, as in metaphor, the unexpected "one-thousandth
part in common" between two unlike things, provided that this
quality be "new, distinguished." The passage continues with the
portion previously cited, about the senses clinging in despair to
the accustomed or scientific "array." While it is theoretically impossible to have a completely unconditioned response to things—
to be free of all memory and cultural influence—yet the unconditioned response remains an ideal for freeing consciousness, like
a tiny aperture admitting glimpses of reality beyond the barriers
of custom and closed systems of thought. The imagination, in its
freedom from temporal and spatial order, allows at least some
element of novelty to enter into one's perception of the world.

According to Abrams, the great obstacle faced by the Romantics
in their desire for reawakened vision was habit or custom:

> The prime opponent-power is "custom"—what Wordsworth in The
> Prelude repeatedly condemns as "habit," "use and custom," "the regu-
> lar action of the world"—which works insidiously and relentlessly to
> assimilate the unique existent to general perceptual categories.[32]

Likewise, Williams, in Spring and All, maintains that the imagination, in its encounter with life, must contend with the accumulated
patterns that make up "tradition." Tradition is condemned when

it automatically conditions one's responses, although Williams, like
Emerson, finds examples in history of inspired imaginative responses to life (like Pere Rasles's uncondescending contact with
the Abnaki Indians in *In The American Grain*) that inspire people
in the present to seek authentic contact with the ground of their
own experience. Usually in *Spring and All,* however, Williams
speaks negatively of tradition as "repetition," "redundancy," "repression," "the handcuffs of art." Tradition is a prescribed "cur-
riculum"; it is a "rock" that must be split by the "seed" of the
imagination. The chief metaphor for uncritical adherence to tradition is "plagiarism."

While acquiescence in tradition represents one form of
blockage to the creative artist, the mere submission to external
reality represents another form of oppression. Echoing Samuel
Johnson, Williams says it is not necessary "to count every flake of
the truth that falls" (*I* 112). Although description, when used,
should be accurate in order to bring in the actual feel of the
external world, literal or copy realism is not the ultimate aim of
Williams' art. Echoing Coleridge, Williams claims that copying nature produces "sham," "lie," and "illusion." The result is "frustration" and "stupor" of the mind.

For Williams as for the Romantics, the agency of renewed perception is the imagination, a recurrent theme in Williams' prose
works as well as his poems. The imagination—the mind's image-
making capacity—has both perceptual and creative functions. It
is important not because it can weave escapist reveries or conjure
up strange creatures from outer space, but because it can realize
value latent in the actual and therefore can bring one into fuller
possession of experience: "Rich as are the gifts of the imagination
bitterness of world's loss is not replaced thereby. On the contrary
it is intensified, resembling thus possession itself. But he who has
no power of the imagination cannot even know the full of his
injury" (*SE* 15). Implicit in what Williams says is the fact that the
imagination links image to thought and feeling and thus makes
possible the most complete expression of human experience.

Some further sense of what Williams means by the imagination
can be gleaned from the metaphors and terms used in the prose
sections of *Spring and All* and the Prologue to *Kora in Hell,* which,
taken together, comprise Williams' major effort to define the
imagination. Echoing romantic precedent, Williams says in *Spring
and All* that the imagination is a "lamp" (active), not a "mirror"
(passive). Although the imagination is a "farmer" or a "fisherman"
making direct, bare-handed contact with the earth and sky, literal

or copy realism is anathema to it; instead of a "reflection," it creates a "play, a dance."

Implying its transcendental function, Williams personifies the imagination as a "saint" mediating between temporal existence and the "eternal," or as a heroic woman who leads us: "Her feet are bare and not too delicate." Imagination is like a natural force—"comparable to electricity or steam" or, more inclusively, it is a special dimension of nature: "transfused with the same forces which transfuse the earth—at least one small part of them" (*I* 121). The imagination deals with life, with the raw material of perception, figured as a "bizarre fowl" of indefinable color, or as an "ocean" that is too vast to "drink" (to classify into categories and concepts, to grasp by the "acquisitive understanding"). Imagination is associated with "vigor," "accuracy," "enlargement," "invention," "revivification," "dynamization"—with Spring, the New World, and freedom.

The Prologue to *Kora in Hell* stresses the power of the imagination to defamiliarize the object, to see it in its nominalist particularity. The Prologue opens with seemingly inconsequential anecdotes about Williams' mother, but it is soon seen that she exemplifies for him the imagination, especially as it seizes the particular in its immediacy and without preconception. Williams' mother is, in effect, a nominalist:

> If a man cheat her she will remember that man with a violence that I have seldom seen equaled, but so far as that could have an influence on her judgment of the next man or woman, she might be living in Eden. And indeed she is, an impoverished, ravished Eden but one indestructible as the imagination itself. (*SE* 4)

The imagination is indestructible in that, barring extreme pain, one can always use it to return to a state of innocence, at least temporarily; it is also indestructible in that it is common to mankind through all ages.

Williams states that his mother sees "the thing itself without forethought or afterthought but with great intensity of perception" (*SE* 5). Then, without transition, Williams turns from his mother to cubist painting, citing the opinion of Duchamp that "a stained-glass window that had fallen out and lay more or less together on the ground was of far greater interest than the thing conventionally composed *in situ*" (*SE* 5). The implied link between Mrs. Williams' enjoyment of individuals without prejudgment and Duchamp's preference for the broken stained glass is an openness to novelty and a freedom from customary response. Williams distinguishes the "true value"—"that peculiarity which gives an object a character by itself"—from the "associational or sentimental," which "is the false" and which "is due to lack of imagination, to an easy lateral sliding" (*SE* 11). This last statement echoes T. E. Hulme's remark in "Classicism and Romanticism" that fresh, vivid metaphor is necessary "to prevent you gliding through an abstract process."[33] Much of the stream-of-consciousness and dadaist-disoriented writing in *Kora* was Williams' attempt "to loosen the attention, my attention" (*SE* 11), to free himself from the conventionally "associational or sentimental" even at the risk of incoherence and obscurity.

3

LANGUAGE AND THE RENEWAL OF PERCEPTION

1. Liberation of the Word: Theory and Practice

In his attempt to break out of the "handcuffs of art" and to confront the universal in its firsthand immediacy, Williams, like other modern poets, faced the problem of how to evoke uniquely personal experience through a public medium. The desire to force the conventions of language to express the private nature of experience provided the drive behind much of the experimentation in modern literature. Hulme gave impetus to this drive in his early, influential essay, "Romanticism and Classicism," when he claimed that the poet's triumph was in forcing language into combinations that would more nearly allow the individual perception to come through:

> The great aim is accurate, precise and definite description. The first thing is to recognize how extraordinarily difficult this is. It is no mere matter of carefulness; you have to use language and language is by its very nature a communal thing; that is, it expresses never the exact thing but a compromise—that which is common to you, me and everybody. But each man sees a little differently, and to get out clearly and exactly what he does see, he must have a terrific struggle with language.[1]

Hulme, influenced by Bergson, believed that only the image, not abstract statement, could express the fluid, multilayered nature of experience. Precision could be gained by fresh, original metaphor—metaphor used to express an unexpected but apt truth about the thing that excites the poet's attention (as when Herrick uses the metaphor "liquefaction" to describe the complex of aural, visual, and tactile sensations produced by the motions of Julia's "silks").

Also implicit in Hulme's Bergsonian theory of art, according to Donald Davie in *Articulate Energy*, is a subversion of conventional sentence structure, because syntax, when used for clear exposition, fails to suggest "the vital complexities" of things.[2] Thus, many writers felt the need, as T. S. Eliot put it, to "dis-locate language" from its ordinary syntactical grooves and meanings. Perhaps no writer felt this need more urgently than Williams did because of his acute sense of the discrepancy between words and things.

Fundamental to Williams' idea of poetry is the dilemma posed by the fact that *word* and *thing* are two independent realities. In *The Great American Novel* Williams faces this dilemma as he contemplates his task as a writer:

> One must begin with words if one is to write. But what then of smell? What then of the hair on the trees or the golden brown cherries under the black cliffs. What of the weakness of smiles that leaves dimples as much to say: forgive me—I am slipping, slipping, slipping into nothing at all. Now I am not what I was when the word was forming to say what I am. (*I* 158)

Because natural things are filtered through the medium of words, their "smiles" grow weak and leave only dimples of their essence behind. The speaker within the passage, a young girl sitting on a bicycle, personifies the alluring world of things speaking to the narrator, the would-be writer. The moment that he uses language to fix her identity she has already changed into something else. On the other hand, were he to abandon words, he might fully possess her, but at the cost of his own identity:

> But if you take me in your arms—why the bicycle will fall and it will not be what it is now to smile greyly and a dimple is so deep—you might fall in and never, never remember to write a word to say good-bye to your cherries. (*I* 159)

The dilemma here is that, in becoming a writer, one falsifies and therefore loses things by fixing them in words; but not to write means acquiescing in a speechless embrace of unintelligible reality. The solution to this dilemma is to be found by approaching both words and things with a sense of wonder and with a vigilant awareness that one's formulations never exhaust the reality of that which is described. In short, the poet must be willing to "dis-locate" language, to push it beyond complacent public meanings and even

beyond his own creations in order to reattach it to things in new
and unexpected ways.

Williams' way of "dis-locating" language may be discussed under
the heading of what he calls in *Spring and All* "the liberation of
the word." The liberation of the word was an attempt to free
poetry from the overcontrol of literary custom, from the habits
and imprecisions of everyday usage and from the unavoidable
abstractness of language itself. Referring to the effects of custom,
Williams states: "In description words adhere to certain objects
and have the effect of the sense of oysters, or barnacles" (*I* 149).
The more the poet becomes aware that *word* and *thing* are two
independent and separate realities rather than stuck together like
barnacle to ship, the greater sense of freedom he has to make
words express unique perceptions. This is not to say that words
imaginatively used lose all touch with reality: "As birds' wings beat
the solid air without which one could not fly so words freed by
the imagination affirm reality by their flight" (*I* 150). Just as birds'
wings, in contact with air, affirm the existence of this invisible
medium, so the poet's flight of words affirms the existence of an
external reality.

Williams was aware, however, that his theory of words was leading him in the direction of "pure poetry," of Poe's conception of
poetry as approximating the indefiniteness of music. In *The Great
American Novel* Williams, albeit in a self-mocking tone that hints
at the limitations of solipsism, expresses a strong attraction to the
seductions of a completely subjective use of language:

> Everything had been removed that other men had tied to the words
> to secure them to themselves. Clean, clean he had taken each word
> and made it new for himself so that at last it was new, free from the
> world for himself. (*I* 167)

Perhaps to be a true poet one must go through this exhilarating,
solipsistic phase of intoxication with words, which is analogous to
infatuation with an illicit lover:

> He had progressed leaving the others far behind him. Alone in that
> air with the words of his brain he had breathed again the pure moun-
> tain air of joy—there night after night in his poor room. And now he
> must leave her. (*I* 167)

The "her" in this passage is "Miss Word," a humorous personification of langauge as his "poetic sweetheart" in contrast to his
wife, who is sleeping in another room and who represents a re-

sponsible, conventional use of words. When he enters her room to boast of his book completed in his glorious isolation with language, her deflating response is merely, "What did you say, dear, I have been asleep?"

In *Spring and All* Williams' flatly rejects solipsism and with it the equation of poetry with the nonverbal arts: "I do not believe that writing is music" (*I* 150). Such a pure poetry "would use unoriented sounds in place of conventional words. The poem then would be completely liberated when there is identity of sound with something—perhaps the emotion" (*I* 150). Thus, in asserting the independent reality of the word, Williams did not want poetry to lose touch altogether with the public meanings of words or with the commonly perceived external world:

> According to my present theme the writer of imagination would attain closest to the conditions of music not when his words are *disassociated* from natural objects and specified meanings but when they are *liberated from the usual quality of that meaning* by transposition into another medium, the imagination. (*I* 150, italics added)

The distinction between "disassociated" and "liberated" may seem to be a fine one, but it is crucial to Williams' theory. Williams wants to free words not from referential meaning altogether but "from the usual quality of . . . meaning" that comes from lazy usage, stereotypes, and the conventions of art. He is attempting to reconcile the demands of realism with the demands of emotional expression, as well as with the demands of a poem as an aesthetic construct distinguishable from prose.

One way to liberate *word* from *thing* is to intensify one's awareness of the phonic and rhythmic textures of words themselves, to savor the sounds of words and their feel in the mouth. Another way is to have knowledge of the origins and history of words so that one is not tied down to current usage. Williams was not indifferent to etymology, and his poetic practice often shows his awareness of a word's earlier meanings or its multiple meanings, as in his use of the word *term* (termination, limited extent of time, fixed date, provisions of a contract) in the title of the poem that confronts human mortality in the image of the brown paper "about the size and bulk of a man" (*CP1* 451).

Williams' fundamental discipline for liberating the word, however, is through a concentrated attention on his uniquely individual perceptions, an effort carried out in large part by what Hulme describes as the poet's "terrific struggle with . . . words" to get "the exact curve of what he sees whether it be an object or an idea in the mind."[3] Williams, in pursuing his individual appropriation of words, is practicing a form of Emersonian self-reliance, learning "to detect and watch that gleam of light which flashes across his mind from within, more than the lustre of the firmament of bards and sages" (147). As an artist, Williams wants "to drive toward his purpose . . . to make: make clear the complexity of his perceptions in the medium given to him" (*SE* 256). The repetition of the verb "make" indicates that Williams had to *make* something—a poem—in order to *make clear* to himself the exact nature of his perceptions. In making a poem, he would take neither the form nor the words for granted. For Williams, it was necessary to test the received meanings and connotations of words against his own firsthand experience with the objects and ideas that the words referred to. This point is expressed in the awkward but exact final prose statement in *Spring and All*:

> The word is not liberated, therefore able to communicate release from the fixities which destroy it, until it is accurately tuned to the fact which giving it reality, by its own [the fact's] reality establishes its own freedom from the necessity of a word, thus freeing it [the word] and dynamizing it at the same time. (*I* 150)

Paradoxically, the liberation of the word from the thing is also a liberation of the thing, and thus an intensification of one's awareness of it. Philip Wheelwright seems to have something similar in mind when, in *The Burning Fountain*, he states that the imagination provides not only a close, intensified awareness of the particular but also a "distancing"—a disengagement from the object, especially from the "practical commonplace aspect of things" that allows a "sudden view . . . from the reverse unnoticed side."[4] According to Williams, awareness of the immediate reality of the thing must free it from the prejudgment imposed on it by its long-standing and habitual association with a word. This also frees the word. The poet who sees beyond what the word-as-stereotype permits one to see, to qualities as yet unnoticed in the thing itself, is freeing both the object and the word from staleness of perception.

It is this sometimes almost perverse seeing beyond the word-as-stereotype that accounts for so much of the freshness and surprise Williams' poetry offers for the refreshment of one's own sensibilities. The imagist propensity for "direct treatment of the thing" becomes in Williams a way of perceiving things in unusual, unexpected, and contrary ways. Loneliness is happiness in "Danse Russe"; spring arrives, not gloriously with flowers springing up around her golden hem, but "sluggish and dazed" ("Spring and All"); winter is enjoyed as exuberantly as if it were spring ("January Morning"); autumn is personified as a woman of doubtful reputation whose "tawdry veined body" emerges when the garment of summer drops off ("Arrival"). The pastoral in Williams is not made up of shepherds and doves, but street cleaners and sparrows. This kind of perversity in Williams—it is more or less a characteristic of modernist poetry—is part of his serious purpose as an artist: to free perception from habitual, dulled ways of looking at things in order to discover as yet unappreciated qualities, and even to discover the universal manifest in the concrete particular.

2. Free Verse

The most obvious way in which Williams liberates the word is in his use of free verse to accommodate a wide range of subjects and levels of English and to permit visual techniques of spacing that, as Eleanor Berry puts it, "de-automatize the process of reading," thereby opening up fresh perceptions of the world reflected in the poem.[5] Any attempt to define Williams' free verse is complicated by the fact that his poems come not only in a variety of forms but also in a variety of styles ranging from the conversational and proselike to the more rhythmically sensuous and lyrical, dense with sound patterns.

In keeping this diversity in mind, one can define Williams' free verse as the kind in which the sentence, clause, or phrase is played off against the line—the basic unit of rhythm, or at least of attention. That is, in Williams' verse, grammatical units may coincide with the line, may end midline, or may be split by the line ending, in which case the line is strongly enjambed. Thus Williams' free verse differs from the other most common kind, that which is patterned after Whitman's free verse with its phrasal repetition, regular midline caesura, and long end-stopped line. Williams' verse is freer, more mobile than Whitman's, suitable to an alert and mercurial but thoughtful movement of consciousness, as opposed to an incantatory movement. But although the line is the basic unit of *visual* measure, Williams, in reading his own poems aloud, does not necessarily pause at the end of a line. Thus, from hearing Williams read his poems, a listener cannot consistently tell when lines or stanzas end.

While enjambment, as others have noted, plays a crucial part in Williams' free verse, one may not agree with Stephen Cushman that "enjambment determines lineation."[6] There must be something more basic that determines the frequent but irregular enjambment in Williams, and this something is primarily Williams' intuitive sense of normative line length for a given poem and secondarily his talent for creating special effects through strategic line breaks.

My impression—reinforced from studying Williams' manuscript drafts—is that the first few lines that Williams puts down, or at least becomes satisfied with, tend to serve as a normative length for the remaining lines. (This is probably the case for many if not most free verse poets.) Except for poems in which irregular spacing creates a "broken" appearance on the page, in the majority of Williams' poems, the lines do not vary greatly in length. Of course, in a short-line poem, a given line may be two or three times longer than its neighbor, but both lines are relatively short and the poem, as they say in workshops, looks "skinny" on the page. It is obvious that Williams sometimes breaks a line because the addition of an extra word would extend it *visually* too far beyond the normative length. This is evident in the first stanza of "The Semblables" (*CP2* 84), a poem written in almost blocklike quatrains:

> The red brick monastery in
> the suburbs over against the dust-
> hung acreage of the unfinished
> and all but subterranean
>
> munitions plant . . . .

If "dust-hung" completed the second line, the line would extend visually too far to the right; if the compound word started the third line, it would likewise push "unfinished" too far beyond the visual norm. One could argue that Williams split the word to bring out the associations of dust with death and hence with the munitions plant, in which case Williams' enjambment would be doing double duty: preserving the visual norm of the stanza and also activating the connotations of a word in the reader's mind.

With *Spring and All* in 1923, Williams made radical or violent enjambment a much more prominent feature of his verse, using line breaks, for example, to split an article or an adjective from its noun, or a transitive verb or preposition from its object. Even then, according to a random and informal survey of post-1922 poems, nearly half to two-thirds or more of Williams' lines continue to be end-stopped: they end on a unit of syntax such as a sentence, a subordinate clause, or a phrase.[7] Of course, tallying the number of endstops is complicated by the fact that some line breaks seem to be on a borderline between enjambed and end-stopped. For example, one of Williams' favorite breaking points, that between subject and predicate, often seems to coincide with a natural voice pause, especially if both of these distinct grammatical units are lengthened with modifiers. Line spacing may also affect one's perception of duration at the end of a line. One reads, for example, a stronger or quicker enjambment in

> Now, the Pink Church trembles
> to the light (of dawn) again

than one does in the lines as Williams actually spaced them:

> Now,
>   the Pink Church
>   trembles
> to the light (of dawn) again
>
>   (CP2 177)

The verb "trembles" seems to hover in its indented space and therefore to take on greater vividness in the mind. Further, as regards oral performance, intonation and tempo greatly influence whether Williams will pause or continue at the end of a line of poetry, a fast tempo and feisty tone, for example, incurring more run-over lines as in "Portrait of a Woman in Bed" (CP1 87).

Even making such allowances, however, the proportion of endstops in Williams seems high—too high to be accidental, as can be seen by comparing their frequency to the much lower frequency of midline caesuras in Williams' poems or to the frequency of endstops found at the right-hand margin of a page of prose. End-stopped lines, including phrase and clause endstops, give a rhythmic stability to poems, with line endings reinforcing both natural voice pauses and grammatical junctures. Thus they make poems less awkward when one reads them on the page. While the end-stopped line is a rhythmic factor in Williams' free verse, there are enough strongly enjambed lines to keep the poems from be-

coming monotonously regular, as is often the case in free verse
where each line is a complete grammatical unit.

The need to stay relatively close to a normative line length accounts in good part for Williams' frequent but random use of
enjambment. Most likely he relied on his ear to achieve an overall
blend of stabilizing endstops and unsettling enjambments. But, if
it is true that the first few lines that the poet settles on establish
the norm, how is that norm, one may ask, suitable to the subject
of the poem and the way the poet treats the subject?

Again, there are no absolute rules for judging the appropriateness of line length in a given poem, but there often does seem to
be a correlation in Williams' best poems between lineation and
content. Short lines, often combined in couplets, seem right for
small subjects as in "Between Walls" and "The Red Wheelbarrow"
or for processes that unfold by small increments as in "The Botticellian Trees" and "It is a Living Coral." In general, Williams
seems to combine the short line with the couplet, tercet, or quatrain when he wants to focus more attention on the details and
individual words relative to the overall narrative or argumentative
progression of the poem. Longer lines seem more suitable when
narrative or argumentative progression predominates over details, as in "Tract" or "Elegy for D. H. Lawrence." Williams also
creates an irregular format through varying the length, indenta-
tion, and grouping of lines to create mimetic effects as in "Rain"
and "The Wind Increases" or to create tones that range from
the playful and exuberant to the exalted and rhapsodic, as in
"Perpetuum Mobile: The City" (*CP1* 430), "Paterson: Episode 17"
(*CP1* 439), and "The Waitress" (*CP1* 279). And of course there
are his mid-1950 poems in the triadic stepped-down line, a form
that in its slow, measured pace is effective for a meditative treatment of subject matter. The ultimate test for the rightness of any
line-stanza format is to rewrite the poem in a different format
and then see what is gained or lost.

Except when he decides beforehand to use a specific form like
the triadic line, the overall shape of Williams' poems seems to be
determined, on the one hand, by a trial and error approach
guided by an intuitive sense of normative line length and stanza
format, and on the other hand by a desire to avoid absolute regularity, whether metrical or visual.

Line breaks, both enjambed and end-stopped, serve three basic
purposes in Williams' poetry. First, by trimming the line to fit a
visual design, especially if stanzas are used, line breaks give the
poem a shaped and, therefore, a crafted look, so that the poem

seems to be an object itself, a newly created and unique form (see chapter 4).

Second, line breaks to a great degree create the rhythm of a poem when read silently, although it may be a different rhythm than Williams gives the poem when he reads aloud. The silent reader is forced to experience a visual break at the end of each line no matter now enjambed the line is, whereas, if one were reading the poem aloud in Williams' manner, one would read on through many if not most unpunctuated line endings (the exception being the predominantly end-stopped line segments of the triadic-line poems.) Thus the silent reading of a Williams poem adds dimensions of meaning that are not available in the audible experience alone.

This dimension of silent reading points out the third function of line breaks: they become a means for liberating the word. By breaking up the sentence into smaller units that resist easy assimilation to a prose sense, the lineation focuses more attention on language itself. Thus by disrupting lazy habits of reading, lineation becomes an instrument in Williams' romantic program of cleansing the doors of perception either to reveal hidden value obscured by fixed custom or to expose destructive, stultifying modes of social existence. Eleanor Berry aptly describes this perceptual function of Williams' lineation:

> The obtrusive enjambments . . . hinder the process of syntactical interpretation [and thus] they de-automatize the process of reading. The language is thus defamiliarized, and . . . where the language is made strange, we find the fictional world it evokes made not less but more vivid to us, and things . . . we take as belonging to the "real world" thereby defamiliarized as well.[8]

This defamiliarization, according to Berry, is also carried out by two other aspects of Williams' visual prosody: the use of regular sight stanzas and, contrarily, the use of typographic irregularity to create a broken appearance on the page. Berry further compares Williams' use of visual design to break up the text with the cubists' goal of freeing the mind from stale mental habits by fracturing and then restructuring the way that reality is represented in painting.[9]

In discussing lineation as a method of defamiliarizing language, Berry, Breslin, and Cushman all distinguish between "systematic" enjambment, which prevents the reader from moving quickly through a poem as if it were prose, and meaningful enjambment used to affect verbal meaning in particular ways, often subverting conventional expectations.[10] Williams is especially fond of rhetorical line breaks that cause the reader to retrospectively reinterpret the line that has just been read, as for example line 6 of "Virtue" (*CP1* 89):

1   Why—
2   it is the smile of her
3   the smell of her
4   the vulgar inviting mouth of her!
5   It is—oh, nothing new
6   nothing that lasts
7   an eternity . . .

While line 6 seems at first to dismiss the woman's exciting sexuality as something ephemeral, line 7 makes one realize that this quality is valuable precisely because it is temporal.

Within the visual boundaries created by lineation and stanza form, audible rhythms and sound patterns play a very important role in Williams' poems, giving pleasure in and of themselves and having considerable mimetic or tonal impact. Probaby most readers familiar with Williams' poetry would agree that the following lines from the conclusion of "Love Song" (*CP1* 79) have his distinctive signature:

a burst of fragrance
from black branches

The imagery of floral odors and dark branches is common enough to Williams, but it is the sound and rhythm of these lines that make them so recognizably his:

/   /
a burst of fragrance
/   /
from black branches

Both lines consist of a complete phrase—a noun phrase and a prepositional phrase—and, except for the extra syllable ("of" in the first line), both lines have the same recognizable cadence. Furthermore, the alliteration of burst, black, and branch- is heavily felt, while a lighter pattern of *f* and *r* sounds is also evident. Williams is a master of sensuous sounding verse when he wants to be, and this traditional aspect of his poetry has perhaps received less attention than his visual prosody and the influence of cubism on his work.

The sentence itself, with its impulse from subject to verb, is undoubtedly an important rhythmic force in Williams' verse, though difficult to analyze. Actually, when extra rhythmic drive is needed, Williams, like many free verse poets, will abandon the full sentence for a pattern of verb phrases and participial phrases, as in "Dedication for a Plot of Ground" (*CP1* 105). However, there are other demonstrable sources of localized rhythm in Williams' free verse (in illustrating these, a slash mark is used to indicate a line break and a double vertical bar to indicate a midline caesura, however slight).

A common form of audible rhythm in Williams' poems is his use of short runs of traditional meter, although the meter is all but disguised by line breaks, caesuras, and variations of the meter itself, as in this example:

> At ten A.M. the young housewife
> moves about in negligee behind
> the wooden walls of her husband's house.

These iambic-tending lines have no more metrical variation than can be found in traditional verse. Such lines occur in Williams too frequently to be entirely random; the meter lies buried in Williams' mind, a holdover from his apprentice work in traditional forms. Just as metrical verse tends to deviate toward the irregularity of free verse, so free verse tends to deviate toward the regularity of metered verse—especially if the poet's ear has been well-grounded in the metrical tradition before he takes to free verse. Short runs of metrical verse are an effective means to gain rhythmic force in free verse, provided that the regularity does not go on too long and that it is disguised or subdued by irregular line lengths, varied pauses, and metrical variations.

A second way in which Williams creates a distinctive poetic rhythm is through the use of cadences—the repetition of identical or nearly identical rhythmic configurations, as in the first two lines of "At the Ball Game" (*CP1* 233):

> the crowd at the ball game / is moved uniformly

Sometimes a cadence is repeated exactly, as when spondees mark off the ends of phrases:

skimming bare trees / above a snow glaze

(*CP1* 152)

Sorrow is my own yard / where the new grass

(*CP1* 171)

A rhythmic configuration may be repeated immediately,

petals aslant ‖ darkened with mauve

(*CP1* 184)

in a tissue-thin monotone

(*CP1* 97)

or several syllables or a line may intervene between the two identical configurations:

If when my wife is sleeping

and the baby and Kathleen

are sleeping

(*CP1* 86)

The above example also has a pattern of anapests:

when my wife

and the baby   and Kathleen

Sometimes the cadence is repeated with slight variation:

the horned branches ‖ that lean / heavily

(*CP1* 107)

how the converging lines / of the hexagonal spire

(*CP1* 104)

Flowers through the window / lavender and yellow

(*CP1* 372)

In the last example, though each line has the same accent pattern, the rhythm is delicately altered because of the variation from the two-syllable "flowers" to the three-syllable "lavender."

Of course one could borrow terms from Greek prosody to label most or all of the cadences being discussed here, but Williams was not consciously trying to work within the classical metrical system. Rather he is, in effect, carrying out Pound's imagist prescription, "to compose by the sequence of the musical phrase." In any case, Williams frequently puts phrases together so that the second musically balances or complements the first:

> the oppressive weight / of the squat edifice
>
> (*CP1* 104)
>
> let it be weathered—like a farm wagon
>
> (*CP1* 72)

In the first example, the balanced phrases each begin as anapests, and each phrase has two main accents. In the second, a nice balance is achieved because there are five syllables on each side of the midline pause, the phrases begin and end with unaccented syllables, and the first and last words of each phrase begin with the same sound.

Two other sources or kinds of rhythm in Williams are accentual meter and phrasal repetition. One finds several poems by Williams in which a significant number of lines have the same number of accented syllables, although the unaccented syllables vary greatly in number and placement. In poems like "To Waken an Old Lady," "Sunflowers," "This is Just to Say," and "The Lonely Street," the ghost of accentual meter acts as a loose rhythmic norm. Here are the first three stanzas of "These" (*CL1* 458):

> are the desolate, dark weeks
> when nature in its barrenness
> equals the stupidity of man.
>
> The year plunges into night
> and the heart plunges
> lower than night
>
> to an empty, windswept place
> without sun, stars or moon
> but a peculiar light as of thought

Six of the nine lines have three main accents, irregularly placed.

The three-stress line provides a pattern that can definitely be heard, although it is not allowed to become as regular as the four-beat Old English line.

Williams, in the manner of Whitman, also makes use of phrasal repetition in some poems, but again modified in such a way as to prevent the pattern from becoming too heavily regular. Consider these three stanzas from "The Catholic Bells" (*CP1* 397) in which Williams calls out for the bells to ring as a celebration of change:

> ring down the leaves
> ring in the frost upon them
> and the death of the flowers
> ring out the grackle
>
> toward the south, the sky
> darkened by them, ring in
> the new baby of Mr. and Mrs.
> Krantz which cannot
>
> for the fat of its cheeks
> open well its eyes, ring out
> the parrot under its hood
> jealous of the child

Had Whitman been writing the poem, it would have looked and sounded like this:

> Ring down the leaves,
> Ring in the frost upon them and the death of the flowers,
> Ring out the grackle toward the south, the sky darkened by them,
> Ring in the new baby of Mr. and Mrs. Krantz . . .

The effect here is more incantatory (and monotonous), because Whitman would begin each line with the same word or same part of speech, and each line would be end-stopped. Williams fits the long imperative statements into a stanza form and breaks them up into shorter lines so that individual phrases and words receive more attention and the rhythmic movement is more varied.

Williams understood that traditional meters and rhyme carried with them habits of tone and feeling that were difficult to avoid, that it was difficult "to escape a mere reversion to classical forms . . . representing other temperaments, other emotional fibers, other adjustments of sense."[11] Williams felt, interestingly enough, that if we were to continue to appreciate the beauty of the older verse, a verse form uniquely suited to our own times would have to be developed: "Yet without a Whitman there can of course be for me no Dante. . . . How else to derive benefit from that which I love, unless I create a new thing of my own."[12] Above and beyond any specific emotion expressed in a traditional poem, the very presence of meter and rhyme conveys a kind of poetry-feeling itself, a special mood or tone reserved for poetic utterance that sets it apart from the expression of fact or feeling in real life. The continuation of the Victorian mode had made poetry rhythmically too predictable. For example, if the first line of a traditional poem was

$$\acute{\text{Flo}}\text{wers thr\'ough the w\'indow}$$

the next line would be expected to have a rhythm like this:

$$\text{W\'eeds outs\'ide the d\'oor}$$

and maybe the whole quatrain to sound like this:

> Flowers through the window,
> Weeds outside the door,
> Vines along the lattice
> And petals on the floor.

Of course this made-up example represents to an extreme a tendency latent in metrical poetry: a hypnotic effect of the meter that in inferior poetry reduces the attention to the thing itself—the objects or scene the words refer to. As a matter of fact, Williams does begin a poem with the first line given above, but he continues in a different way:

> Flowers through the window
> lavender and yellow
>
> changed by white curtains—

> (CP1 372)

The initial tendency toward traditional rhythm is checked by the third line to provide something fresh and different; it is still poetic, but it asks that one look more closely at the phenomenon depicted—the appearance of the flowers altered by billowing movements of the white curtains through which the flowers are seen.

Besides offering new tones and feelings to poetry, free verse made possible the assimilation of a wider range of diction. Free verse offered a vehicle in which words and phrases not sanctioned by the canons of nineteenth-century verse would sound appropriate. Since free verse did not arouse the usual expectations of solemn utterance or dreamy remoteness characteristic of so much of the previous century's serious lyric poetry, it could accommodate words like *newspaper, dime, breakfast, buttocks, baby, dirt-colored,* and *sparrows,* and phrases like "run giggling" and "she'll be rescued." These common words and colloquial phrases can be used in elevated, lyrical free verse, whereas in rhymed poetry they would seem out of place or suitable mainly for light verse and satire. Moreover, while meter and rhyme may result in more perfect word-choice for some poets, for others, fixed forms inhibit the expression of the thing exactly as they felt it and also inhibit the poet's sense of his or her own voice. Clearly, Williams would not sound much like Williams had he written only in fixed forms. Finally, from just a technical point of view, meter and rhyme are such strong prosodic elements that they can easily overwhelm the more delicate effects of cadence, assonance, and other sound patterns.

Although Williams demonstrated considerable skill in his early free verse poems, he soon grew dissatisfied with "free verse." By 1917 he had decided that the term was a "misnomer," that it meant "verse whose proper structure escapes a man's effort to control it."[13] He desired "a new verse form" that was recognizably structured but not rigid: "Its elements must not be too firmly cemented together as they are in the aristocratic forms of past civilizations. They must be perfectly concrete or they will escape through the fingers—but they must not be rigidly united into series."[14] Dissatisfaction with free verse continued throughout Williams' career. John Thirlwall, alluding to the following lines from Williams' poem, "This Florida: 1924" (*CP1* 359),

> And we thought to escape rime
> by imitation of the senseless
> unarrangement of wild things—
>
> the stupidest rime of all

declared that in 1924 Williams "rejected free verse . . . and sought for a controlled measure" that he supposedly did not find until he hit upon the variable foot and triadic line,[15] although not even that form proved to be an ultimate solution to the problem of reconciling spontaneity and form. Pound and Eliot had undergone an earlier disaffection with free verse, but their way of restoring discipline to verse was to return, for a while, to a tightly closed form. Pound's "Mauberley" and Eliot's *Poems* both appeared in 1920, both employing a quatrain modeled after Gautier's. Even later, in *The Waste Land,* Eliot is never far away from traditional meters, particularly the iambic pentameter line, for which reason Williams acutely called Eliot a "subtle conformist." Although Williams disliked the term "free verse," especially since so much flaccid poetry had been written under that name, he did not turn after 1924 to meter and rhyme but continued to write what is commonly called "free verse"—verse without fixed meter and rhyme.

While "This Florida: 1924" may crystallize Williams' dissatisfaction with the laxity of much free verse, it would be incorrect to think that Williams' own verse from 1914 to 1923 was undisciplined and that after 1923 it necessarily became much tighter in form as Williams moved away from imagism toward objectivism with its emphasis on poems as shaped objects. Some of Williams' best free verse before 1923 ("The Young Housewife," "The Widow's Lament in Springtime," "To Waken an Old Lady") has the kind of formal, well-made quality that he was more consciously searching for after 1924, whereas much of his later verse, even when the formal necessity of a stanza design has been imposed on it, is inferior to the best of his early verse. Many of the poems in the variable foot and triadic line, for example, tend to be loose and discursive, sometimes lapsing into cliché: "You cannot live / and keep free of / briars" ("The Ivy Crown," *PB* 125). Williams' early free verse had employed a number of rhythmic devices— short runs of traditional meter, the repetition or balance of musical phrases, the approximation of accentual meter in some poems, and the use of phrasal repetition—not to mention an abundant use of alliteration and assonance that add to the sensuousness of his verse. Williams, in his restless pursuit of new forms, failed to appreciate just how much he had accomplished for lyrical free verse in his early poetry.

Nevertheless, his dissatisfaction was real, and it led him on an obsessive quest for a "new measure," by which he sometimes meant a rhythmically structured line not based on syllable and accent count, and at other times meant a broader principle, "the deeper, more inclusive forms," that would give his poems "unity

of form."[16] With regard to his short poems, the most striking
result of Williams' quest for form is the increasing use of stanza
patterns starting with *Spring and All* in 1923. Before then, most
of his free verse was written with continuous lineation or in stanza
segments of irregular length. The chief exceptions were the
poems in *Spring and All,* of which more than half are grouped
into neat stanzas that, in contrast to the disorganized dadaist
prose, suggest the form-creating power of the imagination, the
theme of the book.

What had been previously an occasional grouping of lines into
stanzas became for Williams the preferred mode. The rough
drafts in The Poetry/Rare Books Collection at the State University
of New York at Buffalo show him more and more composing even
initial drafts in stanza forms. When Edith Heal remarked how
beautiful the poems in *Adam & Eve & The City* (1936) looked on
the page, Williams explained that the poems had been written at
"a time when I was working hard for order, searching for a form
for the stanzas, making them little units, regular, orderly" (*IWWP*
57). Williams thought of his stanzas as part of the corrective to
"free verse." Looking over his *Collected Poems* (1938), Williams said,
gave him "the whole picture." "As I went through the poems I
noticed many brief poems, always arranged in couplet or quatrain
form." Williams added, as if retrospectively seeing his stanzas
evolving into the triadic line, "I noticed also that I was peculiarly
fascinated by another pattern: the dividing of the little paragraphs in lines of three" (*IWWP* 65–66). Williams gave an example of how he had condensed a five-line stanza into a quatrain to
increase the tempo:

The Nightingales

Original version	*Revised version*
My shoes as I lean	My shoes as I lean
unlacing them	unlacing them
stand out upon	stand out upon
flat worsted flowers	flat worsted flowers.
under my feet.	
Nimbly the shadows	Nimbly the shadows
of my fingers play	of my fingers play
unlacing	unlacing
over shoes and flowers.	over shoes and flowers.

Williams might have justified the excision of "under my feet" on
the grounds of its redundancy, but what really pleased him was
"how much better it conforms to the page, how much better it
looks" (*IWWP* 66). Thus it appears that stanza form and line
length were intended to affect both the visual design and temporal rhythm of Williams' poetry.

There is no doubt that Williams simply liked the neat look of
the stanzas on the page. In fact, Henry Sayre, in *The Visual Text
of William Carlos Williams,* argues that regular stanza form in Williams "bears no relation to either sound or sense," but is purely
"arbitrary, imposed upon his subject matter, not organically derived from it."[17] An "organically derived" form would presumably
be generated by spontaneous feeling aroused by subject matter
and would most likely take an irregular shape on the page, not
the shape of neat tercets or quatrains. While Williams' stanzas may
not be organic in this way, they often seem appropriate for the
subject, and they do affect the visual rhythm of a poem—the
rhythm one imagines when reading the poem silently. For example, the short couplets of "It Is a Living Coral" (*CP1* 255), about
the Capitol building and its accumulations of history, suit the
sense of accretion that the poem is about. The even more minimal
couplets of "Between Walls" (discussed in chapter 4) are appropriate to the self-effacing tone and the tiny bits of matter on which
the poem focuses. Well-placed enjambments help to make the
short lines of "Poem (As the Cat)" (*CP1* 352) mimic the cautious,
hesitant movements of the cat climbing over the jamcloset.

The rhythmic effect of Williams' stanzas is not always easy to
discern, but it is evident enough in this Depression-era poem:

Proletarian Portrait

A big young bareheaded woman
in an apron

Her hair slicked back standing
on the street

One stockinged foot toeing
the sidewalk

Her shoe in her hand. Looking
intently into it

She pulls out the paper insole
to find the nail

That has been hurting her

(CPI 384)

Short stanzas in Williams' poems often frame discrete visual impressions so that they have more time to sink into the reader's mind. Furthermore, in the above poem, the first two stanzas establish a rhythmic norm: they are both complete units of description and the shorter line in each stanza is a simple prepositional phrase. Reading the whole poem silently, one mentally hears the wavelike regularity of a long phrase followed by a short one. To continue in this fashion, however, would be monotonous. Instead, Williams begins to vary slightly from the grammatical pattern in the third stanza where the shorter line is just an article and a noun, though almost identical in length to the two preceding short lines. The fourth and fifth stanzas vary considerably more, but still preserve the basic long-line/short-line pattern. (Incidentally, another rhythmic pattern is formed by the trochaic two-syllable words that end each long line except the last.) The last line, because it varies from the pattern by being a single line, stands out with special significance. The variation from the pattern helps not only to bring the poem to a close but to prompt the reader to see special significance in "hurting," universalizing it to the larger sense of hurt felt by the working class during the Depression—a symbolic interpretation in keeping with the poem's original and mock-portentous title, "Study for a Figure representing Modern Culture" (*CP1* 540).

In addition to controlling rhythmic movement, the neatly designed stanza form, almost geometrically precise in its measurement of alternating line lengths, suggests a firmness and stability appropriate to its subject. The firmness of the visual form is reinforced by the pattern of endstops created by complete grammatical units that end each couplet and by the capital letter that begins each couplet to give it the form of a statement if not the structure of a sentence. This is a no-nonsense verse form. The directness and economy of the poem, supported by such strong alliteration as standing / stockinged / street, give it a focused intensity, like that of the strong young woman herself.

The relation between stanza form and subject is not usually as strong in most of Williams' poems as it is in "Proletarian Portrait," although, as argued in the section on free verse, there often seems to be a general appropriateness of stanza and line length to content. But apart from any rhythmic, mimetic, or tonal effects created by line and stanza, their overall purpose is to arouse the reader from the mind-set one has when reading prose, where attention tends to be focused more on deriving information and ideas than on the imagistic and aural qualities of words and the symbolic possibilities of images.

While working on *Paterson* Williams hit upon the highly visual triadic line in a unified verse segment he titled "The Descent" and published in *The Partisan Review* (February 1948) and a few months later in *Paterson* (book 2, 96–97). Williams told Edith Heal that, in looking over "The Descent," "I realized I had hit upon a device," and "my dissatisfaction with free verse came to a head" (*IWWP* 82). Subsequently, Williams made deliberate use of the device for his mid-1950s volumes of poems, *The Desert Music* (1954) and *Journey to Love* (1955). In explaining the verse form to Richard Eberhart, Williams said he might have "half consciously" counted "the measure under my breath," citing as illustration the opening triads of "To Daphne and Virginia":

> (1) The smell of the heat is boxwood
>   (2) when rousing us
>   (3) a movement of the air

Following the example, he instructed: "Count a single beat to each numeral" (*SL* 326–27). Each line is a "variable foot," and the three stepped-down lines comprise a "triadic line." In this particular example, since each variable foot is a complete grammatical unit, there is a pause for grammatical juncture at the end of each line. The sense of hearing measured verse comes not because each line occupies the duration of "a single beat," as Williams thought, but because of the prevailing regularity of end-stopped lines combined with the visual regularity of the three-part stanza.

Cushman ridicules the notion that such lines, which may vary from two to seventeen syllables, could possibly occupy equal spoken durations.[18] On the other hand, some kind of visual norm or parameter for line length seems to be operative, though one is usually not conscious of it until it is violated by a particularly short line consisting, say, of one or two short words. The word or phrase of such a minimal line seems to assume a greater significance because it is not competing with other words for available line space. For example, in the following triad,

> The mind
>   lives there. It is uncertain,
>   can trick us and leave us
>
>   (*CP2* 246)

spatial isolation is used to give the word "mind" greater prominence because of its crucial importance to Williams' theme. (Despite Cushman's thesis that Williams' prosody is not temporal but visual, one cannot avoid experiencing a "pause" after *mind,* whether this pause is temporal or "phenomenological."[19]) Had Williams not wanted to draw such attention to the word, he could have gained a more equitable distribution of words per line as well as better line-phrase coincidence by writing:

> The mind lives there.
>   It is uncertain,
>   can trick us and leave us

The rhythm now seems faster—more routinely even and less thoughtful.

The triadic line was particularly well-suited for the kind of meditative verse Williams wrote in old age. The very regularity of the form, with each line evenly tabulated on the typewriter, is conducive to a mood of rational self-reflection. And yet the lengthening or shortening of a line, the placement of a word or phrase on a given step of the triad, and the breaking of a line at a strategic point all serve to give dramatic emphasis and variation of tempo to the speaking voice. At its best, the form goes beyond arbitrary visual design to affect the tone and rhythm of the words. Consider this short passage written as prose:

> Inseparable from the fire, its light takes precedence over it. Then follows what we have dreaded—but it can never overcome what has gone before. In the huge gap between the flash and the thunderstroke, spring has come in or a deep snow fallen.

Taken from "Asphodel, That Greeny Flower," a poem that looks back on passion as both glorious and destabilizing, these words sum up a hard-won wisdom. As passion (fire) diminishes, reason (light) predominates. But maturity also brings dreaded physical blows (like the strokes Williams suffered in his sixties), though these do not cancel out the glory of what had gone before. Our life, when seen either in a retrospective glimpse or as a moment in cosmic time, may seem no longer than the gap between lightning and thunder, yet in terms of lived experience we have, in that gap, experienced youth (spring) and old age (snow fallen). Now consider the passage as Williams wrote it:

> Inseparable from the fire
>   its light
>   takes precedence over it.
> Then follows
>   what we have dreaded—
>   but it can never
> overcome what has gone before.
>   In the huge gap
>   between the flash
> and the thunderstroke
>   spring has come in
>   or a deep snow fallen.
>
>   (PB 178)

Despite the symbolism, the prose version seems somewhat flat and didactic, whereas, in the form of verse, the passage seems both more grand and more inward. The descending lines create a stately rhythm in which each line or phrase has more time to sink in; thus its weight or import can be more fully felt.[20] For example, "its light" in the first triad, seems to stand out with greater significance and vividness because of its middle position and its brevity. The line break after *flash* in the third triad imitates the time gap between lightning and thunder. One would think to find the phrase "but it can never overcome" as a single unit, but Williams breaks the line between adverb and verb apparently to give some relief from the regularity of end-stopped lines and to put the greater emphasis on *never* rather than on *overcome*.

3. Diction

Williams' free verse and often colloquial or even antipoetic diction could represent experience with a concreteness that most readers of verse in the early decades of this century were not accustomed to. One of Williams' great contributions was to make poetry seem less remote from ordinary experience and, at the same time, to make ordinary experience seem not so ordinary.

Consider, first, this example of Williams' premodernist style from his *Poems* (1909), in which, echoing Keats' "To Autumn," he personifies the beauty of nature as an elusive "nymph":

> Thee once I saw beside a quiet brook
> Where lately thou hadst bathed and troth, thine eyes
> Were clearer than the stream; thy hair which shook
> Unto the grass was as the leaf which tries
> To kiss the water's brim, no more, when gradual currents rise.

These lines contain the kind of inaccurate simile to which Williams would later object (grass does not rise to meet a nymph's hair in the way that a stream might rise and touch overhanging foliage). In contrast to the above, is this imagistic description of a woman:

The Girl

with big breasts
under a blue sweater

bareheaded—
crossing the street

reading a newspaper
stops, turns

and looks down
as though

she had seen a dime
on the pavement

(CP1 444)

The Keatsian nymph in the first passage obviously belongs to the realm of poetry alone, whereas the woman in the second poem, or one like her, might be seen any day on an actual city street. One scarcely realizes that the nymph in the first passage is naked, whereas the "girl" has a definite physical presence. Williams wanted to make the first scene dreamy and lovely, and so he compared the nymph's long hair, which she shakes dry, to a leaf chastely ("no more") trying to "kiss" the water's surface. But where exactly is that leaf—at the tip of an overhanging branch? Williams makes no effort at exact visualization. In the second poem, the woman is not idealized: she has a distinct sexual reality and seems self-assured (she reads a newspaper while crossing the street); ironically, despite her self-confidence and the wealth of her sexual endowment, she is distracted by a gleam from the pavement of something of relatively little worth, like a dime.[21]

"The Girl" has none of the poetic diction that Williams, in the early 1900s, thought poetry must have if it is to be beautiful. The earlier poem is so loaded with archaic words like *thee, thou, troth, hadst* and sanctioned poetic clichés like "quiet brook," "eyes . . . clearer than the stream," and "water's brim," that the reader feels little need to particularize the scene.

Williams' attempt to incorporate American speech rhythms and antipoetic diction into his poetry was part of the general movement—influenced by realism in fiction and by the modernist mistrust of abstractions—to bring poetry closer to the physical and emotional realities of modern life. The modernist revolution in poetic diction may be viewed as an extension of Wordsworth's 1798 revolution against the euphemistic and artificial aspects of eighteenth-century poetry. But since that revolution did not go very far, it is instructive to read through nineteenth-century poetry, playing close attention to the kinds of words favored (and avoided) by poets writing serious lyric poetry.

A random list of the most "poetic" (mellifluous, picturesque, dignified) words includes: rainbow, sunset, melodious, sparkling, silken, mists (but rarely "fog"), dancing, secluded, cliffs, shore, beechen, delved (but not "dug"), dim, shadow, ancient, dewy, murmur, craggy, bower, vernal, flowing. (Most of these words—individually—can be and still are used unself-consciously by poets today.) One can find "babe" but not "baby." One might not expect to find "rot," "slimy," or "skinny"—but they can be found in "The Ancient Mariner" and elsewhere. In fact, the Romantics and the Victorians had a special category, it seems, of poetic diction for things that were ugly, unpleasant, or frightful: drizzling, slimy, ghastly, rotting, groan, moan, abyss, leprosy, blast (for storm), dread, pang, curse, fiend, etc. Williams' vocabulary for the repellent is at least a little more gritty, with words like grubbed, unkempt, fox-snouted, venomous, squat, bedraggled, festering, dog-lime.

Because of the restricted range of nineteenth-century diction and because of an almost unrelieved loftiness or solemnity of tone, poetry came to be, in James Dickey's term, "suspect"—too artificial. In reading through nineteenth-century lyric poetry at any

length, part of the mind tends to turn off because it is simply not
needed. How rare and refreshing it is to come upon something
as particularized as Browning's "yellowing fennel, run to seed" or
"five beetles—blind and green they grope." The particular has
the charm of novelty for us.

Gorham B. Munson was one of the first critics to appreciate
the effect of Williams' inclusion of details that traditional readers
thought unfit for poetry:

> The one gauge is intensity of perception and since the unpleasant has
> great power of impact upon nostrils, ears, eyes, and so on, it follows
> that the unpleasant is generously included in Williams' lines, where
> however it is redeemed by the same exhilaration that a vivid register
> of the pleasing object also creates.[22]

But it is not the unpleasant only that makes Williams' poetry fresh,
but the inclusion of the homely, familiar object or gesture. In this
he was following both Whitman's example and Emerson's precept:
"The meaner the type by which a law is expressed, the more
pungent it is, and the more lasting in the memories of men" (229).

The unpleasant and the common together make up the "antipoetic" in Williams, a term first applied by Wallace Stevens in his
preface to Williams' *Collected Poems: 1921–1931*. Stevens said that
the antipoetic was Williams' means of controlling his "sentimental
side" and thus keeping him in touch with reality. Stevens percep-
tively noted that "the essential poetry" in Williams was "the result
of the conjunction of . . . the sentimental and the anti-poetic, the
constant interaction of two opposites."[23] Williams, however, mis-
construed Stevens to be saying that he was calculatingly using the
antipoetic for effect. Williams said he was tired of everyone echoing Stevens' "dictum that I resort to the antipoetic as a heightening
device. That's plain crap—and everyone copies it" (*SL* 265). Later,
he told Edith Heal: "It's all one to me—the anti-poetic is not
something to enhance the poetic—it's all one piece" (*IWWP* 52).

Indeed, except for poems in which Williams, like Eliot, deliberately juxtaposes the ugly with the exalted for satiric effect, there
is no clashing tension between the antipoetic and the poetic in
Williams' lyrics, but rather a rich harmony. If anything, the inclusion of elevated diction results in an affirmation of value and a
romantic heightening of experience that begins in the ordinary
but becomes something special. Such is the case in "Complaint"
(*CP1* 153), Williams' poem about his experience as a doctor being
called out to deliver a baby. The poem's diction ranges from the

common and the unpleasant—"frozen road," "rigid wheeltracks," "sick," "vomiting"—to the romantic and the mystical: "a room / darkened for lovers," "the sun / has sent one gold needle!"

In "Complaint," Williams solves the modernist problem of bringing poetry down to earth and yet retaining some of the sublimity or at least heightened quality that makes poetry special. In the first five lines, which esteablish the setting and the situation, Williams achieves both dignity of tone and vivid representation with simple, prosaic language:

> They call me and I go.
> It is a frozen road
> past midnight, a dust
> of snow caught
> in the rigid wheeltracks.

Short lines and short declarative sentences add to the impression of an austere, desolate setting. Many of the simple words used here—frozen, road, midnight, dust—have acquired a richness of connotation from traditional poetic usage, thus suggesting a range of feelings: reluctance, obligation, loneliness, purity. At the same time, the words, in their hard factuality, ground the sublime mystery of conception and birth in an awareness of hard realities. The mystery, symbolized by "one gold needle of sunlight" coming through the window slats, seems all the more miraculous in such a hard, frozen setting. The allusion to Zeus appearing to Danae as a shower of gold is both subtle and surprising because of the incongruous juxtaposition of Greek myth with common American folk experience.

While the opening lines above may sound colloquial enough, they do have a dignified, formal quality. A more literally colloquial style might be rendered in a Robert Bly style like this:

> They call me and I go.
> It's past midnight and the road is frozen.
> Snow has drifted into the frozen wheeltracks.

Williams' version is much tighter and less folksy than typical American speech usually is, and therefore one hears the somber assonance of the three long *o*'s in the first two lines, an unobtrusive off rhyme—frozen/go/road—echoed by "snow" in the fourth line. The first two lines, in fact, are nearly metrical:

/   /
They call me and I go.
/   /
It is a frozen road . . .

It would take only a metrical context to bring out the latent accents on *and* and *is*, thereby regularizing the meter and creating
the sound of doggerel which free verse avoids:

/   /   /
My life has sunk so low,
/   /   /
my patients are my load.
/   /   /
They call me and I go;
/   /   /
It is a frozen road.

In addition to the proximate meter, the allusion to Greek myth,
and the visually precise yet romantic image of "one gold needle
of sunlight," other heightening devices are used. The metaphor,
"a dust of snow," is more literary than one expects in colloquial
speech, and the enjambment after "caught" momentarily opens
up several possibilities of meaning before resolving itself in the
next line. Important too are the connotations of the title, "Complaint," with its echoes of the courtly tradition; only here it is not
the male lover lamenting the cruelty of his mistress but the male
doctor experiencing the cold hardship of a midnight journey. It
is also the implied "complaint" of the woman laboring to give
birth to a child, a biological consequence usually obscured by the
courtly tradition.

Another example in which Williams heightens the colloquial by
mixing contemporary idiom with romantic diction is "Danse
Russe" (*CP1* 86). The poem starts out with the mundane observation ("If when my wife is sleeping"), moves to the romantic ("the
sun is a flame-white disc / in silken mists"), and then descends to
the earthy with "my arms, my face, / my shoulders, flanks, buttocks." The most intensely heightened expression, however,
"flame-white disc," is toned down by the precision of *disc* as opposed to more elegant expressions like *orb* or *sphere*.

The use of simple words, besides creating honesty of tone, also
helps Williams to stay close to the familiar physical aspects of the
world. Hard-edged realism, though not an end in itself, was one
quality Williams admired in the poetry of Marianne Moore who
treated words "with acid to remove the smudges" (*SE* 128), that
is, used words with such clear referentiality that "nothing loses its

identity in the composition" (*SE* 129). In "Sea-Trout and Butterfish" (see chapter 2, section 1), for example, language is made
to perform one of its most elemental functions, that of describing
the simple properties of a physical object. Williams' diction in the
descriptive part of the poem ranges from the extremely general
("contours and the shine") to the somewhat more specific ("quick
tails," "silver scales") to the still more specific ("pout-mouthed").
Besides the use of specific and concrete words, the poet has other
ways of particularizing his perception. An especially pronounced
rhythm, for example, can intensify diction by causing the reader
to pay closer attention to the words. The final, emphatic cadence
of "Sea Trout" makes use of alliteration, assonance, and consecutive stress

$$\acute{}\quad\acute{}\quad\acute{}\quad\acute{}$$
the fine fins' sharp spines

to make one feel, through the sound, the sharpness of those
spines.

Another feature of Williams' diction, his abundant use of verbs
and verbals, gives his poetry a kind of dynamic concreteness. It
is revealing to read Williams in the light of Ernest Fenollosa's
"The Chinese Written Character as a Medium for Poetry," which
Williams' friend Pound edited and introduced to the English-
speaking world. According to Fenollosa, things do not exist in
isolation in nature, but are "rather the meeting points, of actions,
cross-sections cut through actions."[24] Therefore, to represent
things in English by nouns and adjectives fosters an impression
that they are static, separate entities. The linking verb "is" also
contributes to this static view of nature, for in English one typically
says "the tree is green," not "the tree greens itself." The Chinese
ideograph, on the other hand, conveys the sense of nature as
activity, as when "spring" is represented by a symbol showing "the
sun underlying the bursting forth of plants." According to Fenollosa, English, through "its splendid array of transitive verbs," can
come close to the ideograph's capacity to represent things in nature as "inter-related processes." "Their power lies in their recognition of nature as a vast storehouse of forces."[25]

Williams, too, recommends that the writer "learn to employ the
verbs in imitation of nature" (*SE* 302), to make "a transit from
adjective (the ideal 'copy') to verb (showing process)" (*SE* 303). In
practice, Williams relies heavily on action verbs and verbals to
convey a sense of energy and life in nature. Williams, describing
the young sycamore, does not say that it "is thinner" at the top

but that "it thins." The present tense verbs and participles describing the tree as it

>   rises
>   bodily
>
>   into the air with
>   one undulant
>   thrust half its height—
>   and then
>   dividing and waning
>   sending out young branches on
>   all sides—

give the impression that the tree is growing as one (in imagination) looks at it, demonstrating that its growth is a continuing process. The fish in "Sea-Trout and Butterfish," though dead, do not seem inert and static, as they might seem if rendered in a factual prose style: "On a white dish are two butterfish with pout-mouths beside a sea trout with orange fins." Williams' verbal modifiers (some of them nouns given the -*ed* form of participles) suggest an active reality: the sea trout and butterfish are *caught, lying,* orange-*finned,* pout-*mouthed.* Even though the fish are dead, something in them continues to sustain vivid qualities that actively strike the senses.

Sometimes through an unexpectedly right word, Williams renews the link between *word* and *thing.* For example, Williams describes the sun as a "flame-white," not a "flaming white," disc. The participle "flaming" would have suggested burning and flickering tongues of flame, whereas Williams, one might infer, wants an image of the sun as it appears at dawn through haze or mist—as a flat, coin-shaped object with a subdued, almost cool brightness, not a vigorous fieryness. Likewise, the geometric, machine-like "disc" has obvious advantages over the more poetic "orb" or the more commonplace "ball" in that it presents the sun as it might actually appear at dawn.

In "Pastoral" (*CP1* 70), the little sparrows are described as hopping "ingenuously." The context of the poem, which affirms the worth of the humble street cleaner over that of the lofty Episcopal minister, helps to draw out the meanings of *ingenuous* as not only "simple; artless; innocent" but, more originally, "of honorable birth, nature, or character; noble." In "Young Sycamore" (*CP1* 266), the word "eccentric," used with a sense of its root meaning to describe the tree peaking in "two / eccentric knotted / twigs," adds to the implication that the farthest reaches of organic growth proceed "out of the center." In speaking of a corpse as a "bastard" ("Death," *CP1* 346) because there is nothing "legitimate anymore in it," Williams gives the terms "bastard" and "legitimate" unexpected extralegal meaning, startling one into an awareness that life is at the essence of human identity and that a corpse is in some sense a sham.

Puns and wordplay are another means by which Williams subverts stock responses and comes up with surprising perceptions. Wordplay calls attention to the words themselves, temporarily unlinking them from their usual connections with things. Williams occasionally uses words in a punning or equivocal sense, as when he says, derogatively, "A bank is a matter of columns" [i.e., architectural and accounting] (*CP1* 126), or "So my life is spent [passed, wasted] to keep out love" (*CP1* 343). In "Tract" (*CP1* 72), Williams refers to nonlocal arbiters and designers of culture as a "troop" of artists, deliberately using the military word (instead of "troupe") to emphasize the invading, authoritarian propensity of the official culture. In "To Elsie" (*CP1* 217), Williams achieves a tri-level pun when he speaks of "young slatterns . . . / to be tricked out that night / with gauds," the expression "tricked out" having connotations of gaudiness, deception, and prostitution. Often Williams' titles have double or triple meanings. The title "The Term" (*CP1* 451), given to the poem about the piece of brown paper run over by a car, seems at first remote from the incident depicted, until one realizes that the poem is concerned with human mortality; then "term"—as lease, contract, limited duration, end of gestation—takes on multiple relevance.

The subject of wordplay leads to Williams' idea of words as objects or things in themselves, having tactile, phonic, and visual qualities and, beyond these tangible properties, having the capacity by their mere proximity to each other in space to interact in one's mind apart from any meaning directed by grammar. To think of words as objects, to savor them, to play around with them and see what effects result when they are placed next to each other, like pigments, is one way to avoid taking the connection between word and thing for granted. Williams' sensuous feeling for words is most obviously evident in his use of onomatopoeia, a common and effectively used device in his poetry. Onomatopoeia helps to bridge the gap between words and things, as in this passage from "The Young Housewife" (*CP1* 57):

> The noiseless wheels of my car
> rush with a crackling sound over
> dried leaves . . .

Here the imitative sounds of *rush* (assisted by the preceding sibilance and breathiness of *z, s,* and *wh* sounds in the first line) and *crackling* bring the reader close to the scene. Winifred Nowottny, in *The Language Poets Use,* explains that making use of the "corporeality" of words is a way "to give the conceptual senses of the words a renewed contact with perceptual experience."[26]

Williams makes use of other phonic and imitative effects besides strict onomatopoeia. His poetry indicates a distinct concern for phonic aptness and sensuous appeal, as in his description of a church building: "the oppressive weight / of the squat edifice" (*CP1* 104). The suggestion of a compact, oppressive heaviness comes, in part, from the percussive force of *pp* and *sq* and the repetition of the hissing *s*—and possibly also the visual shortness of *squat.* Balance, too, plays a part in the appeal of these phrases to the ear, with each phrase carrying two stessed syllables and with the polysyllabic and monosyllabic words linked by a kind of phonic chiasmus:

$$a \qquad b \qquad\qquad b \qquad a$$
the oppressive weight ‖ of the squat edifice

In dismissing conventional funeral practices in "Tract" (*CP1* 72), Williams asserts, "No wreathes please," in which the heavily sibilant internal rhyme reinforces the tone of impatient sarcasm. (The lips draw back in a slight grimace when pronouncing *-eathes* and *-ease.*) In "Young Sycamore" (*CP1* 266), Williams imagines the tree's growth taking place in a moment with "one undulant thrust." One feels the forceful but graceful wavelike movement in this rhythmic phrase. The sound and rhythm of *undulant* imitate its meaning, while its initial vowel sound *uh* links it to the same sound in *one* and *thrust.* Much more might be written on Williams' mastery of imitative and tonally appropriate sound and on the general principles of his free verse. The sensuous, rhythmic vitality of his best poetry distinguishes Williams from many lesser practitioners of free verse.

Before leaving the subject of Williams' diction, any impression that Williams confined himself to the simple words commonly heard in the speech of the common people must be laid to rest. Many of his poems do operate with an austerely simple diction, but generally speaking, Williams' diction is a mixture of the spoken language (from slang to more educated varieties) and written English. His working vocabulary includes a wide range of abstract and polysyllabic words, and his syntax is often quite complex. In the simplest of Williams' imagist poems like "The Red Wheelbarrow," "Between Walls," or "The Term," the vocabulary would, with few exceptions, cause little difficulty for an average sixth-grader. But Williams wrote poems much more complex than these and his vocabulary is not as limited as, say, Hemingway's or Frost's. Besides English, Williams had studied Latin, French, German—not to mention Spanish. His home library contained several books on grammar, etymology, and foreign languages, including Chinese. If Williams used the American speech idiom in his poetry, he certainly did not restrict his vocabulary to the spoken idiom of the uneducated. A random sampling of Williams' early poems offers numerous words rarely heard among the uneducated: blemish, pious, tawdry, tempered, phalloi, avid, discordant, whorls, mauve, flame-green, transpiercing, majolica, isolate (adjective), promiscuity, succumbing, voluptuous, ungainly, excrement.

The real impression of colloquiality in Williams is conveyed not so much through the vocabulary as through the sentence patterns and rhythms with their predominantly normal word order and closeness of subject and verb. Williams' favorite, though not exclusive, opener for a poem is a declarative sentence, often abrupt:

> The Rose is obsolete . . .
>
> I will teach you my townspeople . . .
>
> The little sparrows hop ingenuously . . .
>
> And yet one arrives somehow . . .
>
> Sorrow is my own yard . . .
>
> He's dead . . .
>
> The sea will wash in . . .

These openers command immediate attention—partly because they are so direct and idiomatic and partly becuse they convey a sureness of feeling and point of view. They also confront the reader with the blunt, factual existence of the thing being introduced, implying by the form of the declarative sentence that this thing truly exists.

Yet the poems that begin so simply often go on into greater complexity of syntax and meaning then the simple declarative openers would lead one to expect. Just as Williams' vocabulary is not limited to the most common words of the day, so his syntax has a greater complexity than is normally found in spoken language. Short primer sentences are often followed by a complex trail of phrases and clauses that build up the emotion and complicate the thought, as in this passage from "Seafarer":

> He invites the storm, he
> lives by it! instinct
> with fears that are not fears
> but prickles of ecstasy,
> a secret liquor, a fire
> that inflames his blood to
> coldness so that the rocks
> seem rather to leap
> at the sea than the sea
> to envelope them

Even many of the short imagist poems have an unusual complexity of syntax within their short span. "Between Walls" (*CP1* 453), for example, has a simple vocabulary—walls, grow, lie, cinders, glass, shine—but a complex sentence structure, including two subordinate clauses and inverted word order: "lie cinders." Thus Williams' style is as much influenced by models of written prose as by the American speech he heard around him. Without the complexity of diction and syntax that written models afforded him, Williams would have been a much more limited poet; without his ear for speech rhythms, he would have been a duller one.

4. Metaphor

Williams' attitude toward metaphor and other forms of figurative language is ambivalent. He says, for example, in "Notes in Diary Form," that as a result of the "figures used" in most verse "the general impression of the things spoken of is vague. . . . The truth of the object is somehow hazed over, dulled" (*SE* 67). Such poetry "is a soft second light of dreaming" because "there's too often no observation in it" (*SE* 67). Williams goes on to quote an unidentified passage of verse as admirably exemplifying the absence of figures:

> and the late high growing red rose
> it is their time
> of a small garden

Williams claims that the vividness of this passage is the essence of poetry itself:

> Poetry should strive for nothing else, this vividness alone, *per se*, for itself. The realization of this has its own internal fire that is "like" nothing. Therefore the bastardy of the simile. That thing, the vividness which is poetry by itself, makes the poem. (*SE* 68)

This passage summarizes what many readers and critics have regarded as the essential quality of Williams' poetry—vivid realism. But had Williams limited himself to nonfigurative language, his poetry would be less vivid than, at its best, it is, and certainly less complex in thought and feeling.

Metaphor, as Aristotle recognized, is the poet's greatest linguistic tool for creating freshness of perception. The discovery of new, unformulated resemblances between unlike things is a powerful resource for articulating the exact shade of a physical quality or a state of mind for which no word (or words) used literally would do. Metaphor, in its various syntactical forms (including simile), abounds in Williams' poetry, and one needs only a little familiarity with Victorian and genteel poetry to appreciate the element of novelty in Williams' metaphoric language. Consider a few examples that give us fresh perceptions of physical things: "the sea . . . sways / peacefully on its plantlike stem" (to describe the slow swelling motion of the sea); "fallen maple leaves / still green—and / crisp as dollar bills"; a nervous little girl's "cordy legs . . . writhing / beneath the little flowered dress." Or take the wheelbarrow "glazed" with rainwater. By transferring the quality denoted by "glazed" from pottery and ceramics to the phenomenon of wetness on a wheelbarrow, Williams calls attention to the phenomenon in a novel way, a way that existing literal terms—slick, smooth, shiny, glistening—fail to do.

Williams also uses metaphor to express states of mind and concepts. In "Seafarer" (*CP2* 114), the exhilarating contact with the sea of reality produces "fears that are not fears but prickles of ecstasy," that is, a pleasure that is intensified by the ingredient of

fear. In "These" (*CP1* 458) abstract qualities are implicitly compared to bullets on a battlefield: "emptiness, despair . . . They /
whine and whistle." Williams is describing a state of depression
in which despair and emptiness seem to be not merely a form of
privation but active, threatening, penetrating forces. In another
poem, "The End of the Parade" (*CP2* 20), Williams develops a
witty extended metaphor comparing the decline of the English
poetic tradition to both a sentence falling apart and a parade
petering out:

> The sentence undulates
> raising no song—
> It is too old, the
> words of it are falling
> apart. Only percussion
> strokes continue
> with weakening
> emphasis what was once
> cadenced melody
> full of sweet breath.

"The Botticellian Trees" (*CP1* 348) develops a more elaborate
conceit in which winter branches are visualized as bits and pieces
of the alphabet gradually becoming composed into words and
then bits of grammar until they finally produce the "full song" of
summer foliage. The correspondence between organic growth in
nature and the mental-verbal process that produces a poem is
freshly realized in this poem.

As some of the examples already illustrate, Williams' propensity
for original metaphor leads him into tropes so fantastic or surreal
as to seem illogical. For example, in a trope that is humorous,
grotesque, and grim, Williams personifies death as a bald barber
who cuts "my / life with / sleep to trim / my hair" (*CP1* 212). To
cut *A* with *B* in order to trim *C* seems a roundabout way of pro-
ceeding, but, viewed as a reflection of the Shakespearean paradox
of sleep as restorative and sleep as "death's second self," Williams'
conceit makes sense. Sleep may refresh body and soul, but the
hours spent sleeping are substracted from a total life span, and
so, in a sense, death does trim one's hair.

Both synesthesia and mixed metaphor occur in "At the Faucet
of June" (*CP1* 196), in which a spot of sunlight on a varnished
floor

is full of a song
inflated to
fifty pounds pressure

at the faucet of
June that rings
the triangle of the air

How can a song, which consists of organized sounds moving in time, be "inflated" with air—and inflated not by an air pump but by a faucet that plays musical instruments? Perhaps it all makes sense as an exuberant celebration of the coming of spring, with the birds singing and with the sun intensifying the pressure of growth in the fibers of plant life. "June" is thus a metonymy for the vital forces that pour out of nature in the spring.

One can find statements in Williams' writings attacking "similes"—and, if taken out of context, seeming to imply that Williams opposed figurative language, or at least wished to keep its use to a minimum in favor of a more literal language. In making a case for Williams as a nominalist, Miller cites a passage from the Prologue to *Kora* in which Williams states:

Although it is a quality of the imagination that it seeks to place together things which have a common relationship, yet the coining of similes is a pastime of very low order. . . . Much more keen is that power which discovers in things those inimitable particles of dissimilarity to all other things which are the peculiar perfections of the thing in question. (*SE* 16)

But Williams' objection here is not to similes based on a respect for the integrity of the things compared, but to trite or forced comparisons based on insufficient regard for the real features of the objects compared. In the next paragraph, Williams refers to an objectionable kind of simile-making as a "loose linking" in which "all manner of things are thrown out of key so that it approaches the impossible to arrive at an understanding of anything." Williams himself, however, uses a great deal of figurative language in his poetry, some of it in the syntactical form of similes, as in this striking comparison from "The Catholic Bells" (*CP1* 397):

grapes still hanging to
the vine along the nearby

> Concordia Halle like broken
> teeth in the head of an
>
> old man . . .

The basis for resemblance here is conceptual more than visual:
the sparseness and fragility of grapes and teeth, the agedness of
man and vine, and the inexorable cycle of growth and decay that
unites them both. The comparison helps to individualize both
tenor (the remaining grapes) and vehicle (an aged man's teeth)
by the unexpected rightness of the correspondence between dissimilar things. The power of the simile is further enhanced by
the connotations it borrows from the word "Concordia" as a reminder of the harmony and plentitude that the cycle both creates
and subverts.

Far from discrediting the proper use of metaphor and simile,
Williams goes so far in one passage from the Prologue as to
justify a boldness of metaphor for which Donne and the metaphysical poets have been especially admired in the twentieth
century:

> The imagination goes from one thing to another. Given many things
> of nearly totally divergent natures but possessing one-thousandth part
> of a quality in common, provided that be new, distinguished, these
> things belong in an imaginative category not in a gross natural array.
> To me this is the gist of the whole matter. (*SE* 11)

Williams implies here that metaphor, when rightly used and
rightly understood, is a way of increasing our knowledge by discovering subtle but actual points of resemblance between unlike
things. Nowottny's discussion of metaphor in *The Language Poets
Use* is useful in clarifying Williams' view of how metaphor extends
the range of human perception. "A metaphor," Nowottny writes,
"is thus a set of linguistic directions for supplying the sense of an
unwritten literal term."[27] Nowottny's concise definition becomes
clearer if it is recalled how *glazed* supplied "the sense of an unwritten literal term" for the appearance of wetness on a wheelbarrow's
surface—a phenomenon for which the existing vocabulary
proves inadequate.

Although Nowottny emphasizes the linguistic variety that metaphor makes available, it is clear, too, that such variety makes possible the discovery of new links or correspondences between things.
The enlivening and illuminating power of metaphor is praised in
Williams' poem, "A Sort of Song" (*CP2* 55), in which "the people

and the stones" are reconciled "through metaphor." Without metaphor, a creation of the imagination, external reality—or objects as objects—would, as Coleridge has observed, be dead to us.

In the passage on similes in the "Prologue" to *Kora,* Williams makes it clear that the impulse that leads poets to make similes is sound and normal—to discover unity in being through real correspondences. But the unity achieved in metaphor must not suppress the individuality of the objects brought together for comparison; instead, metaphor should make one more aware of the individuality of those things which it fuses:

> But one does not attempt by the ingenuity of the joiner [craftsman] to blend the tones of the oboe with the violin. On the contrary the perfections of the two instruments are emphasized by the joiner; no means is neglected to give each the full color of its perfections. It is only the music of the instruments which is joined and that not by the woodworker but by the composer, by virtue of the imagination. (*SE* 16)

Valid metaphor, for Williams, is not achieved through an ingenious imposition of resemblance on dissimilar things, but through the discovery of actual likenesses, the test for which is the way that something familiar suddenly becomes vivid to the reader's mind.

One might consider, for example, the metaphor in these lines by Williams:

> Old age is
> a flight of small
> cheeping birds
> skimming bare trees
> above a snow glaze
>
> (*CP1* 152)

The basic comparison encourages the mind to transfer aspects of one phenomenon (small birds in flight) to another (condition of old age). As the metaphor is extended, its component images become subordinate metaphors for different aspects of the condition the poem attempts to define. Physical qualities of the birds— their smallness, their hollow bones, the dry texture of their feathers, their high-pitched voices—evoke the diminished size, fragile bones, dry, papery skin, and higher, weaker voices characteristic of old age in human beings. The bare winter landscape evokes the barrenness of life for many of the elderly for whom existence has become increasingly impenetrable or resistant—as glazed-over snow is resistant to birds seeking nourishment. A good metaphor organizes the contents of memory in a new way. Thus, if one is familiar with both snow glaze and the-seeming-impenetrability-of-the-world-to-the-old (this must be hyphenated because no single word exists for this particular phenomenon), the poet fuses these hitherto separate concepts in one's mind into a new metaphor, providing a fresh understanding of the subject involved.

This discovery of an unexpected similarity between things that have existed separately in the mind until the metaphor brings them together provides a pleasurable surprise and a sense of enlarged knowledge. It is not scientific knowledge; it cannot be measured by surveys or tested in the laboratory—it can be tested only in the minds of readers who examine the metaphor in the light of their own experience and observation and say, "Yes, this comparison strikes me as true." Both the poem as the poet wrote it and the poem as the reader reads it depend on the universality—or at least the typicality—of the quality the metaphor expresses or defines—though that quality might never before have been focused and realized in the particular terms the metaphor offers.

5. The Broken Style: Disordering of the Senses

Something more encompassing than visual form, accurate diction, functional rhythm, and original but exact metaphor is at work in Williams' poetry to create a fresh response to reality. A crucial feature of Williams' poetry is his often disjointed syntax—syntax that involves abrupt juxtapositions and associations as well as disruptions of conventional logic and grammar. As noted earlier, as the diction in "Sea-Trout and Butterfish" is predominantly literal, Williams had to find other means of particularizing his perceptions. While metaphor ("quick tails / whipping the streams") and sound ("fine fins' sharp spines") intensify the particularity of the perceived objects, the most important means of particularization is the disjunctive, elliptical, and slightly ambiguous order of details—testifying to the rapidity of impressions crowding in on the poet's eye and his haste to take them all in lest an inhibiting concern for conventional order limit his sensory awareness.

Besides being used to register the rapid impact of sensations, the disjunctive style is also used to provide multiple perspectives in order to grasp the complexity of the subject or to create surreal psychological or social landscapes. But disjunctiveness is really much more than a method or technique in Williams' poetry; it is at the heart of his definition of poetry, and its chief function is to break up conventional expression so that new associations of thought and feeling might emerge.

As Williams tries to explain it in *Spring and All,* what distinguishes poetry from prose is not a matter of tangible mechanical forms such as audible rhythms or stanza forms but something more subtle. He thought it "ridiculous to say that verse grades off into prose as the rhythm becomes less and less pronounced" (*I* 144). While verse "is likely to be more strongly stressed than . . . prose," one can't assume that the "force" that gave verse such a rhythmic character as it has had in the past "will always reveal itself in that character" (*I* 145). Just as Coleridge in chapter 14 of *Biographia Literaria* attempts to answer the question "What is poetry?" by describing the powers of mind that the poet brings into play, so Williams tries to define poetry according to its origins in the human mind. Williams felt that one could recognize a piece of writing, whether in lines or in paragraphs, in meter or nonmetrical form, as coming from the true "source" of poetry (*I* 145). The terms "force," "reveal," and "source" suggest that poetry comes from a power within but transcending the individual imagination. Williams had a difficult time explaining how one could recognize the genuine thing, often falling back on circular definition: "It has the purpose of poetry written into [it] and therefore it is poetry" (*I* 145). The most specific account he could give of the special essence of poetry was as follows:

> Either to write or to comprehend poetry the words must be recognized to be moving in a direction separate from the jostling or lack of it which occurs within the piece.
> Marianne [Moore]'s words remain separate, each unwilling to group with the others except as they move in the one direction. (*I* 146)

Williams here is speaking of disjunctiveness. In a true poem, the words—because their "jostling" for individual attention gives them a life of their own—may not seem to be moving in "one direction" as they do in prose. However, since a poem is a unified whole, the words do eventually add up to a total meaning. A seeming incoherence resolves itself to coherence. Williams here is defining a poem in terms of simultaneous but incongruous movements, much like Emerson's memorable description of the progress of bold, self-reliant thinking: "The voyage of the best

ship is a zigzag line of a hundred tacks. See the line from a suffi-
cient distance, and it straightens itself to the average tendency"
(153). Each tack is valued for itself and has its own pleasures and
rewards like the separate words and phrases in a poem; Emerson's
"the average tendency" is equivalent to Williams' "the one direction." An Emersonian trust in the vagaries of his own imagination
is what has made Williams so receptive to the influences of surrealism, dada, and cubism.

In 1917 Williams began his experiment in daily automatic writing that resulted in the prose "improvisations" of *Kora in Hell*.
Influenced by Rimbaud, Williams aimed to submit himself to the
free flow of his thoughts, to loosen his attention and to stimulate
his imagination:

> By the brokenness of his composition the poet makes himself master
> of a certain weapon which he could possess himself of in no other
> way. . . . Thus a poem is tough by no quality it borrows from a logical
> recital of events nor from the events themselves but solely from that
> attenuated power which draws perhaps many broken things into a
> dance giving them thus a full being. (*SE* 14)

Brokenness of composition is a weapon against convention and
staleness of thought. Although Williams here plays down the inherent importance of the "events themselves," the larger context
of the Prologue makes it clear that Williams is in no way denying
the objective or intrinsic value of the things or events, but emphasizing the necessity for an imaginative re-ordering of experience
in such a way that the intrinsic values in things and events will be
made manifest.

What Williams meant by "brokenness of . . . composition" and
of the imagination's power to draw "many broken things into a
dance" is clarified by his comments in *Spring and All* on Juan
Gris. Gris, in his cubist paintings, used the "forms common to
experience so as not to frighten the onlooker away but to invite
him" (*I* 107), but these common forms were "in some peculiar
way" detached "from ordinary experience" (*I* 110). They were
detached from their ordinary arrangements in life, broken up,
rearranged, made to interpenetrate: "The cloud laps over the
shutter, the bunch of grapes is part of the handle of the guitar"
(*I* 110). The result is not an "illusion" of reality, but a created
"object" in its own right. Of course, it is still an illusion or imitation
because it has recognizable elements, but it is not a "copy," not
merely an attempt to duplicate a preexisting thing or scene.

Something of the cubist influence is evident in Williams' tendency to view the object from multiple, abruptly shifting perspectives—a tendency found even in poems written in complete sentences and in which line breaks do not disrupt syntax. In "The Yachts" (*CP1* 388), for example, from the opening perspective of the yachts contending safely in the partly enclosed sea, the poem shifts to the dangers of the "ungoverned ocean" that can torture the "biggest hulls." The perspective then shifts from "biggest hulls" to the yachts as "mothlike in mists," but this miniaturization is immediately followed by an enlarged scale: "with broad bellying sails," and the yachts now seem very large in comparison to the "antlike" crew. Also in contrast to the fragility of "mothlike," the yachts now have "sharp prows" that toss green water. In one stanza the yachts are described warmly as "live with . . . grace" and in subsequent stanzas more coldly as "too well made" and "skillful."

These multiple perspectives are not limited to visual and temporal shifts, but include both symbolic abstraction and direct comment. Williams' narrative poems frequently combine narrative movement with time-free symbolism and general comment in order to gain both the vividness of realistic narrative and the complexity of thought and feeling that the subject evokes. Thus because the yachts "appear . . . / live with the grace / of all that in the mind is fleckless, free and / naturally to be desired," they evoke not merely the simple, oft-interpreted social allegory of the rich versus the poor in the 1930s, but something more universal. Like Keats's urn, the yachts represent some timeless ideal that, in its rare beauty, is both desperately appealing and coldly perfect—cruelly unattainable except, perhaps, in art.

As already mentioned, in "Sea-Trout and Butterfish" (*CP2* 353), cubistic brokenness, or disjunctiveness, is a means of registering the full impact of sensory input—although Williams' fragmentations are not nearly so extreme as, say, those in Picasso's 1921 painting, *The Violin*. The poem begins logically enough, but abruptly, with a statement about the most general features of the fish—the qualities one would notice at first glance: "the contours and the shine." The next two details satisfy a need for further general information about the subject. The first of these details is conceptual rather than physical: "caught." The second, "lying," gives the general physical attitude or posture of the object. The next detail is more specific: "orange-finned." But this term is curiously related by syntax to the preceding participle "lying" so that "orange-finned" seems to have verbal force, as if "lying / orange-finned" were an activity, not an inert stasis. Gerard Manley Hopkins, according to W. A. M. Peters, used similar wrenchings of syntax to make us see the "inscape" as an active form.[28]

With the next phrase, "and the two / half its size," the picture becomes more specific as the reader, too, begins to "unravel" the details to form a more differentiated scene. The reader now sees three fish, has some sense of their relative size, and realizes that one of them is orange-finned and the other two, as one reads on, are "pout-mouthed"—the most striking and individualizing term in the poem. In the first three couplets, references to specific physical features (orange fin, pout mouth, silver scales) are mixed in with more general or abstract references to posture, number, size, location, weight—all of which have to do with how the fish occupy space. In effect, there is an irregular mix of Lockean primary and secondary qualities—each equally real. These qualities are laid on with quick brush strokes, the words often related only by juxtaposition rather than grammar: "Silver scales, the weight / quick tails."

Although there is some expository logic to the order of presentation in so far as Williams begins with the most general impressions and moves on to more particular features, the organization of descriptive details appears, on the whole, to be determined by the order of perception, by the sequence in which the qualities of the thing impinged upon the mind. To some extent there is also an association of images, words, and rhythms at work. For example, "orange-finned" and "pout-mouthed" begin and close the second couplet with the same cadence and same phrasing. The "white" of the dish moves easily enough to silver," both being pale colors. The word "scales" may, by unconscious verbal association, lead to "weight"; and once the solidity of the fish has been noted, with their mass pressing down on the dish, it is an easy juxtaposition to the contrasting image, in an imagined retrospect, of the fish whipping the streams with their quick tails. Thus the sequence of perception is affected, in part, by other sequences of association in the composition of the poem.

At a more radical extreme the disjunctive style becomes surreal, as in the last third of "The Yachts" in which the ocean turns into a grotesque sea of desperate, failing human beings. Extreme disjunctiveness is especially frequent in Williams' dadaist period in the middle twenties, as for example in such poems as "Young Love" (discussed in chapter 4) and "The Agonized Spires" (*CP1* 211). In the latter poem, Williams describes a landscape in which "triphammers"

> . . . pulverize
> nitrogen
> of old pastures
> to dodge
> motorcars
> with arms and legs—

Surrealism, mixed metaphor, word play, and nonidiomatic syntax are all at work here. Triphammers cannot logically pulverize nitrogen, a gas, though they can pulverize the land on which nitrogen-producing plants grow. According to Peter Schmidt, the poem deals with the inundation of the countryside by "the rising tide of America's industrial culture."[29]The irrational dadaist syntax, assisted by strategic line breaks, makes possible multiple meanings: road construction pulverizes pastures to make way for Dodge automobiles so that humans must use "arms and legs" in order "to dodge / motorcars." But since the syntax continues past the line break after "motorcars," one is forced to combine the words into another phrasal unit: "motorcars / with arms and legs," suggesting the human appendages are part of the car. Thus "arms and legs" is a synecdoche that reduces humans to a mechanical function and also suggests that the motorcars are half human because people spend so much time in them and are so fascinated by them that they are welded to their cars.

The broken or disjunctive style in Williams is additional evidence of his place within an on-going romantic tradition. Abrams shows how the romantic desire for freshness of sensation took on a more radical form later in the nineteenth century in Baudelaire and Rimbaud, particularly in Rimbaud's theory and practice of the systematic disordering of all the senses as a means of experiencing the unknown. According to Abrams, Rimbaud, by reshaping the romantic concept of the poet as visionary, provided "the rudiments of . . . a genuinely new poetic," the implications of which "are still being assiduously explored by writers in our own generation."[30] Abrams therefore sees a continuity between the romantic desire to shed the lethargy of custom and the postromantic emphasis on "surrealism, free fantasy, automatic writing, and other modes of composition in which control is surrendered to the unconscious mind."[31]

In the hands of inferior poets, incoherence and randomness can become the cheapest way to purchase a dubious kind of originality. Williams recognized the risks involved in the method when he said that the potential "fault" of his improvisations was "their dislocation of sense, often complete" (*I* 117). But the disorderings in Williams' poems are usually unified by a permeating purpose or theme. The disordered sequence of sense data in "Sea-Trout" is evidence of an excitement involved in the act of perception—an excitement accompanying and evoked by authentic contact with something real outside the mind in its singularity and beauty. The disjunctive style—"the brokenness of composition"—is a way of breaking down more orderly and conventional uses of language that condition perceptions and limit responses to the object. Given the dualist tradition that cuts man off from nature, one can more fully appreciate the excitement of authentic contact expressed in Williams' poetry.

6. Symbolism: Representing the Universal

Perhaps Williams' most significant way of liberating the word, of seeing freshly, was to discover the universal in unexpected localizations of the particular. For example, in "The Term" (*CP1* 451), Williams sees an ironic reminder of human mortality—not in the skulls, dust, tombstones, or dying embers of conventional poetic imagery but in a rolling piece of brown paper "about the length / and apparent bulk / of a man" which, however, "unlike a man," rises again after being crushed to the ground.

In "Death" (*CP1* 346), there is a striking and initially irreverent originality in calling attention to a changed circumstance resulting from an indigent man's death: "the dog won't have to / sleep on his potatoes / any more to keep them / from freezing." This detail at once involves humor and pathos, but it soon becomes clear that the poem has an intellectual as well as an emotional dimension, its purpose being to define the essence of life by contrasting it with its opposite—a definition by negation. Williams brilliantly uses pseudosyllogism ("He's a bastard because / there's nothing / legitimate in him any / more"), bold metaphor ("he's / a godforsaken curio"), surreal personification ("love / an inside howl / of anguish and defeat"), and literal fact ("his eyes / rolled up out of / the light") to sharpen an awareness of the gulf between the living and the dead. The last example involves symbolic as well as factual meaning, for the "light" in Williams' symbology stands for that rare and transcendent beauty glimpsed from time to time in all things. One last device is the shift from the pronoun "he," used throughout most of the poem, to "it" in the last three lines as a means of registering the sense of nonidentity once life has departed. The whole procedure of the poem, with its mock-scolding, mock-contemptuous tone ironically intensifying the pathos, is a unique approach to a traditional subject.

This antipoetic and often slangy and irreverent treatment of the subject should not mislead one into thinking that Williams' poems have nothing to do with the transcendent universal. Many readers of Williams are familiar with his oft-quoted slogan, "No ideas but in things," an assertion that first appeared in the lyric poem "Paterson" in 1926 long before Williams adopted it as a refrain in the book-length *Paterson*. The phrase has meant many things to many critics. To some, it is not a statement of metaphysics at all, but of a rhetorical strategy for writing poems: focus on images and avoid abstraction and philosophizing. For others, such as Miller, the phrase indicates something more serious: a nominalist metaphysics in which only particulars are real. Thus construed, the phrase means no ideas, only things. Miller says that Williams' "attitude towards things . . . is Nominalist. Each object is itself and nothing more."[32] Miller uses the term Nominalist as it was used during the medieval controversy over universals, namely to mean that only particulars are real and are all that is known in sense perception, whereas universals are ideas constructed by the mind from what *appear* to be common properties in groups of apparently related particulars.

But nominalism does not do full justice to Williams. At the beginning of *Paterson*, Williams explicitly states that he is looking for larger patterns embodied in local realities: "To make a start, / out of particulars / and make them general." However vivid and particularized an object appears in his poems, its particularity, in his best poems, enriches our knowledge or at least appreciation of the universal which the particular embodies. In "Three Sonnets," Williams, while distorting the sonnet form, makes use of the sonnet's traditional subject, love, to present an argument that assumes a universal essence of woman: "In the one woman / I find all the rest" and "Upon her / their memory clings, each one / distinct, enriching her" (*CP2* 74). The essence found in the one woman is also present in others; his love of these others renews and enriches his appreciation of the essence in her.

For Williams, a particular object, event, or person is often seen as a transient embodiment of the permanent universal: "But often this symbol is suddenly destroyed when we see at last that love is not anything mortal" (*EK* 184). There is a distinct platonic tone to such a statement as this, just as there is a Jungian implication in the declaration that "the imagination / knows all stories / before they are told" ("The Gift," *PB* 61). In "Asphodel, That Greeny Flower," Williams reiterates the platonic doctrine of love as figured forth in *The Symposium:*

> I have learned much in my life
> > from books
> > > and out of them
> about love.
> > Death
> > > is not the end of it.
> There is a hierarchy
> > which can be attained,
> > > I think,
> in its service.
> > Its guerdon
> > > is a fairy flower;
> a cat of twenty lives.
>
> > > > > > > > (*PB* 157)

Although these lines are too abstractly didactic to be first-rate poetry, they serve to illustrate Williams' belief in transcendent universals. Through the love of beauty in things and people, one ascends the "hierarchy," or scale of being, to contemplate the transcendent idea of Beauty, and hence to achieve an intuition of immortality, referred to as "guerdon," "fairy flower," and, more informally, as a "cat of twenty lives."

The vividness of the particulars in Williams' poetry is a guarantee that the mind has, first of all, touched something outside itself—the individual form or inscape of the object described. But important as this contact is, it is not an end in itself. Williams' ultimate goal is "to embody knowledge," and knowledge depends on universals to make the world intelligible. "No ideas but in things" has a familiar Aristotelian ring to it, and Aristotle is generally thought to have believed that there were ideas or essences (forming agents) in things and that the general idea in the mind was identical with or corresponded to the idea active in the thing. According to Aristotle, the mind in recognizing an individual as a member of a species has direct contact with the immaterial form common to all the members and giving them their species identity. Aristotle, however, did not mean that sensory contact with the thing resulted in an easy, comprehensive grasp of the universal embedded in it, but that there was, in Frederick Copleston's explanation, "an objective foundation in things for the subjective universal in the mind."[33]

Williams obviously differs from Aristotle in being uninterested in or incapable of systematizing the universals into an articulated, hierarchical worldview, although Williams made some attempt at systemization in the five essays at the end of *The Embodiment of Knowledge*. Nevertheless, Williams' insistence that "ideas" are derived from and correspond to something actual in "things" is a step back across the dualism of Descartes, Locke, and Hume to the dominant theory of perception that had prevailed from Aristotle down to the seventeenth century, namely that the mind can perceive an objectively existing universal in the particular and that particulars, therefore, are not totally discrete or separate but share in the common, transcendent universal.

Williams—given the organic, evolving character of his cosmos—does not conceive of the universal as something that can be definitively stated. Each manifestation of the universal in a particular involves elements of difference or novelty. But Williams' focus on particulars is a way through to the universal, bypassing—as far as possible—stale, conventional conceptions of what the universal is. Just as Emerson says that symbols "must be held lightly, and be very willingly translated into equivalent terms" (237), so Williams declares: "The natural corrective is the salutary mutation in the expression of all truths, the continual change without which no symbol remains permanent. It must change, it must reappear in another form, to remain permanent" (*SE* 208). Although Williams here is thinking of the form of a poem as well as the observed particulars that go into it, his stance is compatible with the Aristotelianism of a humanist who probably would have disliked Williams' poetry had he been familiar with it. According to Irving Babbitt, the universal "is not to be taken as anything finite, as anything that can be formulated once for all," and "true classicism does not rest on the observance of rules . . . but on an immediate insight into the universal."[34] Such insight depends on the imagination's capacity to perceive the universal in the particular, the ideal in the real. Williams' celebrated commitment to particulars must be seen, then, as a means of beholding the universal in its immediate novelty and vitality, not as an abstraction paled by loss of reference to existence.

The place that universals hold in Williams' worldview will be discussed more fully in chapter 5, "Nature," but here the concern is more with the way in which universals are present in Williams' poems. Williams' insights into the universal are evident both in

poems in which the details are predominantly literal and those in
which the details or images are symbolic. For example, in the
poem about the cat climbing over the jamcloset (*CP1* 352), Williams describes a cautious, deliberate movement that cat owners
would recognize as typical if not universal. Typical too is the comic
aspect of the normally dignified feline caught momentarily in an
awkward situation, with both the right forefoot and hindfoot
down in an empty flowerpot while the other two feet remain some-
where higher up. Although Hugh Kenner argues that the cat is
as much a means of fleshing out a preexisting syntactic pattern
(As . . . first . . . then . . .) as the poem is a means of representing
the cat,[35] it is equally true that a pattern of cat behavior, which
Williams recognized as salient, existed prior to his observation of
the particular cat that occasioned the poem.

The particularity of this poem is not an embodiment of any
great truth, nor did Williams probably think of the poem as being
concerned with anything universal. Nevertheless, in its accurately
observed particulars, the poem does capture something typical.
What the poem provides that differs from actually seeing a real
cat step down from a jamcloset is a selection and arrangement of
words that represent and isolate the most salient features from
the full impingement of sense data one would be taking in if
actually present when the event took place. This selection of detail,
reinforced by the hesitant visual and aural rhythms of the short
lines, is a form of *mimesis* in the Aristotelian sense of the word—
a selection of portions of reality represented by a medium and
organized into a new whole that clarifies and emphasizes the universal—although, in this poem, a very slight universal.

In "the Young Housewife" (*CP1* 57), the writing consists entirely of descriptive and narrative particulars. Some of the observed details, however, are based on inference rather than on
sense impression taken in from the speaker's external point of
view. Such an inferential detail is the fact that the house belongs
to the husband and that the wife typically "moves about" in negli-
gee. The comparison of the young housewife to a fallen leaf also
goes beyond observation of surface detail: it implies an interpretation of the housewife's isolation. Although largely imagistic, the
poem moves from its particulars to general significance through
the juxtaposition of images, the connotations of key words
("walls," "solitary," "fallen"), the explicit comparison of the woman
to a fallen leaf, and the extension of this image into symbolism
in the final image of fallen leaves crushed by the wheels of the
speaker's car.

On the cultural level, the poem implies a social observation about the restriction imposed by custom on a particular woman— a confinement that the young woman seems scarcely conscious of though it is manifest to the reader in the sensuous but listless rhythms of her movement. The possessive form, "of her husband's house," underlines a social and economic fact of the times: both wife and house were normally considered the husband's property. The effect of the social mores of the 1910s is to diminish the wife's freshness so that, though young, she sadly seems a fallen leaf: cut off from the larger organic whole. And the same forces isolate the speaker, "solitary in my car," preventing him from any closer contact with her that might prove enlivening to both of them. It is not with sadistic intent that he drives over the fallen leaves, but with a mocking sense of his own ineffectuality ("I bow and pass smiling") as part of a social system that is silently but surely crushing the young housewife. The ordinarily "noiseless wheels" of his car—perhaps a variant of William James's metaphor for habit, "the great flywheel of society"—rush unavoidably with a crackling sound over the dried leaves in the street. This image, while implying a further stage of devitalization, enlarges the scope of the young housewife's fate to include many others.

But beneath the cultural observation the poem makes, there is a deeper level having to do with the *universal* conflict between the spontaneous, outgoing energies of human nature and the confining structures of forms and conventions. Such a universal idea might not be immediately evident to a first-time reader of Williams, although the idea is fundamental to Williams' worldview, and it is resonant in the image of the fallen leaf that links human to natural processes that transcend the particular cultural situation.

Moving on to a still higher level of abstraction, there are in Williams' poems brief references to transcendent realities of great importance to the poet's sense of the ultimate meaning and value of life. The few abstract words denoting these transcendent ideas—love, beauty, joy, soul, life—are all but buried in the texture of literal and symbolic imagery and the disjunctive progression of thought in Williams' poems. In "Rain" (*CPI* 343), love is first referred to in specific contexts—"your love," "her love"—but towards the end of the poem it is generalized: "love is / unworldly / and nothing / comes of it but love." Love, which Williams conceives as having both a timeless platonic existence and a spatio-temporal one (symbolized by spring rain), flows into the world, manifesting itself both in nature, as Eros compelling the flowers into form and as a nurturing human love offered by women and both desired and feared by men. Beauty is referred to several times in Williams' poems as a timeless, universal, and everpresent reality. In the faces and spontaneous gestures of people at a baseball game, Williams sees a potential for both violence and "beauty / the eternal"; or, when Williams says of the red lily, "in your common cup / all beauty lies," he is not speaking merely figuratively or sentimentally, for he conceives of beauty as a living whole "unexpressed all about me awaiting expression . . . aching to be freed in the semblance of a leaf or anything" (*EK* 164).

The most important way in which the universal is manifest in Williams' poems is in his use of symbolism. The fallen leaf in "The Young Housewife," the spring rain in "Rain," and the piece of drifting brown paper representing human mortality in "The Term" are examples of this symbolism. In "Choral: the Pink Church" (*CP2* 177), the transcendent universal is embodied in an unusually complex and difficult symbolism. "Choral" is one of Williams' most religious and platonic poems, a hymn to the power of universal human love—but the word "love" is not once used in the poem, although "joy" comes in near the very end, as an exclamation. The poem draws upon images from Schiller's "Ode to Joy" and rhythms from the choral adaptation of Schiller in Beethoven's Ninth Symphony. Schiller's ethereal Daughter of Elysium, who represents the joy that accompanies universal love, becomes Williams' pink church that is also, in a surreal fusion of images, a woman's breast, thus retaining some element of Schiller's feminine symbol for joy. In the opening lines of the poem, Williams compares the radiance of the pink church to a dawn in Galilee—alluding to the birth of Christian love as altering the pre-Christian tragic view of life and inaugurating an eventual victory over evil:

> Pink as a dawn in Galilee
> whose stabbing fingers routed
> Aeschylus and murder blinked . . .

The first intuition of this transcendent source of love is, for Williams, an unforgettable moment:

> the thrust of that first light
> was to me
> as through a heart
> of jade—

The poet's whole being was altered inwardly by the light of this love, as translucent jade seems to have its own inner source of illumination. The poem, difficult and strange, makes sense once the universals that its key symbolic images embody are discovered.[36]

The discussion here should indicate that in many poems that seem purely descriptive, the particular details embody universals that give coherence and significance to the particulars—either as literal representations of generic things (cat stepping down from jamcloset) or symbolic representations of more intangible qualities and ideas (a brown paper rolling in the wind, dry leaves crushed by noiseless wheels, a pink jade church). Furthermore, some of the "ideas" in "things" do really seem to be conceived as transcendent, elevated ideals which penetrate the actual world of transient phenomena and give a meaningful order to what might otherwise be sound and fury.

As in the discussion of metaphor in the preceding section, the question again arises as to whether Williams regarded symbolism as compatible with the priority he seemed to place on vividness of representation per se. Just as he opposed "the bastardy of the simile," Williams can also be found vigorously opposing symbolism: "No symbolism is acceptable. No symbolism can be permitted to obscure the real purpose, to lift the world of the senses to the level of the imagination and so give it a new currency" (SE 213). Taken by itself, this passage is a drastic repudiation of symbolism—unless one understands "symbolism" in this context to mean standardized or traditional symbolism—symbols grown stale with use. The larger context of Williams' critical writing, as well as his poetic practice, indicates a more favorable view—one that is consistent with and illuminated by Emerson's discussions of symbolism.

Emerson's Nature (1836), gave American literature the rudiments of a theory of symbolism. "Particular natural facts are symbols of particular spiritual facts," Emerson confidently claimed (31), but to a more skeptical twentieth-century reader, the notion of nature pervaded with human life is likely to seem a pathetic fallacy—a failure to distinguish between subjective human states of mind and objective external phenomena. One balks at the Emersonian notion of sermons in stones. In "The Poet" (1844), however, Emerson gives a more sophisticated account of symbolism. In Nature he had emphasized the fixity of natural symbolism, saying that "there is nothing . . . capricious in these analogies" (32); for example, the "sea-beaten rock" stands for the virtue of firmness (39). But in "The Poet" he states that "all symbols are fluxional" (237). That is, the images expressing a given truth are prone to change, but the truth or universal embodied in the image is permanent:

> The poet by an ulterior intellectual perception, gives them [traditional symbolic images] a power which makes their old use forgotten, and puts eyes and tongue into every dumb and inanimate object. He perceives the independence of the thought on the symbol, the stability of the thought, the accidency and fugacity of the symbol. (230)

But does Emerson mean—and does Williams think—that any fact whatsoever of nature could be used arbitrarily to symbolize any idea or any state of mind? Would the sea-beaten rock be an effective symbol of gaiety or weakness? Both Williams and Emerson would answer, it would seem, that there is some flexibility in the choice of objects (and in the attributes of an object) to embody universal truth, but that the choice cannot be entirely arbitrary. While to Emerson, the sea-beaten rock is a symbol of moral firmness, to Nathanael West in *Miss Lonelyhearts* it is a symbol of a nearly catatonic withdrawal from life: "Miss Lonelyhearts stood it with the utmost serenity: he was not even interested. What goes on in the sea is of no interest to the rock."[37] Nevertheless, both of these symbolizations draw on the actual properties of the rock: its solidity, imperviousness, and firmness.

Although in "The Poet," Emerson often relegates to secondary status the transient image that conveys the universal truth, a careful reading of the paragraph in which he claims that "all symbols are fluxional" reveals that the choice of symbol is not as arbitrary as his tone would suggest. In pointing out that, in the eyes of one person, dawn's "morning-redness . . . comes to stand . . . for truth and faith," Emerson makes the point that other people may justifiably prefer different symbolic images for the same truth: "a mother and child, or a gardener and his bulb, or a jeweler polishing a gem" (237). But note that these images all have a common denominator: they all involve a capable adult who has faith in realizing the full potential of the object being nurtured or worked with. The dawn's "morning-redness" likewise suggests a potential—the hopeful promise of a new day.

To return to Williams, his apparent repudiation of symbolism ("No symbolism is acceptable") is followed in the very next paragraph with a statement about the imagination that is both Emersonian and Coleridgian and that affirms the value of symbolism in literature:

The imagination is the transmuter. It is the changer. Without imagination life cannot go on, for we are left staring at the empty casings where truth lived yesterday while the creature itself has escaped behind us. It is the power of mutation which the mind possesses to rediscover truth. (*SE* 213)

Williams' objection is to fixed and conventional symbols (ready-made symbols such as he thought Eliot had borrowed), not to symbols created from a more direct perception of physical phenomena. Conventional symbols are "the empty casings where truth lived yesterday while the creature itself has escaped behind us" (*SE* 213). But the mind has "the power of mutation . . . to rediscover truth," which is essentially the theme of Williams' poem "The Rose," in which he says that the rose, as conventional symbol, is "obsolete," but that a renewed awareness—Emerson's "ulterior intellectual perception"—of the rose as an object in its own right leads to new, more precise poetic and symbolic uses:

> But if it ends
> the start is begun
> so that to engage roses
> becomes a geometry—
>
> (*CPI* 195)

There is a great deal to say in favor of the view, shared by Emerson and Williams, that nature is an inherent source of symbolism derived from the actual properties of things anterior to language and literary convention. It seems doubtful, for example, that gold could have acquired its preeminent symbolic connotations of sublimity, royalty, and divinity if it were not for its actual qualities: its brilliant sunlike color, its beautiful lustre, its malleability, its resistance to corrosion, and its scarcity. Williams, in fact, uses this very example:

> Gold, by its indestructibility by air or acid, its malleability, its color and its sheen, is the symbol toward which money looks in its turn. And there is nothing that can take its place as an uncounterfeitable, readily available, though rare enough, object of value to pass thus symbolically from hand to hand. The old originators *didn't select gold arbitrarily* to be their standard of exchange. (*SE* 244, italics added)

Similarly, the traditional symbolic associations of the rose with love must have developed in part from European man's response to actual qualities of the rose: its color (the intense red of some

roses forming an association with blood, hence life; the fainter
red of other roses suggesting a delicate blush), its fragrance, the
soft smoothness of its petals and their multifaceted layering, and,
not least, the way the petals unfold to reveal a dark golden center.
These correspondences are evident in another poem Williams titled "The Rose":

> First the warmth, variability
> color and frailty
>
> A grace of petals skirting
> the tight-whorled cone
>
> Come to generous abandon
> to the mind as to the eye
>
> Wide! Wider!
> Wide as if panting, until
>
> the gold hawk's-eye speaks once
> coldly its perfection

The physical qualities of the rose make it, objectively, a fitting
correspondent to, or symbol of, prized human qualities: grace,
generosity, passion, elegance. Many of the key words have dual
reference to both the flower and to human feelings—*warmth, vari-
ability, color, frailty.* The phrase "generous abandon" can describe
both a type of noble human passion and the way the petals of a
rose progressively unfold to reveal the golden center. Although
the rose is, in appearance, a static object, the progress of the description creates the subliminal suggestion of a feminine sexual
climax, from the initial arousal to the peak moment.

A poet must have some awareness of the traditional uses of
symbolic images, but if the stock of symbols is to be refreshed,
the poet must either add to it new images or perceive and use the
old images in fresh new ways. The poet need not be a botanist,
zoologist, or specialist of any kind in order to make effective use
of natural phenomena for metaphor and symbolism; more important is the imaginative power to perceive appropriate analogies
between internal and external phenomena:

> M. Deschanel . . . may have met some English artists who were also
> botanists; but the harm is not in the study of plants, it is in the forget-

fulness of large relations to which minute observation of Nature has occasionally led those who are addicted to it. (*I* 299)

It may be that the more knowledge a poet can incorporate *imaginatively* into his symbols and metaphors, the greater, or at least more interesting, the poet will be; but being learned per se does not make one a poet any more than ignorance does. Through the discovery of actual resemblances between things, the poet enriches our qualitative knowledge of the world and provides a sense of its underlying connectedness.

A thorough discussion and classification of symbolism in Williams' works would involve formidable difficulties beyond the scope of this book because of the complex uses of symbolism in Williams' writing and because the term *symbol* is so loosely defined in twentieth-century critical usage. For example, is "To Waken an Old Lady" a symbolic poem or does it consist of an extended metaphor: "Old age is / a flight of small / cheeping birds . . ."? Or is it an extended metaphor that has such complexity of meaning as to warrant calling it symbolic? There are several other distinctions to think about. Some poems, like "The Yachts" and "The Bull," are devoted entirely to the symbol, whereas, in other poems, the symbol occurs in only a part of the poem, like the severed cod head at the end of "The Cod Head" or like yeast in "Aigeltinger," a highly fecund, varied, evolving fundamental life form symbolic of organic complexities: "Nothing has ever beaten a mathematician / but yeast." One would have to distinguish between poems in which the symbolic image is metonymic—a natural part of the setting in realistic narrative—such as the biological processes in "Spring and All," symbolic of human creative processes, and poems in which the symbol is "metaphoric"—imported or imagined, as in "The Lion," in which the beast drags a woman through the snow. One would also want to explore the extent to which Williams' symbols draw upon literary sources and formal branches of knowledge and to what extent they are the invention of his own mind.

There is finally the question of how Williams' use of symbolism relates him to the romantic tradition. Certainly one feature that Williams has in common with the Romantics is that, like them, he created his own symbology—a system of recurrent symbols: dance, music, light, ground, clouds, sea, rain, blossoming, wind, birds, journey, images of descent, burial, or immersion. Included in Williams' recurrent images are special visionary symbols—light, flame, sun, music, wind—that attempt to embody some ideal dimension of existence. Although Williams uses these symbols in unique contexts, many of them are common to romantic poetry. Wordsworth's "correspondent breeze" also blows through Williams' "The Wind Increases," and Shelley's image of the sun, a symbol for the imagination that links the human and the divine, appears frequently in Williams' work as a symbol of a creative and transcendental power both in nature and in the human mind. Furthermore, Williams' belief that symbolic *imagery* must change in order to reexpress and reenliven permanent *truths* firmly links him to Emerson, who regards revitalization of symbols as the poet's most important task—"re-attaching even artificial things and violation of nature, to nature, by a deeper insight" (229) and perceiving "the stability of the thought, the accidency and fugacity of the symbol" (230).

4

THE IMAGINATION: A FORCE OF NATURE

1. Williams' Organic Poetics

To defamiliarize the familiar in order to see it anew and to perceive the universal in the particular—these two functions of the imagination have already been discussed. But for Williams, the imagination also has a productive function—the creation of organic forms of which the whole exceeds the sum of the parts. Abrams notes that the word *create,* which in our time "has become a colorless, almost dead metaphor," was several centuries ago "new, vital, and—because it equated the poet with God in his unique and most characteristic function—on the verge . . . of blasphemy."[1] The word *create* and its cognates gradually became clichés when divorced from the organic cosmology that gave them significance. Morse Peckham observes that the appearance of organicism in early nineteenth-century thought changed the concept of originality: "If the universe is constantly in the process of creating itself, the mind of man, his imaginative power, is radically creative" and "now the artist is original because he is the instrument whereby a genuine novelty, an emergent, is introduced into the world."[2] With organicism, the injunction to imitate nature no longer means—or no longer *merely* means—to mirror nature, but rather to imitate nature's power to generate new forms.

According to this theory, organically new works of art are "objects" that take their place in a world of other objects. By 1923 Williams, too, came to think of poems as "objects" and later, in 1931, aligned himself temporarily with objectivism, which, he said, "recognizes the poem, apart from its meaning, to be an object to be dealt with as such. Objectivism looks at the poem with a special eye to its structural aspect, how it has been constructed."[3] The theory did not, as will be seen, rule out the referential or

mimetic function of poetry. Rather, the theory called for an immediate focus on the technical problem of getting a poem written,
which generally meant an intuitive feeling for when a word or line
or stanza was right. For Williams, coming indirectly at meaning
through primary attention to technique was one way to avoid stale
expressions of meaning and thus to "represent arrests of the truth
in some particular phase of its mutations" (*SE* 205).

Williams frequently asserted that the artist is cocreator with
nature. In *Spring and All* he said that "the work of the imagination
is not 'like' anything but transfused with the same forces which
transfuse the earth—at least one small part of them" (*I* 121).
Seeming to deny mimetic content to poetry, Williams added: "He
holds no mirror up to nature but with his imagination rivals nature's composition with his own" and "he himself becomes 'nature'" (*I* 121). In 1923, the year *Spring and All* was published (and
several years before Williams would officially align himself with
"objectivism"), he vehemently declared, "in great works of the
imagination A CREATIVE FORCE IS SHOWN AT WORK
MAKING OBJECTS WHICH ALONE COMPLETE SCIENCE
AND ALLOW INTELLIGENCE TO SURVIVE" (*I* 112). As late
as 1949, in "A Beginning on the Short Story," Williams was still
maintaining that "the imagination inflamed, the excitement of it is
that you no longer copy but *make* a natural object. . . . You yourself
become the instrument of nature—the helpless instrument" (*SE*
303). The notion of poetic creation as an extension of natural
process is also explicitly treated in several poems, including "The
Botticellian Trees," "A Coronal," "St. Francis Einstein of the Daffodils," and "The Wind Increases."

The last-mentioned poem illustrates both in form and statement Emerson's memorable formulation in "The Poet" of organic
poetics: "For it is not metres, but a metre-making argument that
makes a poem,—a thought so passionate and alive that like the
spirit of a plant or animal it has an architecture of its own, and
adorns nature with a new thing" (225). In Williams' poem, the
wind is a symbol of natural process that stirs growth in living
things and also generates a corresponding impulse in man towards creative expression:

> The harried
> earth is swept
>   The trees
> the tulip's bright
>   tips

                              sidle and
            toss—

                        Loose your love
            to flow

            Blow!

            Good Christ what is
            a poet—if any
                              exists?

The poem then shifts to a related image, that of the tree, symbolizing the growth of organic expression issuing from one's whole
being as it is intimately rooted in the "ground"—the fertile, immediate, chaotic level of consciousness. The poet whose whole being
is involved in creation is

            a man
            whose words will
                        bite
                              their way
            home—being actual
            having the form
                              of motion

            At each twigtip

            new

            upon the tortured
            body of thought

                  gripping

            the ground

            a way
                  to the last leaftip

                                        (*CP1* 339)

Like the tree putting forth new leaves from the nourishment its
trunk and roots draw up from the ground, the imagination,
rooted in sensory experience, issues forth in words. The words
"bite" and are "actual" because of their sensuous, rhythmic hold

on concrete realities. They have the "form of motion," because they are energized by the life within and convey a sense of the world as process. Just as the leaves are the outgrowth of straining forces within the tree, so words emerge from the "tortured body of thought": a poem emerges from a concentrated and demanding inner struggle toward exact expression, which is to say organic form, with a distinct element of novelty. The unexpected word "tortured" distinguishes Williams' view of artistic creation from a sentimental kind of organicism according to which poetry is a spontaneous, effortless outpouring—as if there were no striving or effort in nature itself.

The irregular but exact placement of the words in "The Wind Increases" is symptomatic of its "constructed," or organic form— to be distinguished from the other notion of organic form as taking shape in a single burst of unreflective and unrevised composition. The visual spacing and enjambment of the lines suggest both fitful movements of the wind and the open spaces through which the winds of creation might be released—a loosening of traditional form to allow new outlets for energy and emotion. The spacing also creates rhetorical emphasis in some cases, as in the single-word lines "Blow!", "bite" and "new." Although organic form cannot be fully explained on functional grounds such as visual mimesis, rhetorical emphasis, and rhythmic movement, in this particular case, the prosodic form seems especially well suited to the poem's expressive content.

The desire to release the form-creating energies underlying existing forms was expressed early in Williams' career, in "America, Whitman, and the Art of Poetry" (1917). This essay, much more balanced and thoughtful than some of Williams' later polemics against tradition, logic, and the university, begins by acknowledging, in effect, some value in tradition: "There is no art of poetry save by the grace of other poetry."[4] Williams then goes on to speak of the forming principles within the constitution of the mind that generate the external forms that poetry has taken. Behind the "aristocratic forms" of "pentameters and . . . quatrains" lay the "democratic groundwork of all forms, basic elements that can be comprehended and used with new force":

> Being far back in the psychic history of all races no flavor of any certain civilization clings to them, they remain and will remain universal, to be built with freely by him who can into whatever perfections he is conscious of.[5]

Williams' Jungian view of the generative forms might have been

worked out more fully in discussions with Kenneth Burke who
seems to have something similar in mind when he says that the
human mind is innately responsive to "such arrangements of subject matter as produce crescendo, contrast, comparison, balance,
magnification, series, and so on."[6] An example of what Williams
might mean by the a priori "democratic groundwork of all forms"
is the principle of variation from a norm. In traditional verse,
meter and stanza provide regularity while metrical substitution,
sentence length, and other factors affecting pace and accent provide the variation. In free verse, end-stopped lines of roughly
equal length and duration are the norm against which enjambent
and irregular length provide variation. Though the method of
achieving variation within regularity may differ, the need for
some interplay between these two factors is universally felt.

Williams' scattered remarks about the creative process itself refer to two different but integrated states of mind: one a fluid,
semiconscious state leading to automatism, and the other an alert
concentration appropriate to craft or making. In "A Beginning
on the Short Story," Williams describes the initial state of consciousness conducive to writing in terms of Keats's poem "Sleep
and Poetry." Williams says:

> At first all the images, one or many which fill the mind, are fixed. . . .
> Then it begins; that happy time when the image becomes broken or
> begins to break up, becomes a little fluid. . . . The rigidities yield—
> like ice in March, the magic month. They coalesce and, finally, merci-
> ful sleep intervenes. Sleep is black. (*SE* 307)

And:

> We are speaking of the resemblances between falling asleep and the
> awakening of the imagination that sometime impossible step to be
> taken before the writing begins (tho' it is wavelike and even during
> the writing, of many qualities, it rises and falls—tho' it remain of the
> same texture). (*SE* 307)

The semiconscious dream state is the subject or mood of several
poems, too: "Portrait of the Author" (*CP1* 172), "A Good Night"
(*CP1* 144), and "Paterson: Episode 17" (*CP1* 439).

Elsewhere, however, Williams stresses conscious craftsmanship
and the idea of a poem as something that a poet makes. In "Author's Introduction" to *The Wedge*, for example, Williams, in making his oft-quoted comparison of a poem to a machine, was
implying that a poem is an efficient construction: "A poem is

a . . . machine made out of words. When I say there's nothing sentimental about a poem I mean that there can be no part, as in any other machine, that is redundant" (*SE* 256). Paradoxically, Williams uses a machine metaphor to say something about organic form, namely that all parts of a poem are essential to its existence as that particular poem. Redundancy is that which is in excess of a poem's specific character as a made object—not necessarily in excess to the treatment of its theme as such, for a poem has an identity or shape that is only partly determined by its theme.

Williams adds that it is not what a poet "*says* that counts as a work of art, it's what he makes, with such intensity of perception that it lives with an intrinsic movement of its own to verify its authenticity" (*SE* 257). Theoretically, a given poem has an intrinsic movement—a movement in time that is recognizable not only as a poetic rhythm but as a rhythm peculiar to that poem. By intensity of perception, Williams means not primarily perception of the subject or scene external to the poem, but principally perception of how the words are moving and interacting, so to speak, as the poem gets written. Williams would probably approve of T. E. Hulme's memorable description of this process:

> A powerfully imaginative mind seizes and combines at the same instant the important ideas of its poem or picture, and while it works with one of them, it is at the same instant working with and modifying all in their relation to it and never losing sight of their bearings on each other—as the motion of a snake's body goes through all parts at once and its volition acts at the same instant in coils which go contrary ways.[7]

This complex interplay of both spontaneous and controlled activity is implicit in Williams' comparison of the creative state to sleep, which is "wavelike . . . *even during the writing,* of many qualities" (*SE* 307, italics added).

Romantic theory makes room for both conscious and unconscious processes, as in Coleridge's famous description of how the imagination is "first put in action by the will and understanding, and retained under their irremissive, though gentle and unnoticed control" (269). Although Williams sometimes speaks as if poetic composition is a spontaneous, unconscious process for him as he becomes the "helpless instrument of nature," his more considered view of the subject calls for a synthesis of conscious and unconscious activity, as stated in his criticism of Kenneth Patchen's poetry:

It's all right to give the subconscious play but not *carte blanche* to spill
every thing that comes out of it. We let it go to see what it will turn
up, but everything it turns up isn't equally valuable and significant.
That's why we have developed a conscious brain. (*SL* 194)

So much happens so fast in the sorting and selecting process of
writing a poem that conscious attention to the theme or to any
single formal aspect can be only part of what is involved; and
much of the time, as Howard Nemerov argues, writing poetry is
a matter of "getting something right in language,"[8] a rightness
that poets often feel at the moment but cannot explain until much
later, if at all. Still, the sense of rightness is not entirely subjective,
for it undoubtedly is based on norms inherited from language
and poetic tradition, although the norms may not be fully analyz-
able and may be rooted, as Williams believes, "far back in the
psychic history of all races."

2. The Poem as an Object

The result of the creative process is an "object"—but what exactly did Williams mean by thinking of poems as objects? Given
Williams' organic poetics according to which artistic creation
brings forth something new in nature, a poem that is a slavish
imitation of established conventions—whether of Victorian or
more recent vintage—would not be a new object, but a carbon
copy. Such a poem would exemplify what Coleridge called "mechanical form"—form determined from uncritical acceptance of
external norms, not thrusting up from within, creating its own
"authenticity" by the poet's urgent need for unique expression.

On the other hand, a poem that was too formless also failed to
achieve the status of "object." In his remarks on objectivism in his
Autobiography, Williams indicated first of all that objectivism was a
reaction to imagism, which, having "no formal necessity implicit
in it," had run out to mere "free verse"—a term that Williams
considered a "misnomer," since verse by definition has "measure"
(*A* 264). By "formal necessity" Williams apparently meant a tension in the design of a poem that made all the parts and their
order necessary, so that a reader feels a sense of completion comparable to that provided by a traditional form like a sonnet. Williams defined an objectivist poem as itself an "object" that
somehow did have formal necessity and was an "antidote . . . to
the bare image haphazardly presented in loose verse" (*A* 265). His

protest here is against imagery that is not charged with significance and against rhythms that are too lax, too close to undistin-
guished prose. Williams' metaphor for the organic unity of a
poem, a "machine made of words," suggests that the "object-ness"
of a poem has to do with its economy, movement, and physicality,
for a poem's "movement" is "intrinsic, undulant, a physical more
than a literary character" (SE 256).

Thus Williams' objectivist view of a poem as an object can be
distinguished from the New Criticism idea of a poem as a tightly
unified *thematic* structure of meanings and images. The New Critics thought of a poem's integrity as inhering in an unalterable
organization of meanings and symbolic images, whereas the Objectivists (Williams, Zukofsky, Oppen, and a few others) thought
of autonomy, or object-ness, as inhering primarily in *prosodic*
structures. Examples that Zukofsky cites are the counterbalancing
of two-syllable words by words of three or four syllables, and the
development of a pattern in which the majority of polysyllabic
words begin with an accent.[9] Aside from the use of regular visual
stanzas, Williams probably did not take such arbitrary patterning
very seriously. Some exceptions are the split units (depends /
upon, white / chickens) in "The Red Wheelbarrow," the monosyllabic words that end the longer lines in "Between Walls," and the
trochaic words that end the longer lines of "Proletarian Portrait."
Objectivism was a movement in the direction of "pure poetry" of
which, Zukovsky said, music is the mathematical limit.[10]

Williams acknowledged that the Objectivists were indebted to
Gertrude Stein for "her formal insistence on words in their literal,
structural quality of being words. . . . It all went with the newer
appreciation, the matter of paint upon canvas as being of more
importance than the literal appearance of the image depicted" (A
265). The reference to words as words and to paint as paint indicates Williams' concern with the medium apart from the message.
In "The Work of Gertrude Stein," Williams praised Stein for having "completely unlinked" words "from their former relationships
in the sentence." "Each under the new arrangement has a quality
of its own, but not conjoined to the burden science, philosophy
and every figment . . . of law and order have been laying upon
them in the past" (SE 116). By treating words as things—as sensuous phonic and visual objects that could be played with and arranged in unusual combinations of sound and syntax—one could
compose them into an original aesthetic object.

Williams' theorizing about the poem as an object doesn't begin
until about 1923. In the Prologue to Kora in Hell, his main concern

is with the power of the imagination to see the object intensely and to detach it from its conventional associations. In the first issue of *Contact* (December 1920), his emphasis is on the indigenous poet's expression of "perceptions rather than . . . standards of attainment."[11] About a month later, in the January 1921 issue, Williams declares in favor of "writing that reveals a high type of discovery" whose "form is of expression and conveyance rather than of structure."[12] But with the fifth and last issue, June 1923, Williams is using language closer to that of his prose in *Spring and All* regarding the poem as a "new form dealt with as a reality in itself" (*I* 133). While Williams maintains that good writing is a "triumph of sense," he adds that "the sense is in the form."[13] Williams does not use the term "object" for poem in *Contact,* but, in reacting to Santayana's criticism that Whitman lacked "thought," he says that Santayana failed to recognize the "masterful comment of [Whitman's] poetical construction itself."[14] Thus Williams' editorializing in the 1923 issue of *Contact* is consistent with the bolder declarations published in *Spring and All* in the fall of 1923.

If Williams came to his "objectivist" theory in 1923, does this mean that poems written prior to that year failed to be "objects," while all of his subsequent poems would pass the object test? Although it is true that Williams became more concerned with the shape of the short poem, casting more than half the poems in *Spring and All* in regular stanzas, many of his earlier poems do have the distinctive physicality of "objects" resulting from their high degree of visual or aural patterning. To mention a few, "The Young Housewife," "El Hombre," "Canthara," "Danse Russe," and "Spring Strains" seem especially well made—distinct from poems at the other extreme that seem more discursive, more concerned with getting something said, such as "Gulls" and "Tract." One might consider "Canthara" (*CP1* 78) for example:

> The old black-man showed me
> how he had been shocked
> in his youth
> by six women, dancing
> a set-dance, stark naked below
> the skirts raised round
> their breasts:
>   bellies flung forward
> knees flying!
>   —while
> his gestures, against the

> tiled wall of the dingy bath-room,
> swished with ecstasy to
> the familiar music of
>   his old emotion.

David Perkins, who uses this poem to illustrate the artistry of free verse, is undoubtedly correct in his observation that "mainly, though not always, the lines are arranged to enact the movement of the voice speaking: they reinforce the natural rhythm by linear notation."[15] That is, about half of the fifteen lines (1–3, 7–9, possibly 10, for rhetorical emphasis, and 11) comprise complete grammatical units after which a pause, however slight, would seem natural. This naturalness, however, detracts from, rather than contributes to the sense of the poem as an object, because line length tends to become merely a notation for the speaking voice. The next part of Perkins' analysis is relevant to the poem's object-ness:

> The enjambment makes for a continuing momentum . . . from the beginning of the poem to the end, yet individual lines are bound together as integral units by assonance and alliteration ("his gestures against the"). A sense of conclusion is obtained by modulating at the end into a regular iambic rhythm and by echoing in the last line the long "o's" from the first line of the poem.[16]

Similar features of the poem's "made" quality include the internal off-rhymes *showed* and *shocked* (each being the fifth monosyllable in its respective line), *while* and *tiled*, *against* and *dingy*, and *swished* and *ecstasy*. The high density of alliteration in the lines

>   . . . stark naked below
> the skirts raised round
> their breasts

the kinesthetic effect of "bellies flung forward," and the cadence of "the familiar music" repeated in "of / his old emotion" also add to the structured feel of the poem.

Perkins' analysis of the poem is intended to show the "formal effects," or "artistry," of free verse, but his concluding comment on "Canthara" indicates that he would regard the poem as somewhat less an object than might be appropriate: "Having noticed these details, however, one should add that the chief use made of the verse form is to avoid clutter, to write with directness and economy."[17] Certainly the conventional progression of the poem from narrative present ("The old black-man showed me") to past ("in his youth") and back to present ("—while his gestures") contributes to the effect of the poem as something said rather than made, but the poem does seem sufficiently tight and sufficiently patterned to be what Williams thought of as an object.

It is probably too restricting to confine Williams' notion of a poem as an object to those poems that have a high degree of visual and auditory pattern. Poems in Williams' "broken style"— characterized by sudden associations of thought, abrupt changes of scene and mood—may also be considered objects if, like a cubist painting, they have their own special coherence and wholeness. In *Spring and All*, poem "IX" (*CP1* 200–2), later titled "Young Love," does not have the shaping form of neat stanzas nor is it especially dense with alliteration and assonance, although repetition of words and brief spurts of cataloging give a rhythmic pulse to the poem. Its surface incoherence and fragmentation, however, may be evidence that the poet's imagination has broken through conventional form to create "a new thing, unlike any thing else in nature, a thing advanced and apart from it" (*A* 241). Its many private references indicate that the poem was written from the "inside," where emotional force generates the form of the poem.[18] The absence of exposition to ease the reader into the poem, to identify the characters, and to set forth the situation allows Williams to concentrate on language that is primarily sensory and emotional rather than expository. Here are the first sixteen lines of the poem:

> What about all this writing?
>
> O "Kiki"
> O Miss Margaret Jarvis
> The backhandspring
>
> I:clean
>   clean
>   clean:yes . . New-York
>
> Wrigley's, appendicitis, John Marin:
> skyscraper soup—
>
> Either that or a bullet!
>
> Once
> anything might have happened

> You lay relaxed on my knees—
> the starry night
> spread out warm and blind
> above the hospital—

Suppose one comes to this poem without any prior knowledge of
Williams. The reader would, first of all, be puzzled by the relevance of the opening question about writing, especially since nowhere else in the poem is there any mention of writing. Also
puzzling would be the names "Kiki" and "Miss Margaret Jarvis"
followed by "The backhandspring." Clearly, this poem does not
have the kind of coherence and order of "Canthara." Gradually,
from the fragments of the poem, a narrative emerges, but inter-
spersed with comments and questions. One can determine that
the setting is a hospital and that the characters in the drama are
involved in some way with it. It can be determined that an intense
affair took place "fifteen years ago," one that ended unhappily.
The elliptical nature of the poem may reflect personal reticence,
but it is also Williams' way of avoiding what he calls "a logical
recital of events."

However, with the aid of biographical information, one can sufficiently grasp the poem's internal coherence to appreciate how
well made the poem is. In 1906, at the age of twenty-three, Williams began his internship at the French Hospital in lower New
York City. It was a time of hard work, long hours, novelty, exposure
to human suffering—and proximity to young "nurses" who "were
kind—but wanted marriage" (A 78). Williams, in his *Autobiography*,
described how, after a patient had died, "you are left with a young
nurse beside you, watching you, and suddenly you are alone with
her" (A 85). He also described how with the nurses, "we'd sneak
out on the roof and hide together behind the water tank at night
and look at the stars"—a detail that gets into the poem (A 85).
Paul Mariani stated that, early in his internship, Williams "had
brushed up against sexual passion and had recoiled from it in
order to 'preserve' himself."[19] In a letter to his brother, Williams
confessed that he had "a weakness wherever passion is concerned"
and that he could "see the terrible results of yielding up to desire,"
which is what he feared he would do "if certain conditions are
present." Because of his dreams of achieving greatness, Williams
felt "I must discipline my affections . . . until a fit opportunity
affords" (SL 14).

Some sixteen or seventeen years later Williams, now entering
middle age, began his poem with the challenging, almost scoffing

question, "What about all this writing?" as if words and his ambition to be a great writer now seem pale beside his memory of an intense affair in his youth. The mere name "Kiki," likely a nickname for Miss Margaret Blake Purvis who is fictionalized as "Margaret Jarvis" in the poem, evokes her presence and the desires he felt at the time.[20] The excitement generated by her presence is suggested by "backhandspring." (In the *Autobiography* Williams recalls an intern trying to do a handstand on the bar of a beautiful patient's bed.) While Williams', or his narrator's, former excitement revives, he also recalls that he strove to be "clean / clean / clean"—the repetition suggesting a self-critical attitude toward his then puritanical self-discipline. Yet without the variety and possibility offered by New York—"Wrigley's, appendicitis, John Marin: / skyscraper soup"—he would have felt suicidal: "Either that or a bullet."

From this jazzy and jagged opening, the poem moves into a nostalgic narration of a time when he was physically close either to "Kiki" (or to someone so special that she is not named, only addressed as "you"). During that enchanted time on the rooftop, "anything might have happened"—including a proposal of marriage? But the next few lines undercut the romantic nostalgia as "unclean" with bitter self-sarcasm directed at the single-mindedness that put abnormal constraint on desire:

> Pah!
>
> It is unclean
> which is not straight to the mark—

Consequently, the poem turns to the anguish that the affair resulted in, and to the guilt that the narrator continues to feel and that he projects onto the surroundings in which the sexual consummation took place:

> In my life the furniture eats me
>
> the chairs, the floor
> the walls
> which heard your sobs
> drank up my emotion—
> they which know everything
>
> and snitched on us in the morning—

Then, on a line by itself, the question,

> What to want?

pinpoints the dilemma of that time: either remain "clean" and
unattached in order to achieve his dreams or yield to passion and
the need for intimacy. The next lines are a judgment on his lack of
intense single-mindedness, ironically compared to drunkenness:

> Drunk we go forward surely
> Not I

His mind then goes back to the hospital routines, which become
mingled with sexual opportunities and then again with the central episode:

> beds, beds, beds
> elevators, fruit, night-tables
> breasts to see, white and blue—
> to hold in the hand, to nozzle
>
> It is not onion soup
> Your sobs soaked through the walls
> breaking the hospital to pieces
>
> Everything
> —windows, chairs
> obscenely drunk, spinning—
> white, blue, orange
> —hot with our passion
>
> wild tears, desperate rejoinders
> my legs, turning slowly
> end over end in the air!

The event is not presented chronologically: the hysterics of the
aftermath come before the sexual act itself. The dizzying, turbu-
lent emotions involved in their passion are rendered through surreal spinning images and expressionistic color imagery, as if a
Chagall painting were set in motion. The narrative is then interrupted by a question—in the present tense, as if the narrator still
has not resolved the dilemma for himself:

> But what would you have?

The next lines suggest the loss of virginity—and the absence of a marriage proposal—that are the causes of the woman's wild grief:

> All I said was:
> there, you see, it is broken
>
> stockings, shoes, hairpins
> your bed, I wrapped myself round you—
>
> I watched.
>
> You sobbed, you beat your pillow
> you tore your hair
> you dug your nails into your sides
>
> I was your nightgown
>   I   watched!

It is clear that the narrator was both physically close, "I was your nightgown," and detached at the same time: "I watched!"—the exclamation suggesting that the narrator is astonished at his lack of sensitivity then.

The poem begins its concluding segment with the narrator's reaffirmation of his ideal, one that he had lapsed from, of a single-minded purity of pupose:

> Clean is he alone
> after whom stream
> the broken pieces of the city—
> flying apart at his approaches

"Clean" here means centered in himself and his purpose, like Emersonian man whose active force allows him both to organize the separate fragments of reality and yet to break free of any fixed order or obstacle that reality may impose. The narrator recognizes, however, that he was not that clean superman:

> But I merely
> caress you curiously
>
> fifteen years ago and you still
> go about the city, they say
> patching up sick school children

She has patched herself up enough to become a public nurse

ministering to sick school children. The poem ends on a note of
regret, of something unresolved, and a sense of the passionless
present in contrast to the unrepeatable passion of the past. In the
televised *Voices and Visions* segment on Williams, the voice-over
narration of the last half of this poem—as the camera moves
through the debris of smashed glass, broken furniture, and paint-
peeled walls of an abandoned building (representing the defunct
French Hospital)—is especially poignant.

Paradoxically, the surface fragmentation of the poem is part of
its quality as a well-made object. The demands of the poem's form
take priority over an orderly imitation of chronological progression. While there is a central episode, it is narrated in segments
that are out of sequence and are further interrupted by stanzas
consisting of questions or comments that are obscure in meaning,
like "In my life the furniture eats me," and quirky in syntax, like
"It is unclean / which is not straight to the mark." The initial
opacity is part of what it means for a poem to be an object. Despite
the fragmentation, the poem has a forward movement, a thrust
from beginning to end, although there is much variation in tempo
and rhythm. Read aloud, the poem has a musical quality unlike
poems in a more meditative or essayist mode such as, to use an
extreme contrast, Elizabeth Bishop's "Some Dreams They Forgot,"
which begins with the very proselike rhythm of

> The dead birds fell, but no one had seen them fly,
> or could guess from where. . . .

That can be compared to

> O "Kiki"
> O Miss Margaret Jarvis
> The backhandspring

The spiky sound of "Kiki," the internal rhyme and alliteration of
"Miss Margaret Jarvis," and the assonance, vividness, and surprise
effect of "backhandspring" are capable of giving much *immediate*
pleasure regardless of the obscurity of the passage.

The line breaks in "Young Love," even more so than those in
"Canthara," are geared to enforce the natural speaking voice, with
natural speech pauses. However, one unusual rhythmic device that
gives pulses of energy to the poem is the use of brief repetitions
and catalogs, usually in units of three. In addition to the catalog
quoted just above there are "I:clean / clean / clean"; "Wrigley's,

appendicitis, John Marin"; "the chairs, the floor / the walls"; "beds, beds, beds," etc. This repetition of rhythmic motifs along with the repetition of images and verbal motifs ("clean"/"unclean") adds much to the constructed quality of the poem, as do its compression and concreteness. Williams would probably regard it as having achieved "object" status more so than the more conventionally lyrical "Canthara."

3. Williams, Aristotle, and Coleridge: Imitation

While much of Williams' theorizing on poetry has to do with defining a poem as a made object apart from the importance or persuasiveness of its content, Williams clearly did not mean to deny poetry a relevance to life by denying it meaning. Just as Coleridge believed that the *"immediate* object" of "a *legitimate* poem" was to give pleasure but its *"ultimate* end" was to provide "truth" (267), so Williams believed that a poem must first succeed as a made object if its embodied truth is to have the quality of discovery. In the context of his definition of a poem as a "machine," Williams stated that only through the "intrinsic form" of a poem can one "make clear the complexity of his perceptions in the medium" (*SE* 256). His stress on formal construction was, in part, an attempt to come at meaning in new and unexpected ways, to keep from slipping into derivative modes of expression: The poet "composes" words "into an intense expression of his perceptions and ardors that they may constitute a *revelation* in the speech that he uses" (SE 257, italics added).

Williams' scattered and contradictory statements about what a poem is reveal an ambivalence that stems from his need to reconcile the poem as prosodic object with the poem as an "imitation" of reality in Aristotle's sense of literary art as an imitation. What Williams has to say about Aristotle indicates that Williams' objectivism was concerned with meaning as well as form, for, in Aristotle's view, a literary work was both an object in itself (he compared it to a living organism) and an imitation of reality beyond itself—namely the universal. That is, for Aristotle, a literary work was not a naive attempt to duplicate events exactly as they had occurred, but an effort to select, arrange, and represent elements of reality so that the representation would be a new whole capable of moving an audience and giving it insight into the probable and necessary.

Although Aristotle's comments on imitation are applied mainly to the genres of tragedy and epic, his theory of imitation is applicable to all genres, including the lyric, which Barbara Herrnstein Smith defines as "the imitation or representation of an utterance . . . in the same sense that a play is the imitation . . . of an action."[21] According to Aristotle, a poetic work does not achieve meaning by simply recounting events in the order and manner in which they have occurred in history; instead, imitation means the creation of a new object that imitates the universal rather than the particular. In the *Poetics,* Aristotle states that this new creation, "like a living organism [*zoan*] . . . may produce its own peculiar form of pleasure."[22] As David Daiches explains Aristotle,

> because the poet invents or arranges his own story, he creates a self-sufficient world of his own, with its own compelling kind of probability, its own inevitability, and . . . because that world is itself a formal construction based on elements in the real world, an illumination of an aspect of the world as it really is.[23]

Williams, in line with both Aristotle and Coleridge, frequently emphasized the crucial distinction between "copy" and "imitation." In his *Autobiography,* he tells of the painter who, when asked to identify something in a corner of his painting, said, "That, Madam, is paint." Williams said that the anecdote dramatized the modernist effort to advance from "the appreciation of a work of art as a copying of nature to the thought of it as the imitation of nature, spoken of by Aristotle" (*A* 240). He added that "the objective is not to copy nature . . . but to imitate nature, which involved active invention, the active work of the imagination." If the painting was "dull" and "unimaginative" because "the elements of paint are emptily used," then "the painting would prove empty even though it represented some powerful dictator or a thesis of Sartre" (*A* 241). "But by imitation we enlarge nature itself, we become nature or we discover in ourselves nature's active part" (*A* 241).

While Williams refers directly to Aristotle, his use of the terms *copy* and *imitate* indicate a probable familiarity with Coleridge. Imitation for both Coleridge and Williams required an active mind on the part of the artist. According to Coleridge, Wordsworth's representation of rustic life was "an *imitation* as distinct from a mere *copy*" because it involved "an imperceptible infusion of the author's own knowledge and talent" (283). Imitation thus required "likeness and unlikeness." "If there be likeness to nature without any check of difference, the result is disgusting, and the more complete the delusion, the more loathsome the effect."[24]

Likewise, Williams declares, "To repeat and repeat the thing without naming it [by an act of imagination] is only to dull the sense and result in frustration" (*I* 115). To "copy" nature is to create an "illusion" that "the ignorance of the bystander" wrongly attributes to "imagination," when it is really the result of "cruder processes" (*I* 107), such as are demonstrated (to use a current illustration with which, one expects, Williams would concur) in those PBS programs that provide instruction in painting landscapes.

Again, linking imitation to Aristotle, Williams says in "A Beginning on the Short Story" that "Art means the skillful lie—what doesn't exist—as Aristotle pointed out"; but this lie had a relation to truth: "It must be so artful with the truth that above and beyond anything else its beauty of style or accurate statement will negate all its petty and thoroughly excusable lies." (*SE* 301). A poem may be an "accurate statement" of some truth despite its distortions of literal or autobiographical fact: "petty . . . lies."

The truth is arrived at obliquely through an imaginative process that requires both a relaxation of inhibitions so that new associations of thought might occur and a concentration on the formal construction of a poem, a focus on getting it "right" so that the poet's attention is not primarily concerned with coherent organization of subject matter as, for example, an essayist might be. In "Against the Weather," Williams speaks paradoxically of the necessity for experimentation with artistic form as a means of sustaining the universal as a living force. There must be "the continual change without which no symbol remains permanent" (*SE* 208). This view is consistent with the one cited earlier regarding Williams' belief in universals:

> But often this symbol is suddenly destroyed when we see at last that love is not anything mortal, that it flows over the forms of the world like water that comes and withdraws. Yet as the objects of life are all we can know love by, this coming and going discloses us to be involved in a destiny more than we can imagine, which must be very marvelous. (*EK* 184)

Much that is central to Williams' thought is present in this passage. First, there is the teleological implication that we become more aware of our purpose through love. Second, there is the belief in both the transcendence of the univeral (its eternality) and its immanence (its continually flowing into actual existence). And third, there is the justification for seeing the universal in particulars ("this coming and going") and expressing these per-

ceptions in artistic forms that represent the universal fused with
the particular into a new whole. Thus a poem, for Williams, is an
"object" in two senses: it is a unified, dynamic pattern of prosodic
elements (visual and aural), some of which may have little to do
with a theme; and it is also—despite surface incoherencies—an
"imitation": a unified representation drawing on the referential
and connotative meanings of words to make a statement of truth.

"Objectivism," for Williams was really but a temporary, semi-
official designation for preoccupations that intensified with *Spring
and All* and persisted throughout his career. By defining a poem
as a shaped or made object, Williams was trying to reconcile his
views that poetry was both a spontaneous, organic extension of
nature and a highly crafted interplay of prosodic, syntactical, and
symbolic structures.

The most obvious way in which Williams was concerned with
form was in his obsessive search for "measure," for a nonmetrical
line that yet carried with it rhythmic necessity. His growing preference for composing in stanza units, his search for a "new measure"
for *Paterson,* and his elation over his invention of the triadic line
and "variable foot" all reflect his desire for the achievement of
organic form over formlessness as well as over prescribed forms.
Stanza formation, pace, line length, spacing, syntax, sound, wordplay, punctuation, visual appearance, the choice and sequence of
images—all were matters that called for disciplined workmanship,
for synthesis into organic form. Williams said that it was "in the
minutiae—in the minute organization of the words and their relationships in a composition that the seriousness and value of a
work of writing exist—*not* in the sentiments, ideas, schemes portrayed" (*SE* 109). "Art" had to be "art" before it could properly
absorb and express ideas and sentiments through its own generic
textures. Williams wanted verse that looked as if something had
been done with it, verse that was more than the unrevised expression of spontaneous feeling—though often his first drafts received
little or no revision. The repetition or patterning of verse elements apart from any thematic or rhetorical function pleased
Williams, who became more and more attentive to visual prosody,
often adjusting line length to fit a visual design.

The following examples of Williams' manuscript revisions are
offered here by way of an appendix to this chapter on the creative
work of the imagination. A close look at how Williams revised his
poems—in so far as his intentions can be inferred from rough
drafts—will help to clarify his insistence on the poem as a made

object and his attention to the "minutiae" of poetry through which the expression of "sentiments, ideas, schemes" could be raised to new levels of freshness and vividness.

The two available drafts of "Between Walls" (*CP1* 453) indicate Williams' imagist concern with direct treatment of the thing perceived as well as his objectivist desire to make an "object" with such concentration on form that it "guarantees the authenticity" of what has been seen and felt. First consider the finished poem, published in 1938:

Between Walls

the back wings
of the

hospital where
nothing

will grow lie
cinders

in which shine
the broken

pieces of a green
bottle

This is as pure an imagist poem as any Williams ever wrote, lacking even the truncated generalization, "So much depends upon," of the earlier wheelbarrow poem (although it contains one slight generalization in the subordinate clause, "where / nothing / will grow"). Since the poem was written during the time when Williams affiliated himself with the Objectivists, one might expect to find a good deal of formal patterning in the poem. Even before the 1930s, however, Williams was experimenting with prosodic patterns, especially the short lines grouped into couplets, triplets, and quatrains in *Spring and All* and, within these groupings, special variations such as the couplet in "The Red Wheelbarrow" with the end of each first line splitting a compound and the second line consistently shorter than the first, or the triplet in "To Elsie" with the consistently short middle line sandwiched between the longer first and third lines.

The most obvious formal feature of "Between Walls" is the patterned visual appearance of the poem on the page: tiny couplets, with the second line even shorter than the spare first line. Such a design acts very much like a convention leading one to expect a minimum of self-assertion, as in Robert Creeley's poems, or, as in imagism, a sharp focus on the image, or both of these attitudes. But Williams seems to have thought of objectivism as involving all kinds of structuring patterns. Rod Townley observes "a set of built structures" in "Between Walls." One of these structures affects the way one visualizes the images in space: the poem focuses the attention "like a zoom lens of a camera,"[25] moving from the hospital wings to cinders to bits of glass. Most often, objectivism seems to have meant aural and visual prosody and the relation of syntax to line. As an example of the latter, Townley notes that the intransitive verb "lie" is "the main fulcrum of surprise"—"it holds the subject motionless within the moving focus of the eye and it retrospectively pulls the title into the syntax of the poem."[26] In Williams' oral reading of the poem, the longest pause is after "will grow," thus marking the turning point from a negative to a positive movement that begins with "lie."

Other visual and aural patterns are evident. For example, the cadence of the title, "Between Walls," is repeated in two subsequent phrases:

the back wings   in which shine

and as the poem reaches closure, the rhythm approximates an accentual meter:

the broken pieces ‖ of a green bottle

The last words in each of the longer lines—*wings, where, lie, shine, green*—receive more visual if not accentual emphasis; furthermore, the alliteration of *wings* and *where* and consonance of *shine* and *green* give these pairs the effect of faint rhymes. The high frequency of plosives (*b, t, k, g, d, p, ch*) and short vowels (especially variants of *i*) give the poem a thin, crisp sound appropriate to the hard-edged distinctness of the images—wings, cinders, broken glass.

With the exception of the minimal stanza form, suggesting an attitude of self-effacement while also, in a stylized way, mimicking small, fragmented objects, the patterns discussed here have little or no mimetic or thematic function but serve primarily to give the effect that this is a poem, a made thing—more highly artificed than ordinary prose or speech.

There are two typed drafts, both double-spaced, of "Between Walls"—an earlier one in the Beinecke Rare Book and Manuscript Library at Yale (below, left) and a later one (below, right, and in the illustration) in the Poetry/Rare Books Collection at Buffalo. A comparison of these drafts reveals more clearly the process Williams went through to achieve both meaning and form. Both drafts have the poem in three-line stanzas, whereas the finished poem is in couplets—an important change.

Between Walls [Yale]	Between Walls [Buffalo]
the back	the back
wings	wings
of the	of the
hospital	hospital
where	where
nothing	nothing
will grow	will grow -
they have	lie→ cinders
strewn	in which
cinders	shine
in which	the broken pieces of
shine	a green
pieces	bottle
of a green	are
bottle	flowering

The first version (Yale MS Za 29) has no hand corrections, indicating that Williams was probably temporarily satisfied. The Buffalo draft (MS A39) consists of thirteen typed lines with penciled markings and words added to the left of the poem and "are / flowering" handwritten (also in pencil) beneath "bottle" and then crossed out. (See facsimile on p. 139.) This draft—if the handwritten additions are ignored for the moment—shows that Williams had taken out "they have strewn" from the third stanza of the Yale version, placed a hyphen (used as a dash or colon) after "will grow," and brought up "cinders / in which" to complete the new third stanza.

Sometime after he typed this version, it seems likely that Williams made the first handwritten addition—"are / flowering" grouped with "bottle" as a tentative part of a fifth and final stanza: "bottle / are / flowering." Later he used pencil to cross out "are / flowering," leaving the metaphor submerged and implicit, with the idea being that what the imagination perceives in some sense blossoms into life. Both Townley and Gross, however, detect a negative tone in the poem. For Gross, the details "add up to a feeling of sudden desolation."[27] Townley says that since there is only "a mockery of the color of growing plants—the feeling is . . . sterile."[28] But the abandoned lines, "are flowering," and Williams' own remarks on the poem indicate that a more positive tone was intended: "All it means as far as I know, is that in a waste of cinders loveliness, in the form of color, stands up alive" (SL 265).

The excision of "they have strewn," which set subsequent modifications in motion, was in accord with imagist principles. Not only is economy improved, but the poem is brought more entirely into the present moment. The human cause of the cinders being where they are is an irrelevant or retrospective intellectual concern that distracts from the poem's impression of immediate perception.

But Williams apparently became dissatisfied with the new third stanza that he had created by excising "they have strewn" and filling the gap with a mere hyphen:

> will grow -
> cinders
> in which

The hyphen is meant to be a pause and a bridge between the negative and positive halves of the poem—between the barren setting and the discovery of shining beauty. Williams evidently felt

Between walls

the back

wings

of the

hospital

where

nothing

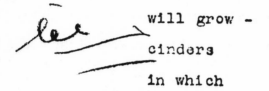

will grow -

cinders

in which

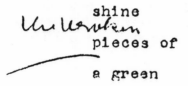

shine

pieces of

a green

bottle

Draft of "Between Walls" showing Williams' hand corrections.

dissatisfied with this abrupt and wordless bridge, and so he added the verb "lie" in the left margin (with a pencil line directing the verb to go between the lines "will grow" and "cinders"). Next he used two sloping, not quite horizontal pencil lines to mark off "in which / shine / pieces of" for regrouping into a separate stanza, the fourth:

<blockquote>

will grow -

lie→

cinders

———

in which

shine

pieces of

———

</blockquote>

This demarcation left him with four remaining lines—"a green / bottle / are / flowering"—to be compressed somehow into a three-line final stanza.

With the addition of "lie" as the main verb of the poem, however, Williams could no longer keep the competing predicate, "are / flowering." He crossed these lines out and, perhaps at this point, wrote "the broken" in the margin but extending part way between "shine" and "pieces of." The addition of "the broken" would give him a final six lines that could then be grouped into his tercet pattern. If he had retyped the poem at this point, the last three stanzas would have come out as follows:

<blockquote>

will grow
lie
cinders

in which
shine
the broken

pieces of
a green
bottle

</blockquote>

By crossing out the explicitly sentimental "are / flowering," Williams left his main idea submerged and more powerful, that idea having to do with the power of the imagination to discover a living, restorative beauty in fragmented things.

But after all the trouble to make the diction right and to maintain the three-line stanza, Williams wound up in the published version with couplets. How does one account for this change? One possible answer is that the poem, compressed from fifteen to ten lines, is vertically shorter and looks more jagged, mimicking to some extent the small, fragmented objects perceived. More important, however, is the tone created by the unassuming couplet form. According to Miller, the recessed second line of each couplet helps to create a "poetry of humility." That is, the stanza form itself subtly indicates a tone—an attitude of self-effacement in which the "richness of the universe" is discovered in "insignificant objects." Sparse lines—composed of bits of grammar surrounded by white spaces—and the absence of capital letters, punctuation marks, figures of speech, and heightened diction all reflect a saintlike "poverty," an absence of egotism such that "when almost everything is removed, the plenitude of what remains shines forth a thousand times brighter." Miller notes how the poem's "meter" contributes to the attitude of selfless attention: "There is a progressive effacement in the rhythm, the first line in each two line unit having as many as five syllables, the second, in all cases but one, only two."[29] Although the rhythm Miller speaks of is more visual than aural, his observation that it expresses a kind of noninterfering selflessness or negative capability makes good sense.

Were the poem to be written in triplets rather than couplets, the result would be simply less interesting, as one can see by comparing the published version to a hypothetical version in which the same words are grouped into triplets:

Between Walls	Between Walls
the back wings of the	the back wings of the
hospital where nothing	hospital where nothing
will grow lie cinders	will grow lie cinders
	in which shine the broken

```
in which                        pieces of a green
shine                           bottle
the broken


pieces of
a green
bottle
```

The triplet version reads monotonously and mechanically. The lines are all about equally end-stopped, and the line breaks (for example the placement of "back" and "wings" on separate lines) achieve nothing useful or interesting. The couplet version, on the other hand, with its subtle variations in line length, enjambment, and emphasis (for example, note how *nothing* stands out) achieves the delicate rhythm Miller speaks of.

The revisions Williams made on "To a Poor Old Woman" show him working for compactness of form and control of tone. A typescript draft (Buffalo MS A358) of the poem is more than a third longer than the published version:

To A Poor Old Woman (draft)	To A Poor Old Woman (*CP1* 383)
munching a plum on the street - she has a paper bag of them in her hand	munching a plum on the street a paper bag of them in her hand
They taste good to her They taste good to her. They taste good to her	They taste good to her They taste good to her. They taste good to her
You can see it by the way she is giving herself to the one, half sucked out,	You can see it by the way she gives herself to the one half sucked out in her hand

Comforted
a solace of ripe plums
seeming to fill the air
They taste good to her

in her hand - a relief
and a delight. Though she
is old and poor
her lusty appetite

lifts her up - a dignity.
Absorbed and relieved
She walks as through
a halo

of ripe plums. A sign!
A sign!
rising ~~to~~ enormous
to the evening sky

The published version begins pretty much as an imagist poem: the object is recorded in the present tense as if being witnessed on the spot. Even the reiteration of how good the plums taste is as much a report of sensory impression as an appraisal of value. The last two stanzas, however, incline more to evaluation and analysis: "You can see it by . . ." and "Comforted" are authorial assessments removed from the immediacy of the first two stanzas.

Williams' revisions of the typescript draft show his continuing adherence to imagist principles of economy and objectivity, evident in the way he toned down his impulse to sentimentalize the old woman by glorifying the eating of plums into a religious experience: "She walks as through / a halo / of ripe plums." Williams deleted most of the last three stanzas and also tightened up the first stanza by excising "she has" and removing the hyphen (dash) between "street" and "a paper bag." The deletion of the subject and verb, "she has," allows the object, "paper bag," to stand out more strongly and also makes it easier for Williams to condense the five lines into four, the norm for the poem. Furthermore, the reduction of "she / has a paper bag of them / in her hand" from an independent clause to a modifying phrase reserves the verb force for the second stanza's "They taste good to her." Williams got the second stanza the way he wanted it on the draft. Had he merely written

They taste good to her
They taste good to her
They taste good to her

the stanza would have been utterly boring. The irregular line

breaks in the finished poem make possible variations in pace and
emphasis, if not for the voice at least for the eye:

> They taste good to her
> They taste good
> to her. They taste
> good to her.

The irregular line breaks above show Williams' desire to move
his poem away from the conventions of prose that facilitate easy
absorption of information to the conventions of poetry that operate to enhance feeling and to arrest the attention in unexpected
ways. This is further evident in Williams' deletion of all punctuation except for one period and in his use of a more radical kind
of enjambment in the finished poem. For example, the finished
poem has two lines that are enjambed after prepositions (*on, by*)
while the draft version has none. One might also note how the
commas in the second stanza of the draft,

> to the one, half
> sucked out,

provide prose pauses that help the reader to bridge the enjambment, whereas the deletion of the commas,

> to the one half
> sucked out in her hand

speeds up the passage and makes it more seamless.

The most radical changes occur in the last three stanzas, which
are condensed into the final stanza of the published poem. Williams must have realized that "a halo / of ripe plums" was a ridiculous image and that "rising enormous / to the evening sky" was
overblown romantic writing. There are also too many words describing the satisfaction the woman is receiving from the plums:
relief, delight, absorbed, relieved. None of these words survives. "Relief" and "Relieved" are replaced by "Comforted," which asserts
something more positive than mere relief. The "halo" becomes
the more abstract "solace"—Williams did not always prefer the
concrete image to the abstract word.

A bite into a ripe plum, because of the way the juices burst and
flood the taste buds, can be a fully absorbing experience for the
moment—a hearty sensual experience the old need not lack. Wil-

liams' evaluation of the experience is more modestly stated in the published poem's "a solace of ripe plums / seeming to fill the air" than in the excessive claim in the draft version that the plums are a "sign" mystically "rising enormous / to the sky." But revision brings loss as well as gain. The unconventional idea that the woman is dignified by her "lust" ("her lusty appetite / lifts her up - a dignity") is appealing and interesting, but is doubtful that it survives, even implicitly, in the finished poem. The imagist preference for concreteness of presentation prevented Williams from making such an idea clear through general statement.

Besides the specific stylistic improvements, the compactness and rhythm of the finished poem give it much more the feel of a well-made poem. Strongly musical phrases add to the sense of the poem as a constructed object. One can note the assonance and alliteration of

$$\text{munching a plum on the street}$$

and how the two consecutive dactyls are closed off with the accented monosyllable "street." It is possible also to see how, in the last stanza, the music seems to strike a new chord with "Comforted," which, since it is the only word on a line by itself, brings the poem to a temporary halt, evaluates all that has gone before, and signals that the poem is about to conclude.

Whereas the revisions of "To a Poor Old Woman" were aimed at achieving economy and better control of tone, Williams' revisions of "The Term" (1938) show a special concern for tempo and rhythm. There are three typed drafts in the Buffalo collection; the first draft (below, left) is titled "A Resurrection." Perhaps Williams felt that the irony of this title was too obvious and heavy-handed for the pathos of mortality, which is the tone inherent in the material:

A Resurrection	The Term (published version)
A rumpled sheet of brown paper about the length	A rumpled sheet of brown paper about the length

and apparent bulk
of a man was
rolling slowly

over and over in
the street as a
car drove heavily

upon it and cr-
ushed it to the
ground. Unlike

a man's body
it rose again as
it was before.

and apparent bulk
of a man was
rolling with the

wind slowly over
and over in
the street as

a car drove down
upon it and
crushed it to

the ground. Unlike
a man it rose
again rolling

with the wind over
and over to be as
it was before.

Consider the published version first. Short stanzas provide sharp frames for detail, while short free verse lines of varied pace provide a hesitant, drifting rhythm for this imagist glimpse into mortality. The irony of the poem lies in the initial identification of a human body with the sheet of brown paper, "the apparent bulk / of a man," followed by a sharp differentiation of the lifeless object, as it undergoes a pseudoresurrection, from a living being, for whom resurrection is much more problematical. The title, a vast improvement over Williams' first choice, is dense in meanings: a *term* is a time for childbirth, a fixed period or lease of time, and the conditions or stipulations according to which something is done or acceded to. Man's "term"—his or her mortal lease on life—is from childbirth to death.

The rhythm, an essential feature of the poem, is perfectly suited to tone and meaning. From the predominantly iambic meter of the first five lines,

A rumpled sheet
of brown paper
about the length

and apparent bulk
of a man was

the poem shifts, signaled by "rolling" at the beginning of line 6, to an undulating mixture of trochees and anapests that mimic the motion of the paper,

$$\overset{/}{\text{rolling}} \text{ with the}$$
$$\overset{/}{\text{wind}} \overset{/}{\text{slowly}} \overset{/}{\text{over}}$$
$$\text{and } \overset{/}{\text{over}} \text{ in}$$
$$\text{the } \overset{/}{\text{street}} \text{ as}$$

and then comes down hard with three heavy consecutive stresses at the beginning of the fourth stanza:

$$\text{a } \overset{/}{\text{car}} \overset{/}{\text{drove}} \overset{/}{\text{down}}$$
$$\overset{/}{\text{upon}} \text{ it and}$$
$$\overset{/}{\text{crushed}} \text{ it to}$$

$$\text{the } \overset{/}{\text{ground.}}$$

After the heavy finality of "ground," the poem returns to the iambic, starting with "Unlike," but then shifts again with "rolling" back to the undulating rhythm of lines 6 to 9 until it comes to rest on the iambic meter of the final line:

$$\overset{/}{\text{Unlike}}$$
$$\text{a } \overset{/}{\text{man}} \text{ it } \overset{/}{\text{rose}}$$
$$\overset{/}{\text{again}} \overset{/}{\text{rolling}}$$

$$\text{with the } \overset{/}{\text{wind}} \overset{/}{\text{over}}$$
$$\text{and } \overset{/}{\text{over}} \text{ to be as}$$
$$\overset{/}{\text{it}} \overset{/}{\text{was}} \text{ before.}$$

   The first five lines of the typescript draft are retained in the published version. The splitting of "cr- / ushed" at the end of a line is startling; and, although it effectively emphasizes the harsh onomatopoeia of the "cr" [kr] sound, Williams might have thought the effect too distracting. The most important change in diction occurs in the fifth stanza, from "man's body" to simply "man," implying the whole human being and giving a dignity to the line, which "man's body" lacked. The most important rhythmic change Williams made was to lengthen the description of the paper's motion by inserting "with the wind" between "rolling" and "slowly" in line 6 of the draft, and "rolling / with the wind over / and over" after "it rose again" in the next to last line. The extra phrases add a necessary retardation and undulation to the flat rhythm of the earlier draft. They lengthen the duration and alter the rhythm of the lines describing the windblown paper so that one feels rhythmically the slow rolling motion and almost casual indifference of this pseudoresurrection.

Unlike the draft of "To a Poor Old Woman," which required drastic cuts, "The Term," in order to achieve its perfections as a made object, had to be lengthened in such a way as to provide the retardation and undulant rhythm that allow the reader's mind to dwell longer on the scene and to absorb its quiet lesson on mortality.

"Sunflowers" (1945), the last and perhaps most complex poem to be discussed here, presented Williams with a different set of problems. The nine drafts of "Sunflowers" show Williams initially composing in stanza units but then reshaping the poem into one segment to meet the demands of economy and cohesiveness. Although Williams, after 1923, generally sought to shape his free verse into stanzas, there were exceptions in which other considerations superseded his desire for a neat visual design.

The second of the nine drafts—Buffalo MS A331 (b)—is a typescript temporarily titled "Fruits and Flowers." The slash marks in this draft (quoted below, at left) indicate Williams' consideration of different line breaks. On the published version, at the right, only the chief accents are marked, not the secondary accents that some readers might find, say, on *-branched* or *-flow-*er. Although the accents are irregularly distributed, a two-stress accentual norm predominates (nine out of thirteen lines), against which three three-stress lines and a single one-stress line are variations:

Fruits and Flowers	Sunflowers
There's a sort of	There's a sort of
multi-branched sunflower	multibranched sunflower

<table>
<tr><td>

blooms hereabouts

when the leaves/begin

first to turn./ In

the rain their/shining

heads droop/beside

the old man/who stumbling

a little/solicitously

carries in/

the overloaded/baskets

of tomatoes/from

the fallen vines,/green

in one basket

and in the other

shining red

</td><td>

blóoms hereabóuts

when the leáves begín

fírst to fáll. Their

heáds leán in the ráin

about an óld mán who,

stúmbling a líttle,

solícitously carries in

his tomátoes from

the fállen vínes, gréen

in óne básket and, in

the óther shíning réds

</td></tr>
</table>

The art of free verse is sometimes evident in the placement of a single word. Had Williams (in the draft) moved "begin" down to the fifth line, as he had thought of doing, he would have disrupted too many prosodic patterns. First, the change would have made the fourth line visually too short for the alternating short line/long line quatrain pattern. Second, placing "begin" down a line would have destroyed the delicate internal rhyme of line 4, "wh*en* the leaves beg*in*." More importantly, the shift of "begin" from one syntactic unit, "when the leaves begin," to the next, "begin first to turn," would have destroyed the cadence of

léaves begín / fírst to túrn.

That Williams, in intermediate drafts, did actually place "begin" on line 5, although finally restoring it to its original place, indicates that the art of free verse is in part a matter of "feel"—of trial and error to find out what sounds right to a well-trained ear.

In the published version, besides the overall structure provided by the unobtrusive two-stress norm and the alternating line-length pattern (a visual pattern carried over from the quatrains in the typescript draft), there are other more localized patterns of rhythm and sound. Short passages of traditional meters are often blended into Williams' free verse, though made less noticeable by line breaks. For example, the pattern of trochees and dactyls in the first three lines of "Sunflowers" becomes more evident when the lines are written as one:

/   /   /   /   /   /
There's a sort of multibranched sunflower blooms hereabouts

The function of these subdued excursions into metrical regularity is to make the verse more rhythmical and hence more charged with feeling, without violating the idiom of prose or of the spoken language.

Another structural pattern in much of Williams' verse is the rhythmically punctuating effect of spondees and of near-spondees (two accents close together).[30] Although these double accents are irregularly placed, they seem almost to form a rhythmic pattern. One can hear it by reading the poem and paying close attention to *heads lean, old man, fallen vines, one basket,* and *shining reds.* In addition, "shining reds" and "fallen vines" echo a cadence established earlier with "leaves begin / first to fall."

Meaning, sound, and stress combine expressively in

/   /   /
Their / heads lean in the rain

to create the kinesthetic sense of leaning. The pressure builds up from a stress pattern of a weak syllable followed by two heavy stresses, two light, then a final heavy stress reinforced by the approximate rhyme of "lean" and "rain."

In addition to the many instances of assonance and alliteration, the frequency of the consonant *n* gives a kind of phonic harmony to the entire poem, with eight of the last seventeen syllables containing the *n* sound. Effective closure is achieved by the rhythmic balance of the final phrases, a balance that's more noticeable when the lines are written as one:

/   /   /   /   /   /
green in one basket and,   in the other shining reds

Rhetorically, the reversal of grammatical structures ("green in one" and "in the other . . . reds") makes for an elegant chiasmus. Rhythmically, the conjunction *and,* with pauses before and after it (the longer pause coming with the comma), acts as a rhythmic pivot point, with three accented syllables on either side of it.

The compactness of the published version compared to the earlier typescript draft is achieved partly through the deletion of the redundant "the overloaded baskets" (third stanza) and the unnecessary "shining" (second stanza), which would have weakened the force of "shining" in the final line. By word count, the finished version (forty-eight words, sixty-nine syllables) is not much shorter than the draft (fifty-two words, seventy-eight syllables). The gain in concentration is reinforced by the compression of the sixteen lines in quatrains to the shorter space of thirteen continuous lines. The deletions of words probably made it difficult for Williams to maintain the symmetrical quatrain pattern. While Williams might have worked at keeping quatrains or converting them to triads (as he did in some drafts), he perhaps felt that the compactness of continuous lineation would emphasize the interrelatedness of the images. Whereas, in Williams' imagist poems, the short stanzas act as frames for visual detail, in this more-than-imagist poem, the interconnections between the symbolic images are as important as their separate visual qualities.

Ultimately, Williams' "Sunflowers" succeeds as a poem for reasons in addition to its visual and aural patterns. It has a symbolic significance that heightens the descriptive details beyond literal fact, and it has an emotional-thematic curve that gives it a sense of completeness—a psychological rhythm that transcends the acoustical rhythm. One way in which a poem is recognized as a poem is that its rhythm is something more than a matter of the audible and kinetic features of language. To cite Elizabeth Drew on this point,

> when we speak of poetic rhythm we mean the whole movement communicated by the words of the poem. Not only the sound movements, the pitch, stress and duration of the syllables, but the way in which the pattern of language directs and controls the ideas and feelings as well.[31]

Likewise, Yvor Winters, although he came to feel that free verse was inferior to metered verse, recognized "a kind of rhythm broader and less easily measurable than the rhythm of the line— the poem exists in time, and if the poet is a good one he takes advantage of this fact and makes the progression rhythmical."[32]

The rhythm Winters speaks of is perhaps evident in the sequence of images representing various stages of growth and decay in a continuing cycle. The poem starts with the blooming of the sunflower in a paradoxical autumn context of falling leaves, aged man, and fallen vines and then moves to the affirmation of the harvest. A new cycle of growth is affirmed with the blooming sunflower just as another cycle is ending with the harvest of ripe and still to be ripened fruit picked from fallen vines by an old man who is at the same stage of the life cycle as the vines. It does not require much familiarity with Williams to see the aging author's personal identification with the old man, still harvesting poems—some ripe, some green—from the fallen vines of old age, the sunflower presiding over this harvest as a symbol of the creative imagination independent of the normal seasonal decline. Some such symbolic meaning accounts for the revision from "droop," with connotations of sickliness, to "lean," with connotations of active power, reinforced by the rhythmic energy and firmness of "their / heads lean in the rain" compared to the slacker "In / the rain their / shining heads droop." Thematic purpose also required such changes in wording as "red" to "reds" to emphasize plenitude, and "of tomatoes" to "his tomatoes" to show personal possession of this plenitude.

5

NATURE: AN OVERVIEW OF
ORGANICISM

The imagination, linked to nature in Williams' view, plays an essential role both in renewing perception and in creating new "objects"—but what is the nature of the Nature that the imagination
discloses in Williams' poetry? One of Williams' projected titles for
his autobiography, "ROOT, BRANCH & FLOWER," serves
equally well as a metaphor for his organic view of nature. Organicism, in its variant forms, links Williams not only to the English
romantic poets and the American transcendentalists but also, in
the revival of the Emersonian-Whitman tradition since the 1950s,
to such diverse poets as Theodore Roethke, A. R. Ammons, Denise Levertov, Robert Bly, William Stafford, and Allen Ginsberg—
many of them influenced by Williams.

The organicism Williams inherited—but made his own—most
probably came from Whitman and Emerson, from the English
Romantics, and from Ezra Pound, who declared in one of his
axiomata that "there is no reason for not applying the term God,
Theos, to the intimate essence" of the universe.[1] Although Pound
fought to rid modern poetic language of romantic excess, in some
fundamental way Pound continued the romantic emphasis on a
bond between man and nature. Perkins describes an organicism
in Pound's work that is close to Williams' view:

> For to his imagination . . . there was a deep, mysterious connection,
> which he expressed in juxtaposed images, between founding a state
> . . . building a Tempio . . . or writing a poem and the fundamental
> creativity of nature, which he thought of as a generalized sexuality and
> symbolized in the goddess Aphrodite and in other myths or mythical
> embodiments of sexuality.[2]

Organicism, however, has a long history which predates romanticism and modern extensions of romanticism. Its most important

early expression was the creationist theory in Plato's *Timaeus* in
which God or some creative force, personified as a Demiurge,
created the universe as "a living creature with soul and reason"
of which "all other living creatures . . . are parts." W. T. Jones,
from whose book *The Classical Mind* this passage is quoted, explains Plato as saying "in *mythical* language" that the universe is
alive in the sense that it has "intelligence" (is ordered) and "is
capable of spontaneous motion," motion that "originates from
within."[3] Aristotle also contributed to organic theory by teaching
that living things have their own internal directive for growth, for
absorbing and organizing material substances to their own ends.
Although Aristotle did not believe in a world soul diffused
throughout the visible world, his idea of a prime mover as an
object of desire or love attracting all things to realize their individual perfections was more compatible with an organic than with a
mechanistic explanation of the universe.

The idea of a world soul was kept alive in platonic and Neopla-
tonic thought down through the late eighteenth century whence
the theory of organicism received new stimulus from progress in
the biological sciences and acquired a greater sophistication in
Kantian and post-Kantian philosophy. Abrams provides a concise
summary of this history:

> Ultimately, the World-Soul was incorporated into the Nature-Philoso-
> phy of the German romantics. In the earlier and cruder versions of
> the concept, sometimes found in Renaissance theory, the world had
> been said to be, in literal fact, an immense animal. . . . When in Ger-
> man theory this concept was subtilized, and the universe held to be
> not literally an animal, but animal-like, and only to the extent that it
> is most appositely described by categories derived from living and
> growing organisms, the old cosmological myth achieved the status of
> a coherent and all-inclusive metaphysics.[4]

From Germany, organic theory was imported into England by
Coleridge and Carlyle, and into America by Emerson. In America
in the twentieth century, the philosophy of organicism was given
a more rigorous character by Alfred North Whitehead. Williams
read Whitehead, apparently with approval, and even recom-
mended the final chapters of *Science and the Modern World* to his
wife (*SL* 79); however, Williams was then in his forties, and his
own world view had been formed long before. Wherever Williams'
largely implicit organicism derived from, there is abundant evidence that he fundamentally conceived of the world organically,
the most obvious indications being his pervasive flower and plant

symbolism and his effort to define the imagination as "transfused with the same forces which transfuse the earth" (*I* 121).

In the following pages, Williams' organic view of the universe will be described and placed within a paradigm drawn eclectically from Plato, Aristotle, Schelling, Coleridge, Wordsworth, Emerson, Whitman, and Whitehead—important contributors to the general theory of organicism. As might be expected, it is difficult to discuss the distinct features of organicism one at a time, since each feature is dependent upon and implies the others. Therefore, a brief preview of the following subsections might help stay the course:

Organicism starts with the basic premise (1) that the universe is a living thing characterized by (2) purposive creative energy, or eros. The notion that the visible universe is living and purposive presupposes (3) a pure potentiality, a fertile a priori ground of being, in which (4) forms are latent and individuation is the realization of inherent form—not merely the result of external circumstances. The whole process of forms being realized is, to borrow a term from Whitehead, (5) "creative advance," or biological and cultural evolution. The total manifestation of this influx of novelty is (6) plenitude—and a concomitant romantic tendency to appreciate novelty and diversity. At the same time, creative advance, since it implies a universe in process, accounts for both (7) imperfection and (8) freedom. Countering and balancing the thrust toward freedom, individuality, and unlimited diversity are the principles of (9) relatedness, (10) correspondence, and (11) universality—or universal essences that give meaning and stability to a world of flux and growth. One universal in particular, (12) Beauty, will receive special treatment because of its special prominence in Williams' cosmology and because it points up the underlying Platonic dimension of Williams' worldview, a dimension that has received insufficient attention.

1. The Universe Alive

The fundamental conception of organicism is that the universe is alive throughout, or at least that it tends toward life. This idea, which received its greatest classical expression in *The Timaeus*, is perennial. Wordsworth, for example, though not wholly giving credence to animism, recorded moments of close affinity with "unorganic natures" when

> with bliss ineffable
> I felt the sentiment of Being spread
> O'er all that moves and all that seemeth still.

At such moments it seemed to Wordsworth that all things looked

> Towards the Uncreated with a countenance
> Of adoration, with an eye of love.
> One song they sang . . .
>
> (*The Prelude*, II, 400–2, 413–5)

With greater vehemence, a modern romantic, Theodore Roethke, asserts: "That stone's alive or I'm not a man!" According to James McMichael, Roethke here recognizes "his own existence as being contingent upon God's immanence."[5] In a similar vein, Williams in "A Unison" (*CP2* 157) intuits a unity of being in which the deceased in a rural family graveyard, along with all of nature, even the stones, are in some sense alive. Like Wordsworth, Williams hears the song of creation:

> Stones, stones of a difference
> joining the others, at pace. *Hear!*
> *Hear the unison of their voices . . .*

And in *Spring and All*, Williams symbolizes life as a "bird" whose "cry reaches to every rock's center" (*I* 98).

According to the most formidable exponent of modern organicism, Alfred North Whitehead, there is no absolute separation between what is commonly regarded as nonliving and living things—although for practical purposes some objects exhibit such a low gradation of life that they are normally considered lifeless. Whitehead, in rejecting the notion that life and matter are separable, states that "the deficiencies in our concept of physical nature should be supplied by its fusion with life" and "the notion of life should involve the notion of physical nature."[6] Much closer in spirit to Williams is Loren Eisley's declaration in *The Immense Journey* that

> if "dead" matter has reared up this curious landscape of fiddling crickets, song sparrows, and wandering man, it must be plain even to the most devoted materialist that the matter of which he speaks contains amazing, if not dreadful powers.[7]

When Williams' "Between Walls," for example, is read in the light of the above statements, the shining bits of broken green glass take on a fuller resonance of meaning. Williams, although seldom stating it explicitly, holds the view of the universe as a living entity. In *Spring and All,* he speaks of life's "colossal surge toward the finite and capable" (*I* 94). Much later in life, in lines that echo Emerson's claim that the poet "knows why the plain or meadow of space was strown with these flowers we call suns and moons and stars" (231), Williams praised René Char for writing of

> sedgy rivers,
> > of daffodils and tulips
> > > whose roots they water,
> > even to the free-flowing river
> > > that laves the rootlets
> > > > of those sweet-scented flowers
> > that people the
> > > milky
> > > > way
>
> (*PB* 87)

For Williams, the "free-flowing" cosmic "river" of life appears to be the fundamental stuff of existence, of which so-called matter is a concresence in varying degrees of animation or fluidity. For both Williams and Emerson, the underlying metaphor or model for this universe is not the machine—a collection of lifeless, separate, interchangeable parts—but the plant, with its vital interrelations between parts, and the whole permeated by an internal organizing power or principle of causation.

2. Purpose and Eros

The most significant implication of the universe as living is that it thereby exhibits something akin to purpose. Life's "colossal surge" appears to be, for Williams, in some obscure way purposeful. One is accustomed in this century to think of only a single kind of causation—mechanical causation, by which energy and motion are transferred from object to object, particle to particle, much like billiard balls in the closed system of the pool table. Such antecedent causation is what Aristotle called the efficient cause, but such a limited notion of causation fails to explain why particles of matter cohere into the forms that populate the world. Aristotle recognized, besides mechanical causation, a final cause or inward

striving toward a goal. According to Abrams, Aristotle's major
contributions to the theory of organicism were

> the concepts that natural things are distinguished from artificial
> things in that they have an internal source of motion, instead of an
> external efficient agent, and that the biological coming-to-be is a pro-
> gressive determination of form unfolding from within.[8]

The idea of a nonmechanical, interior causation leads naturally
to speculation about purpose in nature. Coleridge, for example,
found in nature "something analogous to the causality of the human will, by which, without assigning to nature, as nature, a conscious purpose," man could "yet distinguish her agency from a
blind and lifeless mechanism" (512). More poetically, Whitman,
observing wild wood ducks circling overhead, is inspired to say, "I
believe in those wing'd purposes, / ... and consider green and
violet and tufted crown intentional."[9] Like Aristotle, Coleridge,
and Whitman, some modern biologists are inclined to believe that,
in addition to matter and energy, a purposive, organizing power
must be recognized as a fundamental aspect of the universe.
Ralph S. Lillie in *The General Biology and Philosophy of Organism*
writes: "Conscious purpose, as it exists in ourselves, is to be regarded as a highly evolved derivative of a more widely diffused
natural condition or property, which we may call 'directiveness.'"[10]
Finally, Whitehead asserts that the intuition of internal purpose
or aim is a necessary step beyond the scheme of scientific materialism, for without the assumption of internal purpose "there is no
reason in the nature of things why portions of material would
have any physical relations to each other."[11]

In Williams' world, purpose is often manifest as a striving in
man and nature toward form or identity, a striving that Williams'
precursor, Whitman, called the "procreant urge." In discussing
purpose, however, one must distinguish between an overall cosmic
purpose and a more limited purposiveness evident in individual
things. Williams, at least in his early poetry, is less the prophet of
cosmic optimism than Whitman is, nor does he dwell on anything
like Tennyson's faith in a final goal towards which all creation
moves—although Williams does occasionally adopt the prophetic
mode, especially in late poems. "The Turtle" (*PB* 63), for example,
mixes humor and irony with prophecy to predict that the imagination—symbolized as a turtle of mythical proportions—shall in
future generations triumph over the present mechanical organization of society. Likewise, in "Asphodel," Williams foresees the

triumphant emergence of good in which the transcendent "light" of love and insight "gelds the bomb" (*PB* 179).

Apart from a few prophetic expressions of cosmic optimism, Williams more characteristically discovers purpose as manifest in the immediate texture of existence. What Whitehead calls "subjective aim" and Aristotle terms "final cause"—the lure that attracts things to fulfill their natures—Williams represents with a symbolism drawn from Greek mythology. The notion of immanent causation was grasped imaginatively in early Greek myth in the personification of Eros, "a motive force on a sexual model used to explain the 'marriage' and 'birth' of the mythological elements . . . a species of 'First Mover' in the ancient cosmogonies, and . . . recognized as such by Aristotle."[12] Eros was present at the beginning of creation to bring order out of chaos. While Williams does not use the personification of a masculine Eros in his poetry, the concept of eros is present in many poems, often symbolized as Kora (Persephone) or Aphrodite (Venus), or abstractly indicated by such words as "love," "desire," "appetite."

For example, in "Rain" (*CPI* 343), the life-giving rain is a manifestation of a healing, generative power in nature and in woman:

> The rain
> falls upon the earth
> and grass and flowers
>
> come
>   perfectly
>
> into form . . .

The brilliant syntactical device by which the words *grass* and *flowers*, objects of *falls upon,* become subjects of *come* emphasizes the dual passive-active nature of living things, both acted upon externally and asserting their own intrinsic thrust towards form. While the rain has a direct physical effect on the earth, Williams adds: "But love is / unworldly . . . falling endlessly / from / her thoughts." Although it may seem that Williams is contrasting "love" and "rain," his intent is to make a distinction between rain as the transitory physical manifestation of eros, and love as the eternal source—personified as Aphrodite (whose counterpart is present as an actual woman in the poem). To take a quite different example of eros, in "The Sea-Elephant" Williams is not being merely sentimental when he personifies the beast as saying, "But I / am love. I am / from the sea" (*CPI* 343). Rather, the statement reflects a long-considered view of Williams that at the basis of creation in Eros—a bountiful form of love permeating existence. Just as medieval theologians, according to Arthur Lovejoy, thought of God's love not only as "compassion" but also as "inexhaustible productive energy," so Williams recognizes a creative force in nature that he identifies with love or desire.[13]

The power of eros is exuberantly portrayed in "Spring Strains" (*CPI* 97), where eros is actively present in the mating birds, in the buds "crowded erect with desire," and, on a cosmic scale, in the sun's energy drawing up all nature into form from the formless ground: "Pulls the whole / counter-pulling mass upward" and "locks even the opaque, not yet defined / ground in a terrific drag." Some of the words and phrases used in the poem—*monotone, circles, angles, convergings to a point, dirty orange*—suggest that the poem is in some ways a description of a painting, cubist or expressionist, as well as a description of a scene in nature, hence identifying eros as the energy at work in both artistic and natural production. Williams makes one feel the energies of growth as irrepressible but purposive desire. The tone of the poem is one of excited, amused wonder, the speaker identifying with the process and urging it on.

"Spring and All" (*CPI* 183), a related but much more serious poem, expresses tones of awe, respect, and wonder before the process of life taking on form—of new form emerging from the semiformless mud and compost of a landscape on the verge of a significant change. There is also compassion for the new, delicate sprouts that emerge from the process. The inclusive indefiniteness of the pronoun in "They enter the new world naked" allows the process of birth in the vegetative realm to be associated with that of human birth as well. Furthermore, the prose context of the poem in *Spring and All,* a book devoted to the renewal of the imagination, strongly suggests that Williams had in mind the birth of new forms of poetry as well as of plant life (although this idea is not explicit in the poem). The same creative force operating biologically in nature functions at a higher level in human consciousness to create art. Even at the level of nature the process seems to be teleological or in some sense purposeful. The pseudoactive verb in "It quickens" suggests that the process is in some way active and self-directing. Quickening is the result of organic, intrinsic motivation, not just mechanical causation. The new sprouts "grip down" and "begin to awaken"—to act with a kind of intelligence, to realize "subjective aim," the accomplish-

ment of an inner design. "Spring and All" is not about an entirely
alien, inhuman process; the process is mysterious, but it manifests
something akin to human creative intelligence.

3. The Ground

The universe exhibits life and purpose because it is a manifestation of a creative principle within the ground of being, the ultimate source of being. This source is often represented in
romantic literature as the sea, as in Whitman's "Crossing Brook-
lyn Ferry":

> I too had been struck from the float held in solution,
> I too had received identity by my body . . .

As noted earlier, the sea likewise appears in many of Williams'
poems as symbol of the ground of being: the "ungoverned ocean"
of "The Yachts" (*CP1* 388), the source of life and death in "The
Cod Head" (*CP1* 357), the embracing unity of the sea in "Labrador" (*CP2* 124). In book 4 of *Paterson*, the sea becomes a complex
symbol, source of both the shark (violence) and Venus (love). The
sea, or formless origin, exerts an attraction, a death wish, which
must be resisted:

> our nostalgic
> mother in whom the dead, enwombed again
> cry out to us to return
> the blood dark sea!
> nicked by the light alone, diamonded
> by the light   .   from which the sun
> alone lifts undamped his wings
> of fire!
>
> (*P* 202)

That the dead are referred to as "enwombed again" indicates that
their origin was in the sea. The sea is "blood dark": life-giving
but also holding violence. Yet it is "nicked by the light," the hidden
beauty that marks its spiritual dimension, and the sun, as it often
does in Williams, represents eros or the creative force that brings
form and identity out of the formless potential of the sea. Here
it is also the source of the light that diamonds the sea. Normally,
in Williams, the light (beauty, divinity) is latent within the formless
ground, immanent in things; in this passage, however, separate

symbols—sea and sun—give a more transcendent connotation to
form-creating eros and beauty, as if they are qualities that come
from outside the sea of matter and act upon it or penetrate it,
making it intelligible.

Though the formless ground is itself nonmaterial—like Aristotle's matter, a pure potential for being—its most immediate
manifestation is in the simplest elements of nature and in the
undifferentiated sense impressions and feelings of human beings.
For example, in Williams' poem "The Clouds," the clouds, created
by vapor from the earth, take on half-formed shapes of gigantic
horses in the poet's imagination, symbolizing the emergence of
form or formed perception from the chaos of unformed sensory data:

> caught among low, blocking forms their foreparts
> rise lucid beyond this smell of a swamp, a mud
> livid with decay and life!
>
> (CP2 171)

The imagination here does not impose form on nature; rather,
nature gives rise to emergent forms that are not fully completed
until they pass through the imagination, itself rooted in and part
of nature. The clouds, or partially organized sense data, are

> a rank confusion of the imagination still uncured,
> a rule, piebald under the streetlamps, reluctant
> to be torn from its hold.
>
> (CP2 171)

Although the syntax is difficult here, Williams means that the half-
formed reality (rank confusion) emerging from sense data has yet
to be completed, or "cured" (in the sense of processed), by the
imagination—and the imagination itself may be restored in the
process of giving order to confusion. The rank confusion of
clouds both seeks and resists form—"reluctant to be torn from
its hold" in the ground of being. Though the clouds seem nearly
of indeterminate shape, they are *latent* with order or form—"a
rule"—which the imagination does not deny.

Williams' view of the ground is complex and ambivalent, for the
ground, as Miller has shown, is both the source of renewal and
the drag toward formlessness. The precariousness of a genuine
form is illustrated, for example, in *In The American Grain* by the
beautiful and intricate Aztec civilization, which vanished "at the
very breath of conquest," "sank back into the ground to be reen-

kindled, never, . . . a spirit lost in that soil" (*AG* 32). The ground, thus, is double-valent. As the absorbing void, it is destructive, but as fertile source, it accounts for the influx of novelty into the world, of creative advance; therefore, when cultural forms (marriage, funerals, work, trade, education, poetry) lose touch with the instinctual needs and energies that created them, they become inhibiting and oppressive, or anemic and "genteel." The concept of the "ground," of a fundamental nature underlying the forms and mores of civilization, provides Williams with a perspective for judging the distortions and rigidities that civilization often imposes on nature. On the other hand, the ground, being chaotic and irrational, can dissolve all effort to achieve form, with tragic consequences, as in "The Yachts" where "the whole sea [becomes] an entanglement of watery bodies / lost to the world bearing what they cannot hold" (*CP1* 389).

Williams, on the positive side, believes that each person, each art form, each culture must maintain ongoing contact with the ground of being. For example, in "Tract" (*CP1* 72), Williams exhorts his "townspeople" to remake the funeral ritual so that it accords with their own "ground sense," their indigenous sense of who they are, where they are, and what a funeral is for—to express *their* grief: "sit openly— / to the weather as to grief." In *In The American Grain*, Williams speaks of the ground as the source of a people's distinctive character or spirit—their sense of identity shaped by contact with the particular conditions of their environment. But most early settlers of America, however ingenious they were in solving practical problems, remained aesthetically and morally unchanged by contact with the new ground:

> The problem of the New World was . . . how to replace from the wild land that which, at home, they had scarcely known the Old World meant to them . . . to find a ground to take the place of England. They could not do it. They clung, one way or another, to the old. (*AG* 136)

Williams elaborates on this point in "The American Background," in which he states that the "burning need" for a culture is

> the realization of the qualities of a place in relation to the life which occupies it: embracing everything involved, climate, geographic position, relative size, history, other cultures—as well as the character of its sands, flowers, minerals and the condition of knowledge within its borders. . . . It is the act of lifting these things into an ordered and utilized whole which is culture. (*SE* 157).

Williams finds small, isolated growths of indigenous culture—culture related to the ground—in some examples of American craftsmanship: "the lines of fast ships," "the carved and painted figureheads," "glassware," "the wooden marriage chests of Pennsylvania workmanship," "furniture in white pine and other native woods built by the Shakers" (*SE* 150).

Williams, however, makes clear that local culture, involving a direct and original relationship to the immediate environment, does not mean chauvinistic Americanism or an automatic avoidance of anything old or European. What he desires is culture built on "a relation to the immediate conditions of the matter in hand, and a determination to assert them in opposition to all intermediate authority" (*SE* 143). This could mean, for example, that, while the townspeople in "Tract" are to reject the traditional black hearse and the driver with a top hat, they may, if it suits their ground sense, absorb elements from other cultures: "Walk behind—as they do in France, / seventh class."

The potential for what Williams calls a "related culture"—one emerging from contact with the ground of immediate experience—was thwarted in America by the drive toward wealth. Money cushions one from the necessities of dealing with the environment at first hand, and the drive for money led to the development of huge cities, which meant "the actual decay of the small community," and this Williams regards as "a primary cultural decay" (*SE* 147). The small, local community was sacked "by invisible troops" (*SE* 147), the urban designers of standardized tastes. (In "Tract" Williams says that his townspeople, with their ground sense, "have it over a troop / of artists"—the designers and arbiters of culture who operate from remote urban centers.)

In *In The American Grain,* Williams shows some exceptions to those like Cotton Mather and Ben Franklin who refused to give themselves to the ground of their new existence. While Mather clung to theology and mistrusted the wilderness and while Franklin thought of the New World primarily in terms of practical and economic advantages, Daniel Boone and Sam Houston each, at different times in their lives, formed passionate attachments to the wilderness. Daniel Boone is important, Williams says, not because he made "a path to the west," but "because of a descent to the ground of his desire" (*AG* 136). In the wilderness, Boone, "a great voluptuary," immersed his senses ecstatically in nature, liberating and alienating himself from his inherited culture, including its prejudices against the Indian. Boone's immersion in the wilderness was the first step toward a new form in which life could be more fully expressed.

But neither Boone nor Sam Houston, who made a similar "descent" to the ground, was able to translate his experience into a viable form that could function outside the wilderness. While they stepped outside the repression of inherited forms, their immersion in the wilderness was a kind of regression. Both men were changed by their experiences so that they could never quite fit into civilized society in the same way as before. Although Houston became governor of Texas, a United States senator, a married man, and a member of the Baptist church, still there were moments, as Williams imagines him, "when in deep thought" he "whittled pine sticks" (*AG* 215), as if, Williams implies, he was trying to get back some lost sense of his earlier connection with nature.

For Williams, the authentic poet is one who comes up from an immersion in the ground of his own consciousness beneath the accumulated forms, attitudes, and conventions that constitute civilization at any one place or time: "Whitman had to come up from under. All have to come from under and through a dead layer" and "he who will grow . . . must sink first" (*AG* 213). The poet or person who maintains something of essential innocence will appear to others as lacking sophistication: "where foreign values are held to be a desideratum, he who is buried and speaks thickly— is lost" (*AG* 214). The risk of not conforming to "foreign" or established values is that one appears inarticulate and backward:

> Those who come up from under will have a mark on them that invites scorn, like a farmer's filthy clodhoppers. They will be recognized only from *abroad*, being so like the mass out of which they come as to be scorned from anear. (*AG* 215).

Williams may have had in mind here the early response to his own poetry as naive and roughshod, or his feeling while among exiles and intellectuals during his 1924 trip to Europe, that he was "the brutal thing itself" (*AG* 107). The renewal that comes from immersion in the ground of experience must be followed by a more conscious struggle to achieve form, but a form that reflects something of fresh contact with the ground, with nature— a form "sculpted to the / tune of retreating waves" (*CP2* 394).

4. Form and Individuation

The ground for Williams is the source of individual forms (as distinct from universal forms, which will be discussed later). The forms preexist as a potential in matter. In nature, the latent forms emerge spontaneously as a result of biological forces organized by a latent pattern or form to be achieved. In Williams' organic conception of the universe, true form proceeds from within, from some given core or seed of identity, whether the thing that takes shape be a plant, a human being, a work of art, or an entire culture. Organic identity means exclusion as well as inclusion. Williams says of the Evening Primrose (a four-petaled yellow flower) that "It is a disinclination to be / five red petals or a rose" (*CP1* 161).[14]

This conception of individuality has much in common with views held by Emerson and by Whitehead. In "Self-Reliance," Emerson says that "the power which resides in [each person] is new in nature"; and Williams similarly states, "Each man or woman is born facing a must" (*SE* 301). Williams' belief in an innate core of identity, a "must," likewise accords with Whitehead's view of how identity is shaped:

> I shape the activities of the environment into a new creation, which is myself at this moment; and yet, as being myself, it is a continuation of the antecedent world. If we stress the role of the environment, this process is causation. If we stress the role of my immediate pattern of active enjoyment, this process is self-creation.[15]

Whitehead means that each person is a product of existing bits of the environment—but organized into and shaped by a unique, never before realized pattern, or intrinsic form, aiming at fulfillment. How or why does this individuation take place? For Whitehead, God "is the ground for concrete actuality," providing the particular focus or "limitation" that individualizes each thing.[16] In Williams, there is not quite such an explicit theological explanation for individuation: it just happens because the ultimate ground of being must express itself in individual forms, and this becoming is, as expressed in "Spring and All," one of the most stirring processes in nature or man.

Williams' experience as a doctor, helping to give birth to and care for a great many infants, contributed to his insight that human beings had marked differences even at birth, a stubbornness and tenacity that led him to think of babies as "white mules." Just as for Emerson and Thoreau the cultivation of individuality was aided by solitary walks, journal-keeping, and other solitary activities in which the true self could be discovered, guarded, and unfolded, so in Williams there is what Reed Whittemore discusses as the "stealing *motif*," moments in which Williams, writing in his attic or solitary in his car, withdraws from his social role as doctor, husband, and middle-class citizen.[17] American transcendentalism, like European existentialism, gives priority to authentic individualism, the difference being that the secular existentialist rejects the notion of a given core of identity while at the same viewing man as unavoidably cut off from both nature and other human beings, whereas the transcendentalist shares an ultimate unity with man and nature. Hence in Whitman's "Song of Myself," one of Williams' early enthusiasms, there is a continual movement from self to embrace not-self and back to define self again. This pattern of assimilation and self-assertion is characteristic of Williams' work as a whole.

While each person or creature has an identity or form to realize, identity involves, as will be seen later, relationship to other parts of the universe. This interrelationship acts as a check on the kind of rugged individualism fostered by the mechanistic scheme of existence in which human beings, like atoms, are considered discrete, self-sufficient entities. Although it is more characteristic of Williams to focus on the individuality of things in isolation, this focus does not deny their relationship to the rest of nature. Poems such as "Danse Russe" (*CP1* 86) and "Young Sycamore" (*CP1* 266) illustrate the "self-enjoyment" that Whitehead sees accompanying the realization of inner form. Other poems, such as "The Wanderer" (*CP1* 108) and "Choral: The Pink Church" (*CP2* 177), celebrate identity achieved or maintained within a context of contact, interrelationship, and unity.

Williams finds in nature analogues and support for the achievement and persistence of unique identity. Especially in his formative period, from 1914 to 1921, Williams wrote many poems that reflected his struggle to define himself as a man and a poet. In some of these poems a natural object serves as a symbol of idiosyncratic self-definition. For example, the "crooked, black tree" in "Trees" (*CP1* 98) is "bent . . . from straining / against the bitter horizontals of / a north wind," forces against which it struggles to fulfill its existence. While other "voices" blend "willingly / against the heavy contra-bass / of the dark"—that is, the dark of nonbeing—the black tree persists in its own nature however grotesque and deformed it might become: "but you alone / warp yourself passionately to one side / in your eagerness."

In Williams, the realization of identity is characteristically exemplified or represented as a flowering, as in "Chicory and Daisies" (*CP1* 65):

> Lift your flowers
> on bitter stems
> chicory!
> Lift them up
> out of the scorched ground!

The flowers here transcend their impoverished environment, because they have their own internal thrust toward form. Similarly, Williams' poems often achieve a perfection that transcends the author's personal bitterness and his sense of a deficient environment.

One of Williams' most intense meditations on individuation, or "flowering," is "The Crimson Cyclamen" (*CP1* 419), a difficult poem, but one which the Whiteheadian view of individuation might help to explain. Whitehead says that "the notion of life implies a certain absoluteness of self-enjoyment"; that is, each living thing "appropriates" aspects of process "into a unity of existence," and this appropriation, in Whitehead's context, seems akin to feeling or desire.[18] Williams, using the flower as both instance and symbol, implies that all living things are a manifestation of "passion" (life) emerging and revealing itself through form, achieving a "glory" in blossoming, and then fading back to nonexistence. The poignancy of this theme is intensified by the poem's occasion, the death of Williams' friend Charles Demuth, whose watercolors include one of the cyclamen itself.

After two introductory stanzas celebrating the flowers as "mirrors / of some perfection" where "color has been construed / from emptiness," the poem compares the growth of stem, buds, and leaves to the development of an argument, as suggested by the words *pattern, logic, thought, conclusion,* and *argument.* On each leaf is "a pattern more / of logic than a purpose"; that is, the leaf pattern is more intelligible as an aesthetic design than as something utilitarian. An aesthetic design makes sense to the mind; it has an intelligibility even though leaves are "of roots / dark, complex," and the roots themselves are from something even deeper, "from / subterranean revolutions / and rank odors" where they lie "waiting for the moon," for mysterious forces to stir them to generate the form of the plant. Midway in the poem, however, as the blossom appears, the vocabulary of logic and argument is replaced by a vocabulary of feeling and desire:

> it begins that must
> put thought to rest—

> wakes in tinted beaks
> still raising the head
> and passion
> is loosed—
>
> its small lusts
> addressed still to
> the knees and to sleep—
> abandoning argument
>
> (*CP1* 422)

As with Whitehead, Williams seems to think of life as feeling, or like feeling—something comparable to James's "Pure Experience":

> It is passion
> earlier and later than thought
> that rises above thought

Life is known only through the form of living things, but one also knows or intuits that life itself is a seamless reality, not confined to the particular occasions of "self-enjoyment" in which it is embodied, but transcending these. Implicit in the poem is the assumption that life organizes matter, not that matter produces and shapes life. Life expresses itself in matter as emotion expresses itself in tangible forms—gestures, words, architecture. As in "To a Solitary Disciple" (*CP1* 104), feeling, or life, is sustained and held within form: the moon is held like a living flower within the hexagonal lines, the "sepals," extending abstractly from the spire of the church and representing lines of force, of form-creating energies that go beyond the fixed form of the church. Life and emotion must both be realized in form, but they are not wholly contained by form. There is always an aura or suggestion—in a poem, a flower, or a person—of something intangible and just beyond conceptualization.

The struggle to realize intrinsic identity can, in the case of a neoromantic poet, receive powerful stimulus and encouragement from the observation of nature. For example, Theodore Roethke in "Cuttings (later)" observes the "urge, wrestle, resurrection of . . . / Cut stems struggling to put down feet." The struggle is echoed in the poet's own being: "In my veins, in my bones I feel it." Similarly, the individuation that Williams sees taking place in nature, where "One by one objects are defined," and "rooted, they / grip down and begin to awaken," provides a model and inspiration for his own growth as a poet.

The struggle to achieve identity, however, is not always successful—in fact, is usually not successful, and herein lies a tragic dimension that gives richness and complexity to Williams' view of life. In "Adam" (*CP1* 407), for example, Williams expresses regret that his father, in succumbing to the pressures of conformity, dies unfulfilled—"a desperate, unvarying silence / to the unhurried last." In "To Elsie" (*CP1* 217), the young woman (a ward of the state taken into the Williams' household) is "voluptuous water . . . with broken brain." She is unformed, sexually vulnerable, and doomed to be the prey of "rich young men," or worse. The most striking expression of failed individuation is the "Yachts" (*CP1* 388), where the "watery bodies" (formless like the "voluptuous water" of Elsie) are "lost to the world." The image of sinking back into formlessness is also used in *Paterson* where Williams assumes that human beings, like all growing things, are born with a unique potential: "They begin! The perfections are sharpened." But because "the language"—devitalized by lack of a living literature—"fails them," they will "sink back into the loam / crying out . . . / as they wilt and disappear" (*P* 11). Potential, unrealized, is lost forever.

5. Creative Advance

The forms, existing in potential, issue forth in a vast flow of creativity—symbolized in *Paterson*, for example, as a river bursting at the falls from its primal unity into the differentiation of particulars (which Williams, as a poet, attempts to regather into a new unity). This "upsurge of novelty," to use a Bergsonian term, would be impossible within the strict determinism of a mechanistic cosmos in which the present is merely the sum of the past and the "new" is only a recombination of aspects of the old. In organicism, however, the present moment is only partly shaped by the past: it inherits the past, but is also open to an undetermined future. The universe, in Whitehead's phraseology, is "ever plunging into the creative advance."[19] Creative advance is evolution, but it must be distinguished from a mechanistic explanation of evolution. Classic material science accounts for evolution in purely naturalistic terms: there is no Eros, no divine agency; instead, there are mechanical agencies or efficient causes—like the solar and electrical energies that activated chemical reactions in ocean water to "create" organic molecules from simple lifeless elements.

Yet the idealist-teleological view of evolution, with its roots in Plato's *Timaeus*, actually prepared the way for the empirical, scientific theory of Darwin—and both idealist and naturalist theories of evolution worked to undermine the mechanistic model of the universe that has dominated since the seventeenth century. The Darwinian theory of evolution, which led many writers toward the end of the nineteenth century to view humans as helpless victims of mechanical or inexorable natural forces, later encouraged others, like Whitehead, to criticize mechanism as logically incompatible with evolution, because the premises of mechanism provide no adequate account for life and growth. Hence the organicist replaces the machine, finished and closed, with the plant, living and unfolding, as the metaphor that gives the most comprehensive understanding of the universe.

Although Williams characteristically celebrates the renewal of life in nature, there are few references in his work to a theory of biological evolution as such. Williams was much more concerned with the cyclical renewal of life in nature as a symbol of creative force operating through the imagination, the maker and modifier of art and culture. In *Spring and All*, Williams makes playfully serious use of the idea of evolution. He imagines that the world has been destroyed, and then, within seconds, eons of evolution take place producing a duplicate of the world that was just destroyed. But people do not seem to realize that they now inhabit a new world; they go on as if no cataclysm had occurred—"Only the imagination is undeceived" (*I* 94). Williams' point is that the world, which from moment to moment seems to be the same, is in truth—when perceived with awakened imagination—a new world. In this passage, Williams speaks of evolution in language suggestive of an organic-idealist view of creation in which the infinite manifests itself in the finite: "In that colossal surge toward the finite and the capable life has now arrived for the second time" (*I* 94). Readers will recognize the word "surge," which is used in the poem shortly following this prose passage: "By the road to the contagious hospital / under the surge of the blue / mottled clouds." The prose context of the poem indicates that Williams conceived of the power of nature, the "surge," not only as a cyclically renewing force but as evolutionary as well.

Williams sometimes symbolizes evolution or creative advance as a river, and sometimes as a growing plant. In "The Source" (*CP1* 286), Williams' impersonal eye, noting the distinct features of barn

and trees in a pasture, moves beyond this enclosure to "the profound detail of the woods." Images of simple life forms and breed-
ing places of microscopic life—"mold," "fungi," "water in an old /
hoof print," "Cow dung," "a stone / half green"—begin to increase
as the mind's eye approaches the "source": an underground
spring in whose depth it can see "white sand" bubbling. As the
water begins to flow down "a stair of uneven stones," it begins to
throw up rudimentary forms:

> An edge of bubbles stirs
> swiftness is molded
>
> speed grows
>
> the profuse body advances
> over the stones unchanged

The stream, flowing from its hidden source, symbolizes the living
universe as a "profuse body" advancing from the ground and
becoming "molded" into "profound detail" yet in ultimate substance remaining "unchanged."

The stream image occurs on a much grander scale in *Paterson*
where the life force, symbolized as mysterious waters, evolves and
converges to a river of phenomena from which man and city
emerge. The image of water flowing from an indiscernible source
(as in Henry Vaughn's "The Waterfall") is an effective symbol of
the universe conceived as perpetually emerging from potential
to actual.

The image of a growing plant also conveys this idea, with the
additional emphasis on the form that comes out of chaos. In the
short poem, "Descent" (*CP2* 238), Williams writes:

> From disorder (a chaos)
> order grows
> —grows fruitful.
> The chaos feeds it. Chaos
> feeds the tree.

The poem may be read both as a statement about artistic creation
and, metaphysically, as a statement about the character of the
universe, both emerging out of an initial stage of chaos. The forms
of art and culture are "fruitful" when they emerge from the rich
confusion of possibilities that lie outside complacently accepted

concepts. As a metaphysical statement, the poem alludes again to the "ground"—formless, but holding form in potential.

6. Plenitude

The consequence of creative advance is plenitude—or at least a plenitude in the making. Since the universe is in process, unfinished, there is a continuous emergence of novelty. In Williams' world, life is constantly passing into form and out of form, as in "The Catholic Bells" (*CP1* 397), in which the bells

> ring down the leaves
> ring in the frost upon them
> and the death of the flowers
> ring out the grackle
>
> toward the south, the sky
> darkened by them, ring in
> the new baby of Mr. and Mrs.
> Krantz . . .

Williams welcomes and celebrates this influx of novelty as testimony to a genuine creativity in nature, although his tone is complicated by an awareness that change means loss, too.

Traditionally, plenitude—the fullness of variety—was regarded as the mark of divine creativity in the universe. Lovejoy has shown how the original doctrine of a static plenitude, with the universe consisting of a complete and continuous scale of being, was "temporalized" so that the universe then came to be conceived as an unfolding process achieving plenitude over a long period of time.[20] Since the creationist doctrine of Plato's *Timaeus*, plenitude has been generally regarded as a manifestation of God's uncontainable goodness in its aspect of generative power. Subsequently, the typical romantic response to plenitude has been one of respect, delight, and wonder. As R. H. Fogle observes,

Cultivation of the sense of wonder . . . follows naturally from the richness and complexity of the organic vision, and the sense of potentiality and the aspiration for infinitude are concomitants of organic growth, which in itself has no logical limits.[21]

One of the accomplishments of romanticism was to extend the bounds of sympathy and wonder to the small and the ordinary—

to wheelbarrows, weeds, sparrows, and common men and women both in rustic and in urban settings. The celebration of plenitude often leads Williams to a kind of Whitmanesque cataloging as in "January Morning" (*CP1* 100), "The Catholic Bells" (*CP1* 397), and "The Poor" (*CP1* 452). "It's the anarchy of poverty / delights me," Williams declares in "The Poor." The unregimented neighborhood described in that poem, like "the dress of the children," reflects "every stage and custom of necessity."

But while the conception of plenitude formed the basis for romantic wonder, sympathy, and optimism, it also held some darker implications, as Lovejoy has pointed out:

> The preoccupation of the optimists with the notion of the "fullness" of the organic world sometimes led them . . . to draw an almost Darwinian or Malthusian picture of a Nature overcrowded with aspirants for life and consequently given over to a ubiquitous struggle for existence.[22]

Lovejoy's statement serves as an apt gloss on Williams' "The Yachts," in which the "watery bodies" that struggle in the sea of existence are "lost to the world bearing what they cannot hold." There is no doubt that competition plays a part in the struggle for existence (as cooperation does too). Yet that struggle, for human beings, is potentially mitigated, because humans, more than other natural beings, have a larger degree of freedom with which to give rational, constructive direction to the energies of aggression and self-preservation that stem from nature. That is, as long as organicism makes a place for consciousness as an activity within nature but transcending the mechanical aspect of nature, the Hobbesian vision of life as brute struggle is not inevitable. Although Williams was aware of the blind struggle for existence in nature, as for example in his image of the shark snapping at its own entrails in *Paterson*, he was more impressed with the nurturing and generative rather than the maiming powers of nature. In "To All Gentleness," Williams asks the question, "Violence and / gentleness, which is the core?" His answer (although it switches metaphors) is that "gentleness harbors all violence" (*CP2* 72). Perhaps the ambiguity of "harbors" indicates Williams' ambivalence, for gentleness both conceals violence within it but also circumscribes it. Love, or eros, for Williams is the larger, more encompassing reality. Furthermore, as shall be seen in section 8, Williams believes in free will, which allows humans to consciously choose love.

7. Imperfection

As indicated in "The Catholic Bells," Williams knows that change brings loss and death as well as renewal, but in his overall picture of the universe, Williams tends to be an ameliorist. The dilemma for the romantic idealist is that his or her impulse to celebrate growth towards perfection comes into conflict with the recognition that an achieved perfection is static. Peckham sums up one side of the dilemma, the organicist tendency to accept imperfection as a concomitant of growth: "Anything that continues to grow, or change qualitatively, is not perfect, can, perhaps, never be perfect. Perfection ceases to be a positive value. Imperfection becomes a positive value."[23] But although the Romantic may value imperfection as a sign of continuing growth—of the spontaneous and natural as opposed to the rigid and artificial— still the Romatic cannot be undisturbed by the fact that suffering, too, is the consequence of an imperfect, evolving universe. Various attempts to account for imperfection or evil have included the arguments that evil is privation (absence of good), that evil is necessary to the fullest possible variety of existence, and that evil is only apparent—the result of limited human vision that fails to see the totality of God's design—or what the poet A. R. Ammons calls "Overall." Organicism accounts for evil as a necessary concomitant of the incomplete universe still completing itself. To quote Peckham again:

> In its radical form, dynamic organicism results in the idea that the history of the universe is the history of God creating himself. Evil is at last accounted for, since the history of the universe—God being imperfect to begin with—is the history of God, whether transcendent or immanent, ridding himself, by the evolutionary process, of evil.[24]

Williams, in some of his later poems, appears to affirm a kind of ameliorative evolution. For example, in the "Coda" to "Asphodel," Williams praises the "light," symbol of the source and lure of perfection. In "The Turtle" (PB 63), he prophesies the coming of a new order created through the force of the imagination. Also, the spirit addressed in Paterson is very much like the organicist's God-of-becoming whose potential perfection strives for actualization through nature and man:

                                              But you
                            never wither—but blossom
                            all about me. In that I forget
                            myself perpetually—in your
                            composition and decomposition
                            I find my . .
                                                              despair!
                                                                (*P* 75)

Although the organic universe is in a state of becoming and is
therefore imperfect, there are moments recorded by romantic
poets in which the universe does appear so beautiful as to be
wholly satisfying, thus confirming man's place in it and hinting
also at its ultimately ideal character. In "Self-Reliance," Emerson,
chiding his readers for lamenting the past or overanticipating the
future, reminds them of the perfection of the present:

> There is simply the rose; it is perfect in every moment of its existence.
> Before a leaf-bud has burst, its whole life acts; in the full-blown flower
> there is no more [perfection]; in the leafless root there is no less. Its
> nature is satisfied and it satisfies nature in all moments alike. (157)

According to Hirsch, the Romantic's experience of moments of
perfect harmony with nature, as in Wordsworth's "spots of time,"
is only an intensification of a more comprehensive sense of harmony that the Romantic constantly strives to achieve: "It is a necessary moment, one that sustains Enthusiasm's confidence and
expectancy, but in the general course of experience the beyond
remains unattained."[25] Many of Williams' poems, too, are records
of such perfect but transient moments when the "hidden flame"
or "Beautiful Thing" reveals itself, confirming the essential goodness of creation. Yet, at the same time, the elusiveness of the "rare
presence," as in the above passage from *Paterson,* is a cause for
"despair," although the confidence, in Williams, outweighs the despair.

8. Freedom

Freedom is closely allied with creativity and novelty, for if novelty perpetually emerges into the world, then the present moment
is not wholly determined by the past. Williams asserts the freedom
of consciousness in the living moment when, in *Spring and All,* he
declares his purpose as being "to refine, to clarify, to intensify that

eternal moment in which we alone live" (*I* 89). Through an effort of imagination, it is ideally possible to free perception from the conditioning of the past, as well as from a mechanically projected future. Yet a difficulty arises. While the root metaphor of organicism implicitly repudiates *mechanical* determinism, it introduces another form of determinism—that of unconscious becoming. Abrams points out the deterministic implications of Coleridge's use of the organic metaphor to explain artistic creation:

> For if the growth of a plant seems inherently purposeful, it is a purpose without an alternative, fated in the seed and evolving into its final form without the supervention of consciousness. . . . To substitute the concept of growth for the operation of mechanism in the psychology of invention, seems merely to exchange one kind of determinism for another.[26]

Thus, in Coleridge's view of the psychology of creation, the "justification of free-will is a crux . . . because this runs counter to an inherent tendency of his elected analogue."[27]

One possible answer to this dilemma, an answer that is at least implicit in Williams' assumptions about life and nature, is that the measure of freedom manifested by the emergence of novelty in the natural world is multiplied and raised to a conscious level in human beings who are both passive recipients of the energies of nature but also active and conscious directors of these forces. The reciprocal relation between conscious effort and unconscious force is described in Coleridge's famous definition of the imagination, which, while operating to some extent unconsciously, is a "power, first put in action by the will and understanding, and retained under their irremissive, though gentle and unnoticed controul" (269). According to Abrams, Coleridge used the analogy of organic growth to account for "the spontaneous, the inspired, and the self-evolving" aspects of artistic creation, but did "not commit himself so far to the elected figure as to minimize the supervention of the antithetic qualities of foresight and choice."[28]

Williams does not attack the philosophical issue of freedom directly; furthermore, he is well aware of how much of life is subject to physical necessity and social habit, as in "To Elsie"—"a girl so desolate / so hemmed round / with disease or murder" (*CP1* 218). Yet implicit in Williams' worldview is the assumption that the imagination can, at moments, attain liberation. Even in the stifling environment of "To Elsie" there are "isolate flecks" of possibility for those who have the imagination to seize them. That

humans can at least partially liberate themselves from social habit
is assumed in exhortatory poems such as "Tract" (*CP1* 72) in
which Williams urges his townspeople "to perform a funeral" in
a way that is more in keeping with their local setting and more
satisfying to their inner needs. In "The Ivy Crown" and other late
poems, Williams speaks of love as a conscious choice: "We will it
so / and so it is / past all accident" (*PB* 126). In "The Turtle" (*PB*
63), Williams envisions a time when a newer generation, through
the agency of the imagination, will overturn the present order
and establish a new, less mechanical one. The imagination, symbolized as a mythic turtle, "lives in mud" (nature), "but is not mud-
like," not wholly conditioned by physical necessity. Freedom, as a
metaphysical reality, is directly proclaimed in another poem, "St.
Francis Einstein of the Daffodils" (*CP1* 414):

> the Venusremembering wavelets
> rippling with laughter—
> freedom
> for the daffodils!

The poem is a celebration of Einstein's visit to America in 1921,
but it is also a celebration of a new worldview. Williams sees Einstein's theory of relativity as freeing both man and nature from
the lockstep determinism of the Newtonian universe.

Creative advance, plenitude, novelty, freedom—it may seem up
to now as a description of a cosmos without order, in continuous
and unstable flux. But many versions of organicism incorporate
stable features that add balance and order to the evolving universe. Perhaps the most important of these stabilizing features
are interrelatedness, correspondence, and universal essences.

9. Interrelatedness

Romanticism is often construed as giving free rein to an individualism which, when carried to grandiose Byronic or Faustian
extremes, results in isolation and self-destruction. But there is an
equally powerfull countertendency within romanticism emphasizing the individual's shared identity with nature and with other
human beings. This awareness of shared identity acts as a check
on the destructive potential inherent in romantic individualism.
While romantic organicism places a premium on individual

growth, the logic of the organic metaphor requires a complementary principle of vital relatedness—because a thing cannot be fully itself unless there is a context of other things to which it is related. The life of any single part of a plant—root, stem, leaf, cell, petal— is enhanced by its participation in the whole, and the plant itself exists within a larger environment of soil, sun, bacteria, and so on. Nothing can be fully itself by itself—this principle distinguishes organic individualism (like the inclusive individualism of a Whitman) from laissez-faire individualism premised on a mechanical autonomy of separate parts.

Furthermore, the organic balance between individuality and relatedness is not, ideally, one of compromise so much as one of mutual enhancement: both the individual part and the whole are more fully realized by participation in the life of each other. The extremes of anarchism and authoritarianism are, then, both prohibitive of the fullest organic development. Thus Williams sees "liberty" for the American people as properly having "the significance of inclusion rather than breaking away," and the "real character of the people" being "not toward dispersion except as a temporary phase for the gathering of power, but to unite. To form a union" (SE 208–9). A similar attitude is reflected in Williams' attempt to avoid both the formlessness of free verse and the regimentation of traditional metrics—that is, Williams wants a verse that is more inclusive of prose detail and common language than traditional poetry was, but not so inclusive as to lack a strong sense of being formed.

As noted in chapter 1, Miller stresses only Williams' focus on things in isolation, things revealing their uniqueness. But there is an equally important awareness on Williams' part of the interdependence of things as well. In A Novelette and Other Prose, Williams speaks of a "singleness I see in everything—actual" (I 283). "So all things enter into the singleness of the moment and the moment partakes of the diversity of all things" (I 282). Citing several observations he has made of natural phenomena (how to tell temperature from the way rhododendron leaves shrivel, how sycamores shed their bark), Williams asserts: "These and other things have a relationship with each other simply because both are actual" (I 297). The interrelatedness of things in nature is perceived, in special moments, as evidence of a harmony underlying the variety and flux of the universe. In "Flowers by the Sea" (CP1 378), for example, Williams perceives how a field of wind-tossed flowers resembles the sea and likewise how the nearby sea, swaying or gently swelling, resembles a single flower on "its plantlike stem."

The perceived resemblance no doubt renews Williams' enjoyment of objects previously seen as unrelated. The metaphorical resemblance sharpens his appreciation of form and movement—qualities actually in the field of flowers and in the sea.

Two unusual examples of Williams' sense of interrelatedness in nature are "Primrose" and "The Lily." "Primrose" (*CP1* 161) was mentioned earlier as an example of individuation. The evening primrose, with its "disinclination to be / five red petals or a rose," illustrates Williams' celebration of individual uniqueness. But the flower also exists in an environment, and the poem would be baffling if Williams' view of organic interrelationship were not taken into account:

> Yellow, yellow, yellow, yellow!
> It is not a color.
> It is summer!
> It is the wind on a willow,
> the lap of waves, the shadow
> under a bush, a bird, a bluebird,
> three herons, a dead hawk
> rotting on a pole—

Although these are not the best descriptive lines in the poem, they indicate that the primrose, while unique, is part of all the features of its immediate environment and that these environmental features enter into the poet's perception of the flower. Interrelatedness is additionally reinforced by Williams' selection of details that share correspondent similarities:

> It is a piece of blue paper
> in the grass or a threecluster of
> green walnuts swaying, children
> playing croquet or one boy
> fishing, a man
> swinging his pink fists
> as he walks—

All of these items, including the piece of blue paper if, as indicated earlier, the wind is blowing, involve swaying or swinging movements.[29]

The poem might be compared with Emerson's "Each and All" as a variant of the theme that in an organic universe nothing can be fully itself by itself. Emerson tells how he was disappointed with his captive bird whose song, in its natural setting, had thrilled him: "He sings the song, but it cheers not now, / For I did not bring home the river and the sky." Emerson explicitly states his theme: "Nothing is fair or good alone." Whitehead expresses the same idea in different terms: "There is no possibility of detached, self-contained existence. The environment enters into the nature of each thing"[30]—or, as Williams says, "the moment partakes of the diversity of all things" (*I* 282).

"The Lily" (*CP1* 286) is a more successful effort than "Primrose" in dealing with the theme of individuality within relationship. In "The Lily," Williams has found a subtle way of combining the catalog technique with a kind of suspended syntax—a method that both individualizes the elements in the scene and also brings them together in a perceived unity. The last two stanzas will illustrate:

> It's raining—
> water's caught
> among the curled-back petals
>
> Caught and held
> and there's a fly—
> are blossoming

Williams uses the device of postponing the predicate until the last line so that the separate items in the scene—tiger lily, hummingbird, petals, rain, fly—are held in suspension until unified by the final assertion, "are blossoming." Bits of grammar, including brief independent clauses ("and there's a fly"), form the series of subjects leading to the predicate. These discrete grammatical units help to particularize each item, suggesting that each has its separate, active life yet each is part of a single perceptual event reflecting their interrelation in nature. The harmony in nature is perceived by the poet, who extends it through language into the poem.

Through the exercise of sympathetic imagination, the individual becomes more fully aware of the surrounding world and of the subtle web of relations connecting all things. Therefore the principle of organic interrelatedness can serve as a basis for morality, providing a check on unlimited and indiscriminate use of nature. Williams, in "The Lion" (*CP2* 180), deals with the unsettling effect that abuses of nature and human nature have on the unconscious mind: "Use defames! the attack disturbs our sleep." In the poem, a lion, symbolic of unchecked entrepreneurial forces, drags off a woman (symbolic of nature) into the woods, staining the pure snow with her blood. This ongoing assault by "Traffic, the lion, the sophisticate" cannot be entirely shut out of mind.

Thus Williams' organicism should not be equated with an indiscriminate approval of newness. Williams, in spite of his campaign for innovation in the arts, did not consider all changes undergone by civilization for the better. In "To Elsie," for example, Elsie and her kind suffer "from imaginations which have no / peasant traditions to give them / character." Not all change represents true organic development stemming from a beneficent teleological drive. The test of the organic validity of any cultural form— whether a funeral rite or an office building—is not only the way in which it satisfies immediate utilitarian need, but also the way it fits the environment, including the human environment of aesthetic and emotional needs. Its individuality must not be such that it abuses its supportive context.

10. Correspondence: Nature as Symbol

The principle of organic interrelationship predicates resemblances both between parts of nature with each other and between human states of mind and natural phenomena. Thoreau, in the chapter titled "Spring" in *Walden,* grew ecstatic over the way that the "forms which thawing clay assume" resemble those of leaves, feathers, ice crystals, branching rivers, lungs, the human hand, and so on. This "sand foliage" from a thawing embankment was a "prototype" of organic creation: "The Maker of this earth but patented a leaf" and "there is nothing inorganic." Similarly, Williams recognizes a unity that contains all opposites and correspondences. Addressing some spiritual presence in *Paterson,* perhaps a presence felt in the landscape, Williams says

> You are the eternal bride and
> father—quid pro quo,
> a simple miracle that knows
> the branching sea, to which the oak
> is coral, the coral oak.

(*P* 75)

Perhaps Williams has in mind a correspondence in which the oak, an outgrowth of the earth, is the counterpart of the coral, an outgrowth of the sea; that is, both earth and sea "branch out" in different but parallel ways.

Williams' strong sense of correspondence between natural phenomena and states of human consciousness led Kenneth Burke to admire Williams' power to evoke "the human nature of things."[31] And Williams' use of natural symbolism, like other aspects of his thought, is very much in the Emersonian vein. Emerson, observing felt resemblances between human states of mind and natural objects and events, inferred that this "kinship" presupposed a common origin and that, consequently, Nature was a latent source of symbol or metaphor for Mind. Convinced that nature is the dormant counterpart of mind, Emerson believed that natural images are therefore necessary for the fullest expression of human thought and emotion:

> Nature is so pervaded with human life that there is something of humanity in all and in every particular. (49)

> Every appearance in nature corresponds to some state of the mind and that state . . . can only be described by presenting that natural appearance as its picture. (32)

Williams, too, expresses a sense of nature "pervaded with human life," as in "The Sparrow" (*CP2* 291), which begins with the Emersonian claim that the sparrow "who comes to sit at my window / is a poetic truth / more than a natural one":

                    His voice,
                              his movements,
          his habits—
                    how he loves to
                              flutter his wings
               in the dust—
                    all attest it

Williams' poem is, among other things, a tribute to Keats, echoing in its choice of subject, the famous instance of Keatsian negative capability: "if a Sparrow come before my window I take part in its existence and pick about the Gravel."[32]

Williams, in his identification with the sparrow, uses a language that is not wholly different from what one would use in describing human life:

```
                                      granted, he does it
                to rid himself of lice
                            but the relief he feels
                                      makes him
                cry out lustily—
                            which is a trait
                                      more related to music
                than otherwise.
```

The sparrow, when one enters imaginatively into its life, is more
than a natural or biological fact; it is a "poetic truth," having an
intrinsic value, an inner nature that is on a continuum with human nature and therefore capable of experiencing emotion in
some sense.

Many readers will undoubtedly feel that Williams has overhu-
manized the sparrow, projecting human emotions onto something
that is wholly alien to human nature. The poem might be acceptable to such readers either on the grounds of pure entertainment
or on the grounds that the sparrow is a "symbolic" representation
of typical masculine psychology recognizable in male human beings but not attributable to sparrows except in a fanciful way. On
the other hand, it may be that a modern poet, through the power
of imagination, has realized an actual continuum joining man and
nature. Such an Emersonian (and Aristotelian) belief in continuity
is explicit in Williams *The Embodiment of Knowledge:* "To say that
the inorganic, the organic and the ethical world are absolutely
separate is not true—for an analogy of 'truth' runs thru all three"
(*EK* 132). The truth, then, of both human and sparrow nature is
made more evident by the resemblance the imagination discovers
between them.

Perhaps any use of language to describe that portion of existence where humanity and nature overlap is going to sound too
anthropomorphic. But an ornithologist's scientific account of the
bird would probably lead to falsification by another route—a reductive use of language that ignores the rudimentary aspects of
emotion and volition in living things.

Besides having much in common with Keats in his sympathetic
identification with the life of nature, Williams is remarkably close
to being a Gerard Manley Hopkins—a Hopkins stripped of
Catholic doctrine and Jesuit introspectiveness. It is the Hopkins
who describes nature who is closest to Williams. A divine grandeur that flames out in special moments of perception, the willful
ignorance or suppression of this grandeur, and the inexhaustible
creative life at the heart of nature are themes as dear to Williams

as to Hopkins. Apart from the question of direct influence of Hopkins on Williams, the affinities between the two poets are worth consideration. Both poets have a loving eye for the distinctive, highly individualized character of natural phenomena. Hopkins coined the term *inscape* to refer to the visible manifestation of the unique essence of an individual object (or arrangement of objects in a scene) and *instress* to refer (1) to the teleological force that holds the various parts and qualities of an object into its unique inscape or organic form and (2) to the strong impression made by the inscape on the receptive mind. W. A. M. Peters defines Hopkins' inscape as "the unified complex of those sensible qualities . . . that strike us as inseparably belonging to and most typical of [an] object, so that through the . . . complex of sense-data we may gain an insight into the individual essence of the object."[33]

Inscape, furthermore, was evidence for Hopkins of the presence of God in things, and this in turn led him to conceive of things in nature as "selves":

> Hopkins was acutely aware . . . that, in spite of profound generic and specific differences, man and beast and inanimate nature were all alike "selves" . . . so that *from his angle of vision* there was between man and the rest of creation a difference of degree, not one of kind. In man the self was joined to a free nature, while in all other things the self was not so raised.[34]

Peters uses the term *impersonation* rather than *personification* to suggest that the animation Hopkins gives to natural objects is not merely a literary device but a recognition of things in nature as "selves." Williams, in poems like "The Sparrow," shares something of Hopkins' sense of things as selves. Personification is abundant in Williams: "even the trunk's self / putting out leafheads" (*CP1* 337); "They enter the new world naked, / cold, uncertain" (*CP1* 183); "The little sparrows / hop ingenuously / about the pavement / quarreling" (*CP1* 70). To some extent the pathetic fallacy is evident in these examples—the fallacy whereby nature is made to sympathize with the individual speaker's mood or to reflect human emotion in general. Personification, no matter how subtle and understated, always exaggerates and overhumanizes the life in nature, but it is a necessary device, given the limitations of language, for communicating the intuition that the universe is an organic continuum.

In chapter 8 of *A Novelette*, Williams explores the consanguinity

186 IDEAS IN THINGS

between human life and nature more fully. The chapter, ironically titled "Anti-Allegory," includes extensive descriptions of a teasel, a great mullein, and a walnut tree to illustrate the proposition that "the wintry landscape is a museum of dried vegetation, bearing much the same resemblance to the verdant wealth of summer that a mummy does to a living human being" (*I* 297). These objects are not described in a scientifically neutral manner devoid of personification, yet one is made to feel that such aesthetic qualities as elegance, beauty, "miracle of texture" are not superimposed by the observing mind but inhere in the objects as a latent part of their reality. Furthermore, Williams' description of the gone-to-seed mullein as an "expression of melancholy ruin," although it involves analogy, is not allegorical; that is, it is not based on an arbitrary connection between idea and image:

> The larger outer leaves have faded and lost form, and become mere brown rags, like the tatters of miserable poverty, drenched in the rains of winter, and draggled on the mud of the cold inhospitable earth. Of all the plants that grow, the mullein in its decay comes nearest to that most terrible form of human poverty when the victim has still, to his misfortune, vitality enough for mere existence, yet not enough to make existence either decent or endurable. (*I* 298).

Granted that there is some sentimentality, or pathetic fallacy, in the first part of the description up through "the cold inhospitable earth," the analogy in the second half seems right, seems based on a shared quality of diminishment. That the wintry mullein *comes nearest* to exemplifying a particular stage of poverty implies that it, out of all other natural phenomena, impressed its resemblance on Williams' mind, not that the mind imposed the resemblance on the object. The chapter title, "Anti-Allegory," implies that Williams does not believe he is falsifying the objects of nature by drawing out their latent resemblance to human conditions. The reality of the autumnal mullein and the reality of a certain stage of human poverty are mutually illuminated by their fusion in Williams' metaphoric prose.

For Williams, even inorganic objects, as well as living things, correspond to human states of mind, and the correspondence is not entirely arbitrary:

> Would you consider a train passing—or the city in the icy sky—a love song? It must be so . . . the lights of the city—in the distance that seem to close together at the end of the dark street . . . in themselves equal in

detail the existence of affection—the fact of love and so, deciphered, intensely seen become in themselves praise and song. (*I* 298–99)

Emerson, too, felt that, when objects are "liberated" by being taken up into the poet's organic expression of his idea, their inner natures are "reflected by a melody" so that, for example, "a tempest is a rough ode" or "summer . . . an epic song" (232–33). Williams' association of human feelings with a specific movement or configuration of physical phenomena might be attributed to strong personal emotion or to literary and folk tradition that establishes an association, say, between the approaching/receding sound of a train whistle at night and loneliness or longing. But Williams would maintain, it would seem, that such associations are not merely arbitrary or subjective, that certain physical configurations correspond to certain emotional configurations (as is often evident in abstract painting). Possibly, in the second example above, Williams is thinking of how streetlights appear smaller and smaller and closer together as one looks down a street that narrows to a vanishing point because of perspective. Perhaps this pattern of intensification, of convergence, suggested to Williams something about the nature of love. The latent a priori correspondences between physical and emotional configurations become explicit through the poet's imagination so that subsequently the symbolic correspondences become a polished part of literary tradition.

11. Universals

Williams' comments on universal essences in *The Embodiment of Knowledge* reveal a platonic influence on his early thought. In an allegorical narrative called "Beauty and Truth," Williams tells of two men who seek absolute truth by different paths. For the narrator, the quest is through beauty and art; for his friend, it is through a scientific analysis of the material world. The scientist discovers that "there are but a very few simple and permanent materials out of which all other things are made" (*EK* 164). But this empirical knowledge fails to satisfy him, so the scientist, in effect, turns philosopher when his "elements . . . suddenly appeared to my imagination as an arrangement of some one ground fiber which became known as electron" (*EK* 164). (This is the closest Williams ever comes to describing the "ground" in terms of modern physics.) The elements are further conceived as having within them a "rhythmic order"; consequently, a "form began to emerge." The scientist then comes to a platonic conclusion:

> All nature is but a complex arrangement; that the few elements, perhaps one, governed by law, take on shapes, form, which cannot be directly analyzed, for as forms they have no substance. . . . Form can only be discovered and appreciated, not analyzed. (*EK* 166)

The forms Williams refers to are, in effect, platonic ideas or essences in which individual things participate.

One may prefer to see Williams as more Aristotelian than platonic, because he usually locates the forms or essences within things—but even Aristotle was platonic in so far as he held the forms to be permanent and immaterial. Being immaterial the forms cannot, as Williams says, be "directly [empirically] analyzed," but they can be known initially through the imagination, which holds idea and sensory image together—a fusion from which the intellect can abstract and formulate a general concept of the idea. As with Whitehead or Aristotle, the universal forms are repeatable patterns in things—what Whitehead calls "eternal objects"—that enter into various transient objects called "events" or "actual occasions." Instead of the terms "universal" or "Platonic idea," Whitehead prefers the term "eternal object" because it stresses both the nontemporality of the forms and the objective nature of their existence outside the mind. For example, a certain shade of yellow, the quality of courage, or a species of tree repeat themselves from object to object, from year to year. Although these forms are known only because they have an embodiment in particulars, their existence is not limited to any finite set of particulars. In Whitehead's terminology, the eternal objects are "real" but not "actual," although capable of entering into "actual occasions" such as a specific tree or a specific act of courage.

As discussed in chapter 3, the universals are often indicated by symbols in Williams' work, though sometimes it is difficult to tell just what the universal essence is. For example, in "The Graceful Bastion" (*CP2* 10), a butterfly, though fragile, is "ribbed with steel / wired to the sun / whose triumphant power / will keep it safe." Clearly, Williams cannot mean that an individual butterfly is literally wired to the sun. The poem was published in 1940 and probably written at a time when Williams felt the impending world war as a threat to much that he held dear. The butterfly, then, may symbolize beauty, poetry, or even the forms of nature itself— and the poem then expresses Williams' faith that the ideal essences

or patterns of these things will survive time and the brutality
of war.

There is another symbol in the poem, the sun, which recalls
Plato's symbol for the Good, the Idea from which all other Ideas
are derived. In Williams, the sun is a symbol for creative power
(eros) that is both transcendent and immanent, as in *Paterson*
where sunlight penetrates "the blood dark sea" from which "the
sun / alone lifts undamped his wings" (*P* 202). In "Spring Strains"
(*CP1* 97), the dawn sun counteracts the tendency in material
things to revert back to formless matter: "pulls the whole /
counter-pulling mass upward." In a much later poem, "The Orchestra" (*PB* 80), the coming of dawn is symbolically represented
as an orchestra tuning up. The "cacaphony of bird calls" is likened
to the various instruments "seeking a common tone":

> Love is that common tone
> > shall raise his fiery head
> > > and sound his note.

Love orchestrates order out of chaos. The point here is that recurrent symbols in Williams' work—sun, sea, soil, blossoming, dance,
song—represent an implicit organic world view in which eternal
forms are perpetually being reembodied in particulars.

While Williams believes that the eternal forms or essences are
real, he is careful to insist on respect for the integrity of the
particular and the local in which the universal is discerned. In an
essay on the painter Charles Sheeler, Williams states that the true
artist must "know that every hair on every body, now or then, in its
minute distinctiveness is the same hair, on every body anywhere, at
any time, changed as it may be to feather, quill or scale" (*SE* 233).
And in an essay on Kenneth Burke, Williams writes: "One has to
learn what the meaning of the local is, for universal purposes.
The local is the only thing that is universal. . . . The classic is
the local fully realized" (*SE* 132). In the first statement, Williams
reminds the artist that, while it is necessary to pay minute attention to the particular, one must not forget that the particular
participates in the universal. Not only is there a universal hair-
ness, but it too is part of a larger universal having to do with
epidermal covering. Of course, the example of hair is meant only
to illustrate a point about the nature of universals in general.
In the second statement, Williams emphasizes that the local or
particular has prior epistemological status—but the local is not an
end in itself. It has to be apprehended for "universal purposes."

The question of universals, like that of free will, involves another crux for the organicist. Just as freedom seemed to be denied by the implied unconsciousness lurking in the basic metaphor of the plant, so too any notion of permanence seems difficult to reconcile with the organic conception of the universe as process. In a "universe of emergents," Peckham states, "it therefore follows that there are no pre-existent patterns"; thus Wordsworth compromised and weakened his creative power by retaining "within his new attitude a nostalgia for permanence, an ideal of eternal perfection."[35] Richard P. Adams finds a similar incompatibility between process and permanence in Emerson's writings: "His point of view was not steady enough; it shifted uncomfortably and unpredictibly between something like Platonic idealism and something like romantic organicism, doing justice to neither."[36]

But is a belief in transcendent ideas necessarily incompatible with organic process? According to Perkins, "Romantic organicism" attempted to reconcile the rival claims of idealist and materialist views of reality by "conceiving the cosmos . . . as a process . . . in which the material world, the mental . . . and the Divine mutually . . . interpenetrate." Thus intangible "values . . . are felt as aspects of concrete experience."[37] Coleridge, according to Walter Jackson Bate, tried to reconcile "concrete, organic naturalism [with] Platonic doctrine."[38] That is, while Coleridge, like Plato, believed in the "absolute existence" of universals, he followed Aristotle in believing that "the reality of nature is to be found in a *process* . . . in which the universal and the particular fulfill each other."[39]

This organic synthesis of transcendentalism and empiricism, as described by Perkins and Bate, is relevant to Williams' sense of concrete existence as immanent with value and meaning—"ideas in things"—and likewise his reluctance, in much of his poetry, to perform what Perkins calls the "secondary act of abstraction" by means of which universals are torn from their fusion with concrete reality. For example, one might consider the description in Williams' *Dial* award poem of 1926, "Paterson," the first poem in which the phrase "no ideas but in things" appears:

> The actual, florid detail of cheap carpet
> amazingly upon the floor and paid for
> as no portrait ever was—Canary singing
> and geraniums in tin cans spreading their leaves
> reflecting red upon the frost—
> They are the divisions and imbalances

> of his whole concept, made small by pity
> and desire, they are—no ideas besides the facts—
>
> (CP1 265)

Williams here does not seem quite sure what the observed details of this working-class environment mean, but he has a feeling that they are somehow significant and that by dwelling on them he will find the significance he feels in them. Perhaps the "ideas" latent in these "things" include the universal human love of beauty, the need for expressing that love, and the pathetically inadequate means available to the lower classes in an industrial society for the expression of aesthetic needs.

Further support for the reconciliation of universals with a dynamic organicism might be drawn from Irving Babbitt, although, in his attacks on romanticism, he undoubtedly did not anticipate that his ideas might be supportive of what is best in romanticism. Babbitt's quarrel with the Romantics was that in their glorification of imagination and feeling over reason, they were failing to distinguish the true nature of reason as exemplified by Aristotle; instead, they were reacting to the more formalized, static, and conventional view of reason held by the Neoclassics. For Aristotle, Babbitt says, the "absolute" was not "fixed"; it "is not to be taken as anything finite, as anything that can be formulated once for all," and "true classicism does not rest on the observance of rules or the imitation of models but on an immediate insight into the universal."[40] For Babbitt, the imagination is the instrument by which the "element of vital novelty" that enters into "any particular case" is related to "the ethical or permanent in life."[41] According to Babbitt, the romantic movement went astray in treating novelty as an end in itself, not as a lively manifestation of the permanent. Without access to universals—regardless of whether they can be known apart from things or only within things— organicism becomes a complete relativism, lacking the assurance of genuine knowledge.

12. Beauty: The Platonic Dimension in Williams

One universal is especially important to Williams' view of the world, and that is the universality of beauty. In his attitude toward beauty, as towards other aspects of nature, Williams was anticipated by Emerson who, rhapsodizing on the stars, "these envoys of beauty," said that "all natural objects make a kindred impression" (23) and "there is no object so foul that intense light will not make beautiful" (26). Beauty is a pervasive but elusive dimension of Williams' cosmos, and his stress on the transcendental aspect of beauty links him with platonic tradition. But beauty is immanent, too, and Williams finds epiphanies of beauty in both the animate and inanimate world—and in people as well as things. One such epiphany occurs in *Paterson* where the narrator, walking on former pasture land gone to weeds, is startled by "a flight of empurpled wings / . . . from the dust kindled / to sudden ardor!" (*P* 47). The sudden appearance of these grasshoppers, the purple in their "announcing wings" revealed in flight, is an inspirational moment for the poet. The discovery and expression of such beauty is an index to the hidden but ultimately ideal character of his universe.

The idea of beauty as an emanation revealing the hidden ideality of the world is crucial to *Paterson* where, in the opening statement, Williams announces his quest as "rigor of beauty," the release of beauty "locked in the mind." This declared intent does not mean that Williams is taking the subjectivist position that beauty is merely in the eye of the beholder. The external universe is real for Williams and has a character of its own: it is active, living, evolving—and charged throughout with an elusive beauty that is a sign of its divine or semidivine nature. Nor does Williams' opening statement mean that his quest is merely an aesthetic one, having private relevance only. The revelations of beauty, in which the poet feels a fusion or oneness with the world, are peak moments in a larger struggle to achieve wholeness of self and ultimately a renewal of culture.

The poet of *Paterson* realizes that beauty is discovered in an immediate response to place. He recalls his experience of a "first beauty"—an intuition of the divine beauty latent in the world. All subsequent moments sharing this vision are related to the first one, forming a continuity—as the wives of the African chief in the *National Geographic* photo form a continuity from first to last (*P* 13–14, 21–22). Williams' recollection of a "first beauty" is a modern instance of Plato's anamnesis, the recollection of the soul's preexistence—or at least the recollection of a state of innocence. (In "Struggle of Wings," *CP1* 260, Williams makes playfully serious use of Plato's preexistence myth to represent the birth of poetry and the poetic impulse from obscure origins.) This special or divine beauty has an elusive, evolving "history": it reveals itself only intermittently and cannot be categorized or held in fixed forms. It is a living quality that appears and vanishes—in snow,

bird, daisy, worm, and locomotive (*P* 23). It is present even in
the inanimate that, by virtue of this presence, is not radically or
altogether discontinuous with the animate.

One of the paradoxes of the beauty Williams seeks to uncover
is that men both fear and desire it. In "Paterson: Episode 17"
(*CP1* 439), men fight jealously over a woman who, though slum-
ming, is an embodiment of the "Beautiful Thing." In their jealous
possessiveness, the men break her nose—"for memory's sake / to
be credible in their deeds." It is as if they must bring this goddess
down to a level where she is imperfect and therefore manageable
and accessible to them. Men fear the power beauty might have
over them if they give themselves to it, or perhaps they fear the
power they must give up in order that beauty might be revealed.
On a grander scale, this idea informs Williams' account of the
New World in *In the American Grain* wherein the lure of power
and gold is seen as a perversion of the need to possess a primal
beauty that has been lost to the over-Christianized European soul.
Williams begins his account of Cortez's destruction of Tenochti-
tlan, the beautiful and intricate Aztec city, with this sentence:
"Upon the orchidean beauty of the new world the old rushed
inevitably to revenge itself" (*AG* 27). Later, the Puritans, like the
Spanish conquerors, also exhibit a fear and hatred of life disguised as the need for conquest and control. By these means they
make themselves invulnerable to the beauty that unconsciously
lures them to self-abandonment. They "closed all the world out"
because "the enormity of their task . . . enforced it" (*AG* 112).

The importance of beauty in Williams' cosmos is fully recognized and subtly treated by Miller in *Poets of Reality*, although
Miller flatly denies any transcendental dimension to Williams'
beauty. Beauty, as Miller explains Williams, is immanent: hidden
in the "ground" and revealed only in the moment that a form
emerges from it. In this way, Miller integrates the three elements
of Williams' cosmos—ground, forms, and beauty. But the "hidden
flame" or "rare presence" (Williams' terms) is "covered up as soon
as the form gets fixed in a shape. Only in the moment when the
flower rises from the ground is a brief glimpse of the presence
released. For this reason validity lies in the process of flowering
and not in the flower full blown."[42] By "form" in this metaphorical
context, Miller undoubtedly means not so much a biological form
but a man-made form (for example, a new mode in art), which,
while still fresh, releases the "presence"—or the "form" might
be a special formation of perception rising spontaneously and
revealing the world's beauty. "The Lily," to use a previously dis-

cussed poem, provides an example of form in both senses. The poem is about a moment in which interrelated aspects of nature are unified into a single perceptual configuration ("are blossoming"), and the poem itself, with its unusual syntax, exhibits something innovative in form that makes it possible to more fully realize the moment and to communicate it to others. But though the forms that release beauty grow dull and stale and gradually disappear, beauty as a transcendent reality is never exhausted.

Miller's essay was written before the publication of Williams' *The Embodiment of Knowledge*, which, although it confirms much of what Miller has to say, gives a much more transcendental character to the nature of beauty as Williams conceives it. In the essay called "Beauty and Truth," Williams tells how the lover of beauty, being moved by its presence in nature, attempts to reproduce it through some artistic medium. He discovers that only when he stops trying so hard to capture beauty directly and instead concentrates on the problems of his medium does he begin to have any success. But, even when he succeeds in producing "masterpieces," he feels that beauty has eluded him. He concludes:

> Nature is not beauty, then, but it is beautiful. Then it expresses beauty: beauty is in nature, it is in a tree but it is not a tree. What is this beauty then but a ghost? The idea seems preposterous, funny even. Beauty has no [material] form but it is expressed in form. . . . It is then, in indefinite part, unexpressed all about me awaiting expression. . . . Why it is here in me fairly aching to be freed in the semblance of a leaf or anything. In me is beauty such as nature elsewhere never dreamt of. . . . I no longer see trees but beauty in form of trees and thus a new life. All nature now becomes a symbol for me to use. (*EK* 163–64)

Williams emphasizes that beauty has a transcendent dimension, that it is not entirely within nature: "Beauty has no form but it is expressed in form." Beauty is in man as well as in nature, "awaiting expression," having an active character of its own. It can be expressed only indirectly, through symbolic form, but it can never be exhausted by any finite set of expressions.

Since beauty is never exhausted in nature or in human works, the artist is never content with existing expressions of it. Miller demonstrates how, in Williams' view, cultural and artistic forms that lose touch with the "ground" cease to have vitality, because they do not express the radiant beauty latent in the ground. Miller does not mean, it is presumed, that an authentic masterpiece delights with its beauty only one time, but that the *general* style or

mode in which the work was conceived eventually fails to reflect
the intensity of life that once gave rise to the style. Given Williams'
sense of the organic, evolutionary character of life, one can see
how this would be so. Once received forms have lost connection
with the needs and conditions that figured in their creation, they
can become oppressive and enervating. Williams symbolizes this
idea, for example, in "The Lion" (*CP2* 180), in which the beast,
representing the authority of established custom, drags off to the
woods and devours a woman—representing nature and its generative impulse—staining the snow with her blood. The lion has
"thick muscles" and a "head / like a tree-stump, gnawing." The
conceptual basis for the simile here is more important than the
visual resemblance, for the stump represents the repressive force
of once-living institutions cut off from their source in nature.

Although Miller asserts that Williams is antiplatonic and beyond
romantic transcendentalism, Miller's description of Williams' cosmos—with its "forms" latent in the "ground" in which also lurks
a "hidden" but "universal beauty" (Miller's term)—is certainly not
materialistic in its implications. As Miller elaborates on the third
element in Williams' cosmos, the "hidden flame," he asserts that
"there is no surreptitious return to Platonism or to any form of
transcendentalism," for "Williams' flame is entirely within
things."[43] Yet, as is evident in *The Embodiment of Knowledge*, Williams thought of beauty as having an existence that transcends
the particulars in which it is immanent.

Although the terms Williams uses to denote beauty—"hidden
flame," "rare presence," "radiant gist"—suggest immanence, it is
an immanence of something so rare and special as to possess a
transcendental dimension. In his *Autobiography,* Williams attempts
to account for his obsession with these moments of revelation:

> We catch a glimpse of something, from time to time, which shows us
> that a presence has just brushed past us, some rare thing—just when
> the smiling little Italian woman has left us. For a moment we are
> dazzled. What was that? We can't name it; we know it never gets into
> any recognizable avenue of expression; men will be long dead before
> they can have so much as ever approached it. . . . So for me the prac-
> tice of medicine has become the pursuit of a rare element which may
> appear at any time, at any place, at a glance. (*A* 360)

Williams is convinced that the rare presence is not merely a product of his own imagination: "It is actually there, in the life before
us, every minute that we are listening, a rarest element—not in
our imaginations but there, there in fact" (*A* 362). Finally, this rare

beauty transcends its particular occasions in people and things: "It will not use the same appearance for any new materialization. And it is our very life. It is we ourselves, at our rarest moments, but inarticulate for the most part" (*A* 362). Miller, although seeing nothing platonic in the passage, is right in saying that "these sentences touch the center of Williams' thought and are his most open expression of the third element in the trinity of forces constituting his world."[44]

There are several reasons why Platonism in Williams has not received the recognition it deserves. First of all, Platonism, as evident in Miller's tone, is largely out of favor in the intellectual life of the twentieth century. The dominant twentieth-century literary and philosophical forms from naturalism to existentialism to deconstructionism stress that the universe is inscrutable or absurd, that there are no intelligible forms inhering in existence—only what the human mind or human language imposes. Secondly, it may seem incongruous to speak of Platonism in connection with a poet who often rails against otherworldliness and who is most noted for his sharp focus on the actual and for his creation of an earthy persona who gets high sniffing "the souring flowers of the bedraggled / poplars" ("Smell," *CP1* 92), a gesture that seems decidedly out of character with Platonism. Furthermore, one can find prose statements by Williams that appear to be incompatible with any form of Platonism, such as the oft cited "no ideas but in things" or "I utterly reject metaphysics" (*Int* 65). Some poems, too, contain statements inimical to any sort of transcendentalism, any belief in a reality beyond the senses. "The Clouds" (*CP2* 173), while not absolutely ruling out the possibility of immortality, deplores current versions of "spiritualism" as an escape from humanity and from "the obtrusive body." Many poems affirm flux as the basic fact of existence: "The change reveals—change" ("Catastrophic Birth," *CP2* 55) or "the phase is supreme!" ("To All Gentleness," *CP2* 71).

While Williams characteristically focuses on the here and now, on process rather than permanence, a more inclusive view shows that, for Williams, the world perceived in process was permeated with a rare and absolute quality of beauty. Williams generally shuns the vocabulary traditionally used to express a sense of divinity—words like "God," "Spirit," "Oversoul," "Divine"—because these words have lost much of their meaning for the modern reader and tend to make the immanent value that Williams celebrates seem remote and irrelevant. Williams desired a fresh contact with the living source from which great religions have arisen—only to fall, as Raymond Blakney puts it, "each into its own parochial form and idiom . . . its own shell which encases one or two germs of the one universal life."[45] Emerson had warned in "Self-Reliance," "If . . . a man claims to know and speak of God, and carries you backward to the phraseology of some old mouldered nation in another country, in another world, believe him not" (157).

Williams, without perhaps fully realizing it, had found a fresh poetic idiom for expressing his sense of the special character of the universe, for which terms like "God" and "Divine" have become nearly dead metaphors for some and institutionalized abstractions for others. There was, as Miller notes, a reluctance on Williams' part to name the nameless, to use terms whose connotations had congealed. Like the ancient Hebrews, Williams thought it irreverent, if not dangerous, to try to fix the nameless in a name. The desire to avoid the traditional form of Christian address to the Deity is evident in revisions Williams made in the last lyrical passage of book 2, *Paterson*. The passage is a prayer, ambiguously addressed to a "you"—the presence of beauty personified:

> Why should I move from this place
> where I was born? knowing
> how futile would be the search
> for you in the multiplicity
> of your debacle. The world spreads
> for me like a flower opening—and
> will close for me as might a rose—
>
> wither and fall to the ground
> and rot and be drawn up
> into a flower again. But you
> never wither—but blossom
> all about me. In that I forget
> myself perpetually—in your
> composition and decomposition
> I find my   .   .
>   despair!

(P 75)

According to Sister Bernetta Quinn, the microfilm version of the *Paterson* manuscript indicates that the passage was originally intended as an address to "God."[46] Miller finds support in the excision of "God" for his antitheistic interpretation of Williams, noting Williams' "reluctance to identify the radiant gist with

God."[47] But it is just as noteworthy that Williams came so close to identifying the rare, intuited beauty with the traditional concept of divinity. Certainly the tone of the passage is that of reverent prayer addressed to a personal being. Furthermore, the passage goes beyond a pantheistic naturalism, for though the being or entity addressed in the poem is present in nature, it is not of the same, perishable substance as the phenomena of nature.

Although Williams avoids religious diction, if not a religious tone, in the above passage, he later introduces the evangelist who states the spiritual message of book 2 in a simple, dignified Protestant preaching idiom, paralleling Williams' more lyrical expression of the theme. The evangelist (bald like Williams' Sunday school teacher who read Plato to his class, ML 203) is sympathetically portrayed: with humility but with homespun eloquence he speaks of "the riches of all the ages" (P 66). The "blessing" proclaimed by both Williams and the bald preacher in their different ways is ironically contrasted with the material wealth envisioned by Alexander Hamilton as he dreams of harnessing nature to industrial production: "Here was water-power to turn the mill wheels and the navigable river to carry manufactured goods to the market centers" (P 69).

Williams' reference to a "first beauty" links him then, via Emerson, all the way back to Jonathan Edwards, who preached of a "divine and supernatural light" that altered one's consciousness and was bestowed without the intervention of the visible church (and that ultimately could not be monopolized by the church). In *Paterson,* Williams suggests that the capacity to intuit the transcendent beauty is inborn:

> which is to say, though it be poorly
> said, there is a first wife
> and a first beauty, complex, ovate—
> the woody sepals standing back under
> the stress to hold it here, innate . . .

(P 22)

All attempts to contain this quality in any single human construct are futile, because it is

> a flower within a flower whose history
> (within the mind) crouching
> among ferny rocks, laughs at the names
> by which they think to trap it.

(P22)

Like a "first wife," the awakening to this sense of beauty holds a special place in the memory of the protagonist. The "flower within the flower" is the platonic ideal within the actual: beauty made immanent. It is what Williams calls in one of his late poems "a sound addressed / not wholly to the ear," something beyond the senses ("The Orchestra," *PB* 81). The recollection of the "first beauty" plays an important part in Williams' worldview: it is what keeps human beings from the despair that inevitably accompanies the confinement of the spirit within an empirical-mechanistic worldview.

Williams' intuition of a transcendent dimension to experience by no means makes him a mystic, if by that term one means someone whose experience of the ineffable makes this world seem unreal, a burden or an obstacle between the human and the supernatural. Williams' mysticism, if that term is appropriate, is a *via affirmativa*, not the *via negativa*, or the darkening of the senses of the later T. S. Eliot. Although there is less emphasis on recollection in tranquillity, the special moments in Williams constitute a value similar to what they did for Wordsworth as interpreted by Hirsch:

> It is true that the mystical moment may constitute Enthusiasm's most complete fulfillment, but it is a moment which is rarely attained and which quickly disappears. In the general course of experience, the Enthusiast senses his separation from things, and, therefore, from God. Such separation is the wellspring of his incessant striving, and the moment of mystical fusion is a vanishing point which lends a confident tone to the process of striving as such.[48]

In *The Embodiment of Knowledge,* Williams allegorizes such an encouraging moment as an "experience on the mountain," a moment of intense feeling earned by the poet's "labor" of praise and appreciation. It is a moment that "hold[s] in concentrated form the whole meaning of life" and which is a "promise" that makes "labor endurable" (*EK* 180).

While Williams characteristically feels a quiet kinship with natural things, it is only infrequently in his poems that he expresses an overwhelming sense of fusion with the divine life in nature. One of these poems, "A Unison" (*CP2* 157), is ecstatic to the point of inarticulateness. In the poem, Williams recalls a visit made with a friend to a rural cemetery. The recollection now appears as a Wordsworthian "spot of time," a recollection, enriched by memory, of a moment of fusion with something transcendent. The experience seems to deny a radical separation between the living and the dead. The whole scene—natural setting, tombstones, and the buried dead—seems alive: "*Listen! Do you not hear them? the singing?*" The poem asserts one of the fundamental tenets of an idealist-organicism, the notion of a living universe: hence immortality.

Williams occasionally resorts to a religious diction to express his reverence for the untranslatable quality of beauty in things. The apples in "Wild Orchard" (*CP1* 239), for example, are "enshrined." Ordinary objects possess a "small holiness" in "Approach to the City" (*CP2* 108). The shining, tall white grass in "The Province" (*CP2* 158) exemplifies, in its gracefulness and beauty, "the principle / of the godly." Williams links beauty with life and divinity, for the grass is "lifeless / save only in / beauty, / . . . the eternal." Williams' use of the lower case on "godly" indicates his desire to dissociate the word from its Hebraic-Christian cultural background and to give it a more universal meaning.

In addition to the more or less explicit reference to a divinity or a divine principle in nature, Williams more often indicates this ideal quality in images of light. Miller has noted that "images of substantial light are dominant in the poet's approaches to a name for the rare presence."[49] In using light as a symbol of immanent divinity, Williams is drawing on a long symbolic tradition. In the Gospel of St. John, God's ever-present revelation is likened to "light" that "shines in the darkness." Plotinus symbolically conceived of Plato's Idea of the Good as an emanation of light radiating outward from a center into the darkness of matter. Wordsworth, in the platonic tradition, speaks of nature as once, for him, "appareled with celestial light." Closer to Williams' sense of the beauty immanent in things is Gerard Manley Hopkins: "The world is charged with the grandeur of God. / It will flame out, like shining from shook foil."

Light in Williams' earlier poetry is not often consciously associated with the transcendent, yet it does seem to be the mark of some rare quality in things. In "Complaint" (*CP1* 153), a poem in which Williams describes a house call to deliver a baby, the mystery of conception is symbolized by "one gold needle" of sunlight penetrating the darkened room through the window slats. In "The Pot of Flowers" (*CP1* 184), the flowers have emerged from the darkness of nonexistence, symbolized by the "wholly dark" pot, to the realm of transcendent beauty manifest in the petals "radiant with transpiercing light." In an environment of social and physical degradation in "To Elsie," there is a slight redeeming hope in the "isolate flecks" of beauty, as elusive as "deer" in "fields of goldenrods" (*CP1* 218). The "contours and the shine" of the fish in "Sea Trout and Butterfish" (*CP1* 353), the scintillance of the yachts in "The Yachts" (*CP1* 388), and the glaze on the wheelbarrow, and the shining bits of broken glass are all indicators of the rare presence. In "The Crimson Cyclamen," as the flower comes into form—that is, as matter becomes intelligible—it ecstatically (in the poet's mind) reaches "upward to / the light! the light! the light!" (*CP1* 423).

In addition to images of light, Williams uses images of music as a metaphor for the beauty and perfection that the world aspires to realize. This metaphor has already been seen in "A Unison" where even the stones sing the praise of creation. In "Ol' Bunk's Band" (*CP2* 149) Williams hears in jazz its African ancestral origins, the

> ancient cry, escaping crapulence
> eats through
> transcendent—torn, tears, term
> town, tense . . .

The music emotionally derives from the suffering and limitations suggested by the unusual catalog—"torn, tears, term / town, tense"—but transcends these limitations to put the players and the sympathetic listener on another plane of existence where, despite the gauntness and "crapulence" of old age, "These are men!" In "The Orchestra," the instruments rise above their cacophony to seek a "common tone" identified as the majestic platonic reality of "Love" that "shall raise his fiery head / and sound his note" (*PB* 80).

The major use of music as a symbol of a universal harmony occurs in "The Desert Music" in which Williams inwardly hears an "insensate music" that begins to awaken his own creativity. This spiritual music has its imperfect counterparts in the screaming of the sparrows, the chatter of vendors and begging children, the music from night clubs and street musicians. A jaded striptease dancer, however, has a style or presence that "lifts" her above "the lying / music" of the orchestra to "another music" (*PB* 115–16) so that she becomes an emblem for Williams of a leap beyond the deficient harmonies of actual sounds to the exalted music that is

wakening in him. This "changeless . . . music" holds him, at
times, entranced:

                                        the music! the
            music as when Casals struck
            and held a deep cello tone
            and I am speechless

This transcendent music is latent in formless but potentially fertile matter symbolized by the egg-shaped figure in rags, its knees
tucked up in embryonic position, leaning against a bridge girder
at the entrance to Juarez: "The music / guards it." This music is
"a benumbing ink that stains the / sea of our minds—to hold us
off" (*PB* 120). That is, there is something inviolate about this
nearly formless figure; its mystery is not easily penetrated. The
music seems to emanate from the figure: it is "shed / of a shape
close as it can get to no shape." As the music becomes more actual
and insistent at the end of the poem, Williams feels empowered
to begin to write: "Now it is all / about me. The dance! The verb
detaches itself / seeking to become articulate" (*PB* 120). The final
lines, in which Williams wonders at the human capacity to hear
"that music" and "sometimes record it," imply that the music has
an objective existence that transcends the self.

   The scattered but important references in Williams' work to
transcendent realities point to a general realm of spirit, a realm
of "light," grasped initially through sensory and emotional experience filtered through the imagination. Of course, any theory of
transcendent forms, if it is to hold good, must admit forms for
such things as dung, boredom, overcrowding, treachery, despair,
and ugliness; but in the hierarchy of forms, the most valued and
most deserving of actualization are what they have most commonly been—truth, beauty, goodness. It is Williams' intuitive
faith—driven back by twentieth-century skepticism to a new starting point in the immediacies of sense experience and driven also
to disguise itself in a complex symbolism—that one can and does
touch such an ideal dimension of value, that it exists independ-
ently of the mind, and that one's intuition of it is not an illusion.

   This belief or faith reaches something like a final statement in
the "Coda" to "Asphodel, That Greeny Flower," written during
convalescence when Williams often felt that the end was near.
This intuitive knowledge of an ultimate goodness is simply given,
a part of being human, though often obscured by the heat and
passion of living:

> Inseparable from the fire
> > its light
> > > takes precedence over it.

The "light," which through most of life is "inseparable from the fire," or the passions that involve one wholly in concrete existence, begins, in old age, to take "precedence" over the fire. The ending of "Coda" combines the transcendental image of light with allusions to music to symbolize some ultimate source of beauty, order, and immortality:

> > It is all
> a celebration of the light.
> > All the pomp and ceremony
> > > of weddings,
> "Sweet Thames, run softly
> > till I end
> > > my song,"—

Williams, reflecting back on his own marriage ceremony, came to see pageantry and ritual, much of which he had criticized in his earlier attacks on convention, as mankind's intuitive, groping effort to objectify some nameless source of glory and harmony.

6

THE LATE YEARS AND THE LEGACY

The transcendental idealism that had been the dominant assumption behind Williams' worldview gave way in his very last years to a more limited and withdrawn attitude toward life. Perhaps because of illness and old age, Williams was feeling, as Wallace Stevens had come to feel in "The Course of a Particular," that "being part [of everything] is an exertion that declines."[1] Absent from *Paterson 5* and from the late short poems of *Pictures from Brueghel* are Williams' earlier themes—ideas in things (universals), the imagination as a force of nature, the identification of nature's creative proceses with man's. Nor is there any celebration of the "light" as in the "Coda" to "Asphodel." Instead, Williams seems to have turned to a religion of art: to celebrate the creation of art as the only kind of meaning or immortality available to man. More than half of the twelve poems that make up Williams' last sustained sequence, "Pictures from Brueghel," contain references to art and the artist. The fourth poem of the sequence, based on Brueghel's "The Adoration of the Kings," places the work of art itself above the religious subject that is its occasion. According to Williams, Brueghel painted the story, including

> the downcast eyes of the Virgin
> as a work of art
> for profound worship

> (*PB* 6)

The syntax—"work of art / for profound worship"—permits the reading that the work of art itself is what is most worthy of worship.

Aestheticism—a regard for art as the highest human value— was always a potent attitude in Williams. But, whereas earlier he had held a kind of Emersonian view that artistic creation was part of the divine or natural efflux, in his last years he came to see art as more autonomous—to see mind not as integrated with nature but as separate, creating its own autonomous order. "Deep Religious Faith," published in 1954, contains one of Williams' last expressions of the idea that artistic creation is linked with organic forces in nature: what "drives" him, he says, is

> All that which makes the pear ripen
> or the poet's line
> come true!
>
> (*PB* 95)

But in *Paterson 5,* published in 1958, Williams comes to conclude that one can know nothing but "measure," which sounds very much as if it means that the order the mind itself imposes on experience, as in a work of art, is the only absolute order that can be known. Hence Williams, in his final years, appeared to move closer to the position of Wallace Stevens whose poem, "Men Made out of Words," was typical of the nominalism so common in modernist thought.

Yet there are ambiguities in *Paterson 5*—or perhaps an unfinished dialectic—with regard to the relationship that art has with external reality. On the one hand, art and nature form a seamless whole as Williams moves without transition from describing what Auduborn saw in the woods of Kentucky—"buffalo / . . . a horned beast" and "the chicadee / . . . its neck / circled by a crown!"—to describing the Unicorn "lying wounded on his belly" and bearing "a collar round his neck" (*P* 211–12). In the beautiful catalog of the flowers in the Cloisters tapestries (*P* 235–37), Williams' description is so exact, intimate, personal, and sensuous (even referring to the odors of the flowers) that he could be describing an actual field or meadow as well as a work of art. On the other hand, Williams, who had earlier criticized the abstract expressionism of Jackson Pollack for its "incompleteness" (*RI* 206), now accords him the highest praise:

> Pollack's blobs of paint squeezed out
> with design!
> pure from the tube. Nothing else
> is real   .   .
>
> (*P* 213)

But then this recommendation of abstract "design" over representational content is immediately followed with an emphatic imperative to get close to the actual world:

> WALK in the world
>   (you can't see anything
> from a car window, still less
> from a plane, or from the moon!? Come
> off of it.)

Williams praises Peter Brueghel's *Nativity* for being "authentic /
enough, to be witnessed frequently / among the poor" (*P* 226)
but also for being visionary: "—they had eyes for visions / in those
days" and "Brueghel the artist saw it / from the two sides," the
material and the visionary (*P* 227–28).

Thus it is not fully clear that Williams' transcendentalist pro-
pensities had entirely faded away. In the short poems of his last
years, he continues to express a love of nature and his fellow
human beings. Love continues to be, if not a transcendent principle as in the "Coda" to "Asphodel," an important imperative
for Williams—love for his wife, for women, for nature, for his
grandchildren, for mankind in general. The fact that Williams
kept experimenting with poetic form—using short, irregular lines
unpunctuated and broken so as to create ambiguities and double
meanings—is in the spirit of transcendentalist individualism and
creative originality.

One might expect of a transcendentalist some intuitive faith in
a life beyond death, though such faith is hard to find in the wintry
images of these final poems. In one poem the snow muffles

> the world
> to sleep that
> the interrupted quiet return
>
> to lie down with us
> its arms
> about our necks
> murderously a little while

>   (*PB* 16)

Here death is ambivalently portrayed as peace-giving and affec-
tionate ("its arms / about our necks") but also murderous. The
"uninterrupted quiet" is the nothingness that underlies all existence—the formless ground of being. In this poem, Williams
thinks only of its absorptive character, not, as in earlier poems, its
generative power. In another poem, Williams emphasizes only the
comforting peacefulness of death:

> all crevices are covered
> the stalks of
> fallen flowers vanish before
>
> this benefice all the garden's
> wounds are healed
> white, white, white as death
>
> (*PB* 56)

To regard death as a healing "benefice"—a blessing—is somewhat closer to the transcendentalist vein, although not nearly so confident as Whitman's declaration in section 6 of "Song of Myself" that "the smallest sprout shows there is really no death, / And if there was it led forward life."

Perhaps the most explicitly transcendental late poem is "The Rewaking" (*PB* 70). Significantly placed last in the collection of Williams' final poems in *Pictures from Brueghel,* "The Rewaking" hints at the possibility of a divine love:

> Sooner or later
> we must come to the end
> of striving
>
> to re-establish
> the image of
> the rose

The rose, with meanings accrued from Dante and Eliot, is very likely a symbol of the divine—a higher reality that Williams feels he must finally and fully acknowledge, "but not yet"—not while secular human love (for his wife) can still "rekindle / the violet to the very / lady's-slipper" (*PB* 70).

The idealism implicit in the major portion of Williams' work is, as one hopes this book has shown, a major dimension of that work—and crucial to the fullest understanding of the poems. The unity of man and nature, the imagination as an agency of higher truth and active creation, the universe as form-creating process, the power of the universal in the particular—these ideas link Williams with Emerson and with much of romanticism in general. The life-affirming transcendentalist tradition, which became a minor current toward the end of the nineteenth century, seemed almost to vanish in the high tide of modernism with its skepticism and pessimistic portrayals of modern man's inner and outer landscapes. The example of Williams has done much to help revive this tradition. Williams extended the poetic impulses and the spiritual intuitions of Wordsworth, Emerson, and Whitman even further than they did into the illumination of the ordinary and the near-at-hand. However much Williams has been routinely and superficially imitated by lesser poets, without his experimentations with verse form and language, American poetry would simply have gone stale.

It is true, as critics such as Yvor Winters have pointed out, that transcendentalism in its most extreme glorifications of individualism tends to discredit the past indiscriminately. Williams himself has often indulged in easy and careless dismissals of anything that smacks of tradition. But Williams—whose later poems are filled with references to earlier poets, artists, and thinkers—increasingly learned to respect what was good (in his judgment) in the past and to use what he could for his own artistic purposes. Another dangerous tendency in transcendentalism—the tendency that has been vulgarized by the slogan "do your own thing"—was, in Williams, integrated with his search for form as something that can be felt and shared by others, with his respect for the actual qualities of things and people, and with his respect for the universal embodied in the particular.

Williams' transcendentalism or romanticism, toughened by contact with modernism, helps to keep alive a tradition that provides confidence that the imagination can give meaning to the individual life and can act as a force of renewal both for the individual and for culture. Williams believed that the social function of authentic art begins subversively with the freeing of the individual from conditioning imposed in infancy—a conditioning epitomized by the adult saying "that if he can catch the young before the age of six . . . or younger he doesn't care what shall happen to him later" (*SE* 270). To Williams, "Nothing . . . so reveals the essential depravity, the basic starvation of the adult mind as that common saying" (*SE* 270). Thus there is "the necessity for revelation" that will "restore values and meanings to our starved lives" (*SE* 271). Even artists like Proust and Rousseau who show themselves or their fictional characters as "deformed" human beings can have a liberating effect: "Fear deformed us and we reveal to you the depths of our deformity. We do not like our deformity. Look what might have been!" (*SE* 271).

Beyond redemption of the individual, Williams believed that the poet was responsible for "the most vital function of society: to recreate it" (*SE* 103). For Williams, the reformist power of poetry was rooted in the poet's apprehension of the active universal and the ability to communicate the universal in such a way that people would be drawn to it and engaged by it. The poet was in a unique position to do this because, like Emerson's "American Scholar," or "Man Thinking" who "guides men by showing them facts amidst appearances" (73), the poet was "a universal man of action" (*SE* 197) and "the truthfulest scribe of society" (*SE* 193). The artist's aspirations "must come from a sense of totality; the whole; humanity as a whole" (*SE* 192), but, at the same time, the artist must be independent enough to articulate these latent aspirations even if initially they are "antagonistic to the people's wishes" (*SE* 185).

By restoring society to a concrete sense of the universal underlying existing forms, the artist gives people a perspective for assessing the extent to which these forms serve their fundamental purpose or have become bloated or have been deflected from it:

> Being an artist I can produce . . . universals of general applicability. If I succeed in keeping myself objective, sensual enough, I can produce . . . the concretions of materials by which others shall understand and so be led to use—that they may better see, touch, taste, enjoy— their own world *differing as it may* from mine. (*SE* 197–98)

By keeping poetry close to the material world, Williams hoped that his poems would have an inviting familiarity that would make readers more receptive to the ideas and attitudes embodied in them and therefore more aware of possibilities for changing society:

> He [the artist] does not translate the sensuality of his materials into symbols but deals with them directly. By this he belongs to his world and time. . . . His work . . . holds the power of expansion at any time— into new conceptions of government." (*SE* 197)

Although Williams appears to denigrate "symbols" here, his objection to symbolism, as has been maintained in chapter 3, is more semantic than substantial: he objects to "crude symbolism," to overused and conventional symbols too abstracted from immediate sensory experience. Clearly the full impact of symbolic images, when Williams uses them, comes from vivid representation of the thing fused with the intellectual power of the idea. Furthermore, by revealing the universal in concrete particulars familiar to all, art would give people of diverse backgrounds a sense of common humanity:

Without conceptions of art the world might well be and has usually
been a shambles of groups lawful enough but bent upon nothing else
than mutual destruction. . . . They lack that which must draw them
together. (*SE* 199)

Williams' art, then, aims to serve a number of purposes. It helps
his readers to rediscover their own lost "revelations." It inspires
them to "see, touch, taste, enjoy—their own world." Further, it
teaches them to discover the universal energies and necessities for
fulfillment that have given rise to cultural forms—it makes them
think about why we have literature, why we have marriages, education, laws, governments, towns, manufacturing and business, and
how well the existing forms of these institutions are performing
their functions. In short, Williams, through his art, performs the
age-honored functions of literature—to teach and delight—although Williams would probably prefer to have "delight" come
first in this formulation.

NOTES

Chapter 1. Williams: a Visionary Poet

1. Vivienne Koch, "Prefatory Note," *Briarcliff Quarterly* 3, no. 2 (1946): 161.
2. In *William Carlos Williams* (Norfolk, Conn.: New Directions, 1950), Koch defines Williams' stance as "essentially [that of] rational humanism." In discussing "Rain," for example, she makes an absolute distinction between the "non-material . . . autoletic nature of 'love'" and "the purely physical renewal of nature by the rain" (72), thus construing Williams as a dualist. (For an alternative view, see the discussion of the poem in chapter 5, section 2.)
3. Kenneth Burke, "William Carlos Williams: Two Judgments," in *William Carlos Williams: a Collection of Critical Essays*, ed. Joseph Hillis Miller (Englewood Cliffs, N.J.: Prentice-Hall, 1966), 56.
4. Richard Macksey, "'A Certainty of Music': Williams' Changes," in *William Carlos Williams: A Collection of Critical Essays*, ed. Joseph Hillis Miller (Englewood Cliffs, N.J.: Prentice-Hall, 1966), 132.
5. Ibid., 135.
6. Joseph Hillis Miller, *Poets of Reality: Six Twentieth-Century Writers* (Cambridge: Harvard University Press, 1965), 328–31 passim.
7. Ibid., 332.
8. Ibid.
9. Joseph Hillis Miller, "Introduction," in his *William Carlos Williams: A Collection of Critical Essays* (Englewood Cliffs, N.J.: Prentice-Hall, 1966), 3.
10. Ibid., 8, 12.
11. Miller, *Poets of Reality*, 288.
12. Ibid., 359.
13. Ibid., 307.
14. Ibid., 343.
15. Samuel Taylor Coleridge, "On Poesy," in *Criticism: The Major Texts*, ed. Walter Jackson Bate (New York: Harcourt Brace, 1952), 396.
16. Hyatt Waggoner, *American Poets: from the Puritans to the Present* (Boston: Houghton Mifflin, 1968), 382.
17. Ibid., 380.
18. Hyatt Waggoner, *American Visionary Poetry* (Baton Rouge: Louisiana State University Press, 1982), 5.
19. Ibid., 6.
20. Ibid., 43.
21. Ibid., 96.
22. Ibid.
23. Joseph Hillis Miller, *The Linguistic Moment: From Wordsworth to Stevens* (Princeton: Princeton University Press, 1985), xvi–xvii.
24. Ibid., 353.
25. Ibid., 366, 386–89.

26. Ibid., 388.

27. Ibid., 356.

28. James Breslin, *William Carlos Williams: An American Artist* (1970; reprinted Chicago: University of Chicago Press, 1985), 34.

29. Ibid., x.

30. James Breslin, *From Modern to Contemporary: American Poetry, 1945–1965* (Chicago: University of Chicago Press, 1985), 146.

31. Carl Rapp, *William Carlos Williams and Romantic Idealism* (Hanover, N.H.: University Press of New England for Brown University, 1984), 65.

32. Ibid.

33. Ibid., 13.

34. Ibid., 19–20.

35. Ibid., 20.

36. Ralph W. Emerson, *Selections from Ralph Waldo Emerson*, ed. Stephen Whicher (Boston: Houghton Mifflin, 1957), 24. Unless otherwise stated, all subsequent references to Emerson are to this edition.

37. Rapp, *Williams and Romantic Idealism*, 23.

38. Ibid., 24.

39. Ibid., 82.

40. Ibid., 84.

41. Ibid., 87.

42. Ibid., 89.

43. Ibid., 91.

44. Ibid., 84.

45. Alfred North Whitehead, *Science and the Modern World* (New York: Macmillan, 1928), 131–32.

46. Ibid., 133.

47. M. H. Abrams, *Natural Supernaturalism* (New York: Norton, 1971), 69.

Chapter 2. Overcoming Dualism

1. Hyatt Waggoner, *The Heel of Elohim* (Norman: University of Oklahoma Press, 1950), 21.

2. F. Scott Fitzgerald, *The Great Gatsby* (New York: Scribner's, 1925), 162.

3. Saul Bellow, *Humboldt's Gift* (New York: Viking Press, 1975), 202.

4. Joseph Wood Krutch, *The Modern Temper* (New York: Harcourt, 1929), 50.

5. E. D. Hirsch, *Wordsworth and Schelling* (New Haven: Yale University Press, 1960), 20.

6. William Wordsworth, *The Poetical Works of William Wordsworth*, ed. Thomas Hutchinson, rev. Ernest de Selincourt (London and New York: Oxford University Press, 1961), 590. All subsequent references to Wordsworth are to this edition.

7. John Dewey, *Experience and Nature* (New York: Columbia University Press, 1929), 4a. For a fuller study of the affinities between Dewey's philosophy and Williams' views of mind and perception, see Stanley J. Scott, *Frontiers of Consciousness* (New York: Fordham University Press, 1991), 109–29.

8. Mary Warnock, *Imagination* (Berkeley: University of California Press, 1976), 26.

9. Ibid., 56, 61.

10. Ibid., 47.

11. The parallel to Aristotle's view of perception is striking. According to Aristotle, "the thinking part of the soul . . . must be capable of receiving the form of an object, that is, must be potentially identical in character with its object without being the object" (A. J. Smith's translation in W. T. Jones, *The Classical Mind* [New York: Harcourt Brace Jovanovich, 1970], 241).

12. The idea that nature fulfills or completes itself in human perception likewise has an antecedent in Aristotle's view of perception. In W. T. Jones's summary of Aristotle, "Until it is actually perceived it is only . . . potentially an object of perception. Thus perception is a dual actualization—an actualization of the object as an object of perception and an actualization of the sense organ as a percipient" (*Classical Mind*, 239). The idea of human perception as creating or completing the world is both very old and very new, for in quantum physics, according to John D. Wiley, Jr., "particles" are the form human perception gives to "waves of probability—potentials—that don't even become particles until some kind of counter—such as our eye—detects them and in that act transforms potential into something 'real'" ("Phenomena, Comment and Notes," *Smithsonian* 11, no. 11 [Feb. 1981]:32).

13. Ralph Waldo Emerson, *Emerson's Essays* (New York: Thomas Y. Crowell, 1961), 382.

14. Poetry/Rare Books Collection, University Libraries, the State University of New York at Buffalo, Micro Roll 21.

15. Frederick Copleston, *A History of Philosophy,* (Garden City, N. Y.: Doubleday, 1962–67), 7, pt. 1:135.

16. John Herman Randall, *The Career of Philosophy* (New York: Columbia University Press, 1965), 2:250.

17. Coleridge, "On Poesy," 396.

18. Walter Jackson Bate, *Criticism: The Major Texts* (New York: Harcourt Brace, 1952), 396 n. 9.

19. William James, *Essays in Radical Empiricism* (1912; reprinted Cambridge: Harvard University Press, 1976), 8.

20. Whitehead, *Science,* 133–34. When, in 1934, Williams described how his "nameless religious experience" had left him feeling "as much a part of things as trees and stones," he was perhaps echoing a passage he had read in *Science in the Modern World* in 1927: ". . . we are *within* a world of colours, sounds, and other sense-objects . . . such as stones, trees, and human bodies" (129).

21. Ibid.

22. John Locke, *Essay Concerning Human Understanding,* ed. Peter Nidditch (Oxford: Clarendon Press, 1975), 10.

23. Whitehead, *Science,* 112.

24. Ibid., 121, 136, 127. M. H. Abrams points out in *The Mirror and the Lamp* (New York: W. W. Norton, 1958) that the "greater number" of "important romantic theorists," including Wordsworth, regarded science and poetry as "complementary ways of seeing," holding "that while analysis yields truths, this is not the whole truth" (308–9).

25. Abrams, *Supernaturalism,* 375.

26. Ibid., 377.

27. Ibid.

28. Ibid., 395.

29. Ibid., 391.

30. Ibid., 385.

31. Samuel Taylor Coleridge, *The Selected Poetry and Prose of Samuel Taylor*

Coleridge, ed. Donald A. Stauffer (New York: Random House, 1951), 264. Unless otherwise stated, all subsequent references to Coleridge are to this edition.

32. Abrams, *Supernaturalism*, 379.

33. T. E. Hulme, *Speculations; Essays on Humanism and the Philosophy of Art*, ed. Herbert Read (London: Routledege & Kegan Paul, 1936), 134.

Chapter 3. Language and the Renewal of Perception

1. Hulme, *Speculations*, 132.

2. Donald Davie, *Articulate Energy* (New York: Harcourt Brace, 1955), 7–10.

3. Hulme, *Speculations*, 132.

4. Philip Wheelwright, *The Burning Fountain* (Bloomington: Indiana University Press, 1968), 41.

5. Eleanor Berry, "Williams' Development of a New Prosodic Form—*Not* the 'Variable Foot,' but the 'Sight Stanza,'" *William Carlos Williams Review* 7, no. 2 (July 1981):23.

6. Stephen Cushman, *William Carlos Williams and the Meanings of Measure* (New Haven: Yale University Press), 19.

7. Cushman considers line breaks between clauses and phrases to be weak enjambments, whereas Berry treats them as endstops.

8. Berry, "Sight Stanza," 23.

9. Ibid., 26.

10. On systematic enjambent, see Berry, "Sight Stanza," 23, and Cushman, *Meanings of Measure*, 18–19. Cushman classifies meaningful enjambents as "mimetic" when they imitate actions in the external world (35–37), "expressive" when they indicate the speaker's emotional state (106–7), and "representational" when they indicate something about language itself (36). For excellent discussions of the effects created by lineation and typography, see Breslin, *William Carlos Williams: An American Artist* (1970; reprinted Chicago: University of Chicago Press, 1985), 80–86, and Cushman, chapters 1 and 2.

11. William Carlos Williams, "America, Whitman, and the Art of Poetry," 1917; reprinted *William Carlos Williams Review* 13, no. 1 (Spring 1987):1.

12. Ibid.

13. Ibid., 2.

14. Ibid.

15. John Thirlwall, "Ten Years of a New Rhythm," in William Carlos Williams, *Pictures from Brueghel and Other Poems* (New York: New Directions, 1962), 183.

16. Williams, "America, Whitman, and the Art of Poetry," 3. See also the last chapter in Cushman, *Meanings of Measure*.

17. Henry Sayre, *The Visual Text of William Carlos Williams* (Urbana: University of Illinois Press, 1983), 3.

18. Cushman, *Meanings of Measure*, 83.

19. Ibid., 22.

20. Cushman aptly describes the triad as having an "epigraphic quality" and sees it as the modern equivalent of the "elegiac couplet, expanding the typographic alternation of longer with shorter lines to distribute an utterance more evenly," ibid., 88, 92.

21. See Dickran Tashjian, *William Carlos Williams and the American Scene, 1920–1940* (Berkeley: University of California Press, 1978), 119. According to Tashjian, at the time the poem was published in *William Zorach: Two Drawings; William*

Carlos Williams: Two Poems (1937), Williams quoted the poem and wrote the following statement about it "in a little magazine [*The Patroon*] of a local college":

> This girl is caught in the economic embarrassments of the age. . . . But there is a dignity in this girl quite comparable to that of the Venus [de Milo]. . . . Why not imagine this girl Venus? Venus lives! She thought she saw a dime on the pavement and leaned—or turned around to pick it up. But being short-sighted she was mistaken. It wasn't a dime it was a gob of spit.

Tashjian is referring to an earlier and slightly longer version of the poem than the final version that appeared in *The Collected Poems* (1950). Litz and MacGowan cite this early version in their notes to *CP1:*

THE GIRL

with big breasts
in a blue sweater
was crossing the
street bareheaded
reading a paper
held up close
but stopped, turned
and looked down
as though
she had seen a coin
lying
on the pavement—

(CP1 546)

Williams' comments indicate that the poem has a social dimension not readily evident to a reader without the inside information that the comments provide. The comments also indicate that Williams sometimes has a definite "idea" in mind when he appears to be presenting only the "thing." With the added context that Williams provides, one might now plausibly infer that the woman is reading the help wanted ads (the longer version emphasizes that the paper is "held up close") and that her distraction by what appears to be a dime is symptomatic of her economic predicament. The poem thus becomes all the more ironic in that a Venus, a goddess, is reduced to such need that she imagines seeing a coin in the streets. Yet there seems to be a confidence in the woman comparable to that of the "big young bareheaded woman" in "Proletarian Portrait" (*CP1* 384), also published in the mid-1930s. Technically, the shorter version of the poem (*CP1* 444) shows many improvements. The use of "under" for "in" is both more visually precise and more tactile. "Dime" is more specific than "a coin," and the redundant "lying" is deleted. The shift to the present tense gives the poem the immediacy of a glimpse.

22. Gorham Munson, "William Carlos Williams, a United States Poet," in *William Carlos Williams,* ed. Charles Tomlinson (Middlesex: Penguin, 1972), 99.

23 Wallace Stevens, "William Carlos Williams," in *William Carlos Williams: A Collection of Critical Essays,* ed. Joseph Millis Miller (Englewood Cliffs, N.J.: Prentice-Hall, 1966), 62–63.

24. Ernest Fenollosa, *The Chinese Written Character as a Medium for Poetry,* ed. Ezra Pound (San Francisco. City Lights Books, 1936), 10.

25. Ibid., 29.

26. Winifred Nowottny, *The Language Poets Use* (London: Athlone Press, 1962), 4.

27. Ibid., 59.

28. W. A. M. Peters, *Gerard Manley Hopkins* (London: Oxford University Press, 1948), 69–196 passim.

29. Peter Schmidt, *William Carlos Williams: the Arts and Literary Tradition* (Baton Rouge: Louisiana University Press, 1988), 162.

30. Abrams, *Supernaturalism*, 415–16.

31. Ibid., 418.

32. Miller, *Poets of Reality*, 307.

33. Copleston, *A History of Philosophy*, 1, pt. 2:45.

34. Irving Babbitt, *Rousseau and Romanticism* (1919; reprinted New York: Meridian Books, 1955), 28.

35. Hugh Kenner, *The Pound Era* (Berkeley: University of California Press, 1971), 399–400.

36. Donald W. Markos, "Embodying the Universal: Williams' 'Choral: The Pink Church,'" *William Carlos Williams Review* 13, no. 2 (Fall 1987):25–31.

37. *The Complete Works of Nathanael West* (New York: Farrar, Straus, 1957), 134.

Chapter 4. The Imagination: A Force of Nature

1. M. H. Abrams, *The Mirror and the Lamp* (New York: Oxford University Press, 1953), 272.

2. Morse Peckham, "Toward a Theory of Romanticism," *PMLA* 66, no. 2 (1961):11–12.

3. *Princeton Encyclopedia of Poetry and Poetics*, ed. Alex Preminger (Princeton: Princeton University Press, 1974), 582.

4. Williams, "America, Whitman and the Art of Poetry," 1.

5. Ibid., 2.

6. Kenneth Burke, *Counter-Statement* (1931; reprinted Berkeley: University of California Press, 1968), 46.

7. Hulme, *Speculations*, 139–40.

8. Howard Nemerov, "Poetry and Meaning," in *Contemporary Poetry in America*, ed. Robert Boyers (New York: Schocken Books, 1974), 1.

9. Louis Zukofsky, "Comment," *Poetry* 37, no. 5 (1931):275.

10. Louis Zukofsky, *Prepositions* (1967; reprinted Berkeley: University of California Press, 1981), 19.

11. William Carlos Williams, *Contact* (Dec. 1920):1.

12. Williams, *Contact* (Jan. 1921):1.

13. Williams, *Contact* (June 1923):1.

14. Ibid., 3.

15. David Perkins, *A History of Modern Poetry from the 1890s to the High Modernist Mode* (Cambridge, Mass.: Belknap Press, 1976), 316.

16. Ibid.

17. Ibid.

18. See Breslin, *An American Artist*, 42, 56.

19. Paul Mariani, *William Carlos Williams: A New World Naked* (New York: McGraw Hill, 1981), 56.

20. See William Carlos Williams, *CP1*, 503.

21. Barbara Herrnstein Smith, *Poetic Closure* (Chicago: University of Chicago Press, 1968), 15.

22. Aristotle, *Poetics,* trans. Hamilton Fyfe (Cambridge: Harvard University Press, 1932), 91.

23. David Daiches, *Critical Approaches to Literature* (Englewood Cliffs, N.J.: Prentice-Hall, 1956), 37.

24. Coleridge, "On Poesy," 395.

25. Rod Townley, *The Early Poetry of William Carlos Williams* (Ithaca: Cornell University Press, 1975), 118.

26. Ibid.

27. Harvey Gross, *Sound and Form in Modern Poetry* (Ithaca: Cornell University Press, 1975), 120.

28. Townley, *Early Poetry,* 156.

29. Miller, *Poets of Reality,* 345–46.

30. I am indebted to Douglas L. Peterson for this observation.

31. Elizabeth Drew, *Discovering Poetry* (New York: W. W. Norton, 1933), 97.

32. Yvor Winters, *In Defense of Reason* (Denver: Alan Swallow, 1947), 12.

Chapter 5. Nature: An Overview of Organicism

1. Ezra Pound, *Selected Prose, 1909–1965,* ed. William Cookson (London: Faber, 1973), 49.

2. Perkins, *History of Modern Poetry,* 485.

3. Jones, *The Classical Mind,* 200–1.

4. Abrams, *Mirror,* 185.

5. James McMichael, "The Poetry of Theodore Roethke," *The Southern Review* 5, no. 1 (Winter 1969):6.

6. Alfred North Whitehead, *Modes of Thought* (New York: Macmillan, 1938), 205.

7. Loren Eisely, *The Immense Journey* (New York: Random House, 1946), 210.

8. Abrams, *Mirror,* 185.

9. Walt Whitman, *Complete Poetry and Selected Prose,* ed. James E. Miller, Jr. (Boston: Houghton Mifflin, 1959), 33.

10. Ralph S. Lillie, *The General Biology and Philosophy of Organism* (Chicago: University of Chicago Press, 1945), 196.

11. Whitehead, *Science,* 118.

12. Francis E. Peters, *Greek Philosophical Terms* (New York: New York University Press, 1967), 62–63.

13. Arthur Lovejoy, *The Great Chain of Being: A Study of the History of an Idea* (1936; reprinted New York: Harper, 1960), 62.

14. Sayre interprets these lines to mean that "the primrose seems to be . . . everything in summer but a rose and itself" (*Visual Text,* 22). However his interpretation apparently fails to take into account that the poem, although titled "Primrose" (a flower that belongs to the genus *Primula*), really seems to describe the Evening Primrose of the genus *Oenothera,* characteristically a four-petaled yellow flower, although there are many species.

15. Whitehead, *Modes,* 228.

16. Ibid., 257.

17. Reed Whittemore, *William Carlos Williams: Poet from Jersey* (Boston: Houghton Mifflin, 1975), 147–54.

18. Whitehead, *Modes*, 205.

19. Ibid., 206.

20. Lovejoy, *Great Chain of Being*, 244.

21. R. H. Fogle, *The Romantic Movement in American Writing* (New York: Odyssey Press, 1966), 4.

22. Lovejoy, *Great Chain of Being*, 218.

23. Peckham, "Toward a Theory of Romanticism," 10–11.

24. Ibid., 11.

25. Hirsch, *Wordsworth and Schelling*, 16.

26. Abrams, *Mirror*, 173.

27. Ibid., 124.

28. Ibid., 224.

29. I was led to look for these correspondences by Sayre's observation that "Primrose" exemplifies Williams' appropriation of the cubist idea that unity could be created in a work of art by the repetition of common abstract forms (*Visual Text*, 20).

30. Whitehead, *Modes*, 188.

31. Burke, "Two Judgments," 56.

32. John Keats, *Complete Poems and Selected Letters*, ed. Clarence Thorpe (New York: Odyssey Press, 1935), 526.

33. Peters, *Hopkins*, 2.

34. Ibid., 7.

35. Peckham, "Toward a Theory of Romanticism," 11.

36. Richard P. Adams, "Emerson and the Organic Metaphor," *PMLA* 69, no. 2 (1954): 121.

37. David Perkins, *English Romantic Writers* (New York: Harcourt, 1967), 14–16.

38. Bate, *Criticism: The Major Texts*, 360.

39. Ibid., 359.

40. Babbitt, *Rousseau and Romanticism*, 28.

41. Ibid., 270.

42. Miller, *Poets of Reality*, 332.

43. Ibid., 333.

44. Ibid., 355.

45. Raymond Blakney, *Meister Eckhart* (New York: Harper and Row, 1941), xiv.

46. Sister Bernetta Quinn, *The Metaphoric Tradition in Modern Poetry* (New York: Gordian Press, 1955), 109.

47. Miller, *Poets of Reality*, 336, n. 24.

48. Hirsch, *Wordsworth and Schelling*, 31–32.

49. Miller, *Poets of Reality*, 334.

Chapter 6. The Late Years and the Legacy

1. Wallace Stevens, *Opus Posthumous* (New York: Alfred A. Knopf, 1957), 96.

WORKS CITED

Abrams, M. H. *The Mirror and the Lamp.* New York: Oxford University Press, 1953.

——. *Natural Supernaturalism.* New York: Norton, 1971.

Adams, Richard P. "Emerson and the Organic Metaphor." *PMLA* 69, no. 2 (1954): 117–30.

Aristotle. *Poetics.* Translated by Hamilton Fyfe. Cambridge: Harvard University Press, 1932.

Babbitt, Irving. *Rousseau and Romanticism.* 1919. Reprint. New York: Meridian Books, 1955.

Bate, Walter Jackson. *Criticism: The Major Tests.* New York: Harcourt Brace, 1952.

Berry, Eleanor. "Williams' Development of a New Prosodic Form—*Not* the 'Variable Foot,' but the 'Sight Stanza.'" *William Carlos Williams Review* 7, no. 2 (July 1981): 21–30.

Bellow, Saul. *Humboldt's Gift.* New York: Viking Press, 1975.

Blakney, Raymond. *Meister Eckhart.* New York: Harper and Row, 1941.

Breslin, James. *From Modern to Contemporary: American Poetry, 1945–1965.* Chicago: University of Chicago Press, 1984.

——. *William Carlos Williams: An American Artist.* 1970. Reprint. University of Chicago Press, 1985.

Burke, Kenneth. *Counter-Statement.* 1931. Reprint. Berkeley: University of California Press, 1968.

Coleridge, Samuel Taylor. "On Poesy." In *Criticism: The Major Texts,* edited by Walter Jackson Bate. New York: Harcourt Brace, 1952.

——. *The Selected Poetry and Prose of Coleridge.* Edited by Donald A. Stauffer. New York: Random House, 1951.

Copleston, Frederick. *A History of Philosophy.* 8 vols. 1946. Reprint. Garden City, N.Y.: Doubleday, 1962–67.

Cushman, Stephen. *William Carlos Williams and The Meanings of Measure.* New Haven: Yale University Press, 1985.

Daiches, David. *Critical Approaches to Literature.* Englewood Cliffs, N.J.: Prentice-Hall, 1956.

Davie, Donald. *Articulate Energy.* New York: Harcourt, 1955.

Dewey, John. *Experience and Nature.* New York: W. W. Norton, 1929.

Drew, Elizabeth. *Discovering Poetry.* New York: W. W. Norton, 1933.

Eisley, Loren. *The Immense Journey.* New York: Random House, 1946.

Emerson, Ralph W. *Selections from Ralph Waldo Emerson.* Edited by Stephen Whicher. Boston: Houghton Mifflin, 1957.

——. *Emerson's Essays.* New York: Thomas Crowell, 1961.

Fenollosa, Ernest. *The Chinese Written Character as a Medium for Poetry.* Edited by Ezra Pound. San Francisco: City Lights Books, 1936.

Fitzgerald, F. Scott. *The Great Gatsby.* New York: Scribner's, 1925.

Fogle, Richard. H. *The Romantic Movement in American Writing.* New York: Odyssey Press, 1966.

Gross, Harvey. *Sound and Form in Modern Poetry.* Ithaca: Cornell University Press, 1975.

Hirsch, E. D. *Wordsworth and Schelling.* New Haven: Yale University Press, 1960.

Hulme, T. E. *Speculations; Essays on Humanism and the Philosphy of Art.* Edited by Herbert Read. London: Routledge and Kegan Paul, 1936.

James, Williams. *Essays in Radical Empiricism.* 1912. Reprint. Cambridge: Harvard University Press, 1976.

Jones, W. T. *The Classical Mind.* New York: Harcourt Brace Jovanovich, 1970.

Keats, John. *Complete Poems and Selected Letters.* Edited by Clarence Thorpe. New York: Odyssey Press, 1935.

Kenner, Hugh. *The Pound Era.* Berkeley: University of California Press, 1971.

Koch, Vivienne. "Prefatory Note." *Briarcliff Quarterly* 3, no. 2 (1946): 161–62.

———. *William Carlos Williams.* Norfolk, Conn.: New Directions, 1950.

Krutch, Joseph Wood. *The Modern Temper.* New York: Harcourt, 1929.

Lillie, Ralph S. *The General Biology and Philosophy of Organism.* Chicago: University of Chicago Press, 1945.

Locke, John. *Essay Concerning Human Understanding.* Edited by Peter Nidditch. Oxford: Clarendon Press, 1975.

Lovejoy, Arthur. *The Great Chain of Being: A Study of the History of an Idea.* 1936. Reprint. New York: Harper Torchbook, 1960.

Macksey, Richard. "'A Certainty of Music': Williams' Changes." In *William Carlos Williams: A Collection of Critical Essays,* edited by Joseph Hillis Miller. Englewood Cliffs, N.J.: Prentice-Hall, 1966.

Mariani, Paul. *William Carlos Williams: A New World Naked.* New York: McGraw Hill, 1981.

Markos, Donald W. "Embodying the Universal: Williams' 'Choral: The Pink Church.'" *William Carlos Williams Review* 13, no. 2 (Fall 1987): 21–31.

McMichael, James. "The Poetry of Theodore Roethke." *The Southern Review* 5, no. 1 (1969): 4–25.

Miller, Joseph Hillis. "Introduction." In *William Carlos Williams: A Collection of Critical Essays.* Englewood Cliffs, N.J.: Prentice-Hall, 1966.

———. *The Linguistic Moment: From Wordsworth to Stevens.* Princeton: Princeton University Press, 1985.

———. *Poets of Reality: Six Twentieth-Century Writers.* Cambridge: Harvard University Press, 1965. Reprint. New York: Atheneum, 1974.

Munson, Gorham. "William Carlos Williams, a United States Poet." In *William Carlos Williams,* edited by Charles Tomlinson. Middlesex: Penguin, 1972.

Nemerov, Howard. "Poetry and Meaning." In *Contemporary Poetry in America,* edited by Robert Boyers. New York: Schocken Books, 1974.

Nowottny, Winifred. *The Language Poets Use.* London: Athlone Press, 1962.

Peckham, Morse. "Toward a Theory of Romanticism." *PMLA* 66, no. 2 (1951): 5–23.

Perkins, David. *English Romantic Writers.* New York: Harcourt, 1967.

———. *A History of Modern Poetry from the 1890s to the High Modernist Mode.* Cambridge, Mass.: Belknap Press, 1976.

Peters, Francis E. *Greek Philosophical Terms.* New York: New York University Press, 1967.

Peters, W. A. M. *Gerard Manley Hopkins.* London: Oxford University Press, 1948.

Pound, Ezra. *Selected Prose, 1909–1965.* Edited by William Cookson. London: Faber, 1973.

Princeton Encyclopedia of Poetry and Poetics. Edited by Alex Preminger. Princeton: Princeton University Press, 1974.

Quinn, Sister Bernetta. *The Metaphoric Tradition in Modern Poetry.* New York: Gordian Press, 1955.

Randall, John Herman. *The Career of Philosophy.* 2 vols. New York: Columbia University Press, 1962–65.

Rapp, Carl. *William Carlos Williams and Romantic Idealism.* Hanover, N.H. and London: University Press of New England for Brown University, 1984.

Sayre, Henry. *The Visual Text of William Carlos Williams.* Urbana: University of Illinois Press, 1983.

Schmidt, Peter. *William Carlos Williams, the Arts and Literary Tradition.* Baton Rouge: Louisiana State University Press, 1988.

Scott, Stanley J. *Frontiers of Consciousness.* New York: Fordham University Press, 1991.

Smith, Barbara Herrnstein. *Poetic Closure.* Chicago: University of Chicago Press, 1968.

Stevens, Wallace. *Opus Posthumous.* New York: Alfred A. Knopf, 1957.

———. "William Carlos Williams." In *William Carlos Williams: A Collection of Critical Essays,* edited by Joseph Hillis Miller. Englewood Cliffs, N.J.: Prentice-Hall, 1966.

Tashjian, Dickran. *William Carlos Williams and the American Scene, 1920–1940.* Berkeley: University of California Press, 1978.

Thirlwall, John. "Ten Years of a New Rhythm." In William Carlos Williams, *Pictures from Brueghel and Other Poems,* 182–84. New York: New Directions, 1962.

Townley, Rod. *The Early Poetry of William Carlos Williams.* Ithaca: Cornell University Press, 1975.

Waggoner, Hyatt. *American Poets: from the Puritans to the Present.* Boston: Houghton Mifflin, 1968. Reprint. New York: Dell, 1970.

———. *American Visionary Poetry.* Baton Rouge: Louisiana State University Press, 1982.

———. *The Heel of Elohim.* Norman: University of Oklahoma Press, 1950.

Warnock, Mary. *Imagination.* Berkeley: University of California Press, 1976.

West, Nathanael. *Complete Works of Nathanael West.* New York: Farrar, Straus, 1957.

Wheelwright, Philip. *The Burning Fountain.* Bloomington: Indiana University Press, 1968.

Whitehead, Alfred North. *Modes of Thought.* New York: Macmillan, 1938.

———. *Science and the Modern World.* New York: Macmillan, 1928.

Whitman, Walt. *Complete Poetry and Selected Prose.* Edited by James E. Miller, Jr. Boston: Houghton Mifflin, 1959.

Whittemore, Reed. *William Carlos Williams: Poet from New Jersey.* Boston: Houghton Mifflin, 1975.

Wiley, John P., Jr. "Phenomena, Comment and Notes." *Smithsonian* 11, no. 11 (Feb. 1981): 30–38.

Willey, Basil. *The Seventeenth Century Background.* 1935. Reprint. Garden City, N.Y.: Doubleday Anchor, 1953.

Williams, William Carlos. "America, Whitman, and the Art of Poetry." 1917. Reprint. *William Carlos Williams Review* 13, no. 1 (1987): 1–4.

———. Editorial comment in *Contact* 1, 2, 5 (Dec. 1920–June 1923).

———. *Poems.* Privately Printed, 1909.

Winters, Yvor. *In Defense of Reason.* Denver: Alan Swallow, 1947.

Wordsworth, William. *The Poetical Works of William Wordsworth.* Edited by Thomas Hutchinson, revised by Ernest de Selincourt. London and New York: Oxford University Press, 1961.

Zukofsky, Louis. "Comment." *Poetry* 37, no. 5 (1931): 268–84.

———. *Prepositions.* 1967. Reprint. Berkeley: University of California Press, 1981.

INDEX

Abrams, M. H., 101, 154, 158; on accommodating romanticism to a later age, 29; on Coleridge and organic determinism, 177; on romantic modes of perception, 50–51; on romantic poets and science, 213n.24

Abstract expressionism, 205

Actual occasion, 188

Adams, Richard P.: Emerson's compromised organicism, 190

Aesthetic design in nature, 36; in "The Crimson Cyclamen," 168

Aestheticism in Williams, 18, 30, 204–6

Alienation, 20, 29, 31–32. *See also* Cartesian dualism; Cosmic chill

Allegory, 186

Ammons, A. R., 21, 153, 175

Anamnesis, platonic doctrine of, 192, 199

Antipoetic diction, 79, 103; accommodated by free verse, 72; in "Complaint," 81–83; Wallace Stevens on, 82

Aphrodite, 153, 159, 215n.21

Aristotle: final cause, 157–58, 159; imitation (of the universal), 132, 133; metaphor, 91; organic conception of the universe, 154, 155, 157; organic continuum, 184; perception, 213n.11; *Poetics*, 132; universals, 104–5; Williams on, 132, 133

Audubon, John James, 205

Automatic writing, 98, 119

Aztec civilization, 162–63

Babbitt, Irving: and universals, 105, 191

Bate, Walter Jackson, 42, 190

Baudelaire, 101

Beauty: and "Beautiful Thing," 176; epiphany of, in *Paterson*, 192–93;

and "a first beauty," 16, 192, 198; and Edwards' divine and supernatural light, 15, 198: expressed in artistic form, 194; feared and desired in "Paterson: Episode 17," 193; as immanent and transcendent, 161, 194, 195, 197–99; as hidden flame, 176, 184, 193, 198; immanence of, implied by Williams' terms, 195; intuition of its transcendence, 198; Miller on, 18, 22; and need for renewed expression of, 192, 193, 194–96; objective existence of, 36–37, 195; as platonic or transcendent, 28, 102, 104, 108; and Platonism in Williams, 191–203; as rare presence, 18, 20, 27, 49, 138, 141; as ubiquitous and inexhaustible, 194, 198; as universal, 36–37, 155, 191–203; and universe as living, 193

Beethoven: Ninth Symphony, 108

Beinecke Rare Books and Manuscript Library, Yale, 137

Bellow, Saul: on egocentric perception in *Humboldt's Gift*, 31–32, 33

Bergson, Henri, 56, 170

Berry, Eleanor: on lineation in Williams, 61, 65, 214n.10

Bishop, Elizabeth, 130

Blake, William, 32

Blakney, Raymond, 197

Bly, Robert, 153

Boone, Daniel, 164–67

Breslin, James: enjambment in Williams' poems, 65, 214n.10; *From Modern to Contemporary*, 22; *William Carlos Williams: an American Artist*, 22, 214n.10; and Williams as antiromantic, 22

Broken style, 96–102; in "The Agonized Spires," 100–101; as central to Williams' definition of poetry, 96–

230